AF292562

SCUM OF THE EARTH

SCUM OF THE EARTH

A TRUE STORY FROM THE MARGINS

RAKSHIT SONAWANE

HARPER

NON-FICTION

First published in India by Harper Non-fiction 2025
An imprint of HarperCollins *Publishers*
HarperCollins *Publishers* India, Cyber City,
Building 10-A, Gurugram, Haryana – 122002, India
www.harpercollins.co.in

2 4 6 8 10 9 7 5 3 1

Copyright © Rakshit Sonawane 2025

P-ISBN: 978-93-6989-553-3
E-ISBN: 978-93-6989-821-3

The views and opinions expressed in this book are the author's own and the facts are as reported by him, and the publishers are not in any way liable for the same. This book includes accounts of real events and individuals. Any resemblance to actual characters, events or private exchanges is coincidental and liberties have been taken for facilitating narrative clarity and flow. Some names, locations and identifying characteristics have been changed to protect the privacy of individuals. The author and publisher disclaim any liability for losses, damages and expenses arising from misinterpretation or misidentification of characters or events as real.

Rakshit Sonawane asserts the moral right
to be identified as the author of this work.

All rights reserved. No part of this publication may be reproduced, stored in a retrieval system, or transmitted, in any form or by any means, electronic, mechanical, photocopying, recording or otherwise, without the prior permission of the publishers.

Without limiting the exclusive rights of any author, contributor or the publisher of this publication, any unauthorized use of this publication to train generative artificial intelligence (AI) technologies is expressly prohibited. HarperCollins also exercise their rights under Article 4(3) of the Digital Single Market Directive 2019/790 and expressly reserve this publication from the text and data-mining exception.

Typeset in 10.5/13 Adobe Garamond Pro
by HarperCollins *Publishers* India Pvt. Ltd

Printed and bound at
Replika Press Pvt. Ltd.

This book is produced from independently certified FSC® paper to ensure responsible forest management.

HarperCollins *Publishers*, Macken House, 39/40 Mayor Street Upper, Dublin 1,
D01 C9W8, Ireland

To my father, Dhondiram Hanumant Sonawane, and the millions of foot soldiers who made Dr B.R. Ambedkar's non-violent social revolution possible

PART ONE

The Slum

CHAPTER 1

It was a scorching Sunday afternoon. A schoolboy was sitting on the threshold of his home, dangling his feet over the stairs below, enjoying his weekly holiday. The inside of the house felt like a furnace as the tin-sheet walls had heated up. The sunlight filtering in through the numerous tiny holes in the walls lit up the dust particles dancing in the air.

Located in a slum on a hill, the house offered a panoramic view of a part of Ghatkopar, a Bombay (now Mumbai) suburb. Irregular rows of huts were perched along the length of the hill, below which was a bylane with a dead end. The landscape in front of the boy was dominated by multi-storeyed buildings that looked like huge concrete boxes with pigeonholes, towering over perennial streams of vehicles swirling around. These structures stretched far and wide till the horizon was sealed by a wall of hazy mountains. At their foothills were industrial structures, with chimneys jutting out of their triangular roofs, billowing smoke in shades of grey.

An aircraft emerged from behind the mountains, gradually descending to a lower altitude. As it approached the hill, the boy could see the landing gear, the wings, the windows and the colourful insignia on its vertical tailfin. It flew overhead, engulfing the locality in a shrill, noisy vibration. It was a fascinating world, so captivating that it seemed to exist in some other dimension.

'Avinash, don't just sit there. Come in and study,' Godavari, the boy's mother, said. 'Your fourth-grade examinations are approaching.'

He looked over his shoulder. She had just returned from her job as a domestic worker and was pumping air into the kerosene stove.

'Complete your homework before it gets dark. You have school tomorrow,' she said.

He shook his head in displeasure. 'Later,' he said.

'Your father will return home now—hurry up.'

'I'm waiting for him,' he replied. 'He said he would bring me apples today.'

'Apples?'

'Yes,' he said.

'Is that so?' she asked, knitting her eyebrows. 'I have a little surprise for you.'

'What is it?' he asked.

'Wait till your father returns,' she said.

Avinash thought about what it could be. Sometimes, she would bring leftover food, worn-out garments or a broken toy from the houses she worked in.

'Is it a toy?' he asked.

'No.'

'Clothes?'

'No.'

'Something to eat?'

She nodded with a smile. Avinash went inside the house.

'There was a birthday party in one of the houses I work in,' she said, opening the cloth bag she normally carried. Plunging her hand inside, she came up with a small, colourful carton. When she opened it, he saw a piece of cake layered with chocolate and white cream inside, its aroma filling the house. He took a deep breath with a broad smile as she closed the box and put it back into her bag.

'Wow!' he said, stretching his hand out for the cake.

'Wait till your father gets home,' she said. 'Then we'll share it.'

He nodded, but the aroma was tempting. 'Let me at least smell it,' he said. Opening the bag again, he poked his nose inside to inhale the chocolatey sweetness.

'Enough,' she said, taking the bag away. 'Now do your homework!'

Avinash opened his schoolbag and took out some books, but as usual, he did not feel like opening them. He went to the door and looked out. The shadow of the house had crept down the stairs, reaching the bottom one. This was usually when his father came home. He went inside and sat down with a book open in his lap, pretending to read.

After what seemed like ages, he heard footsteps outside. His father, Dagadoo, appeared at the door in his watchman's uniform. He came in head-first, appearing to get taller with each step he took.

Dagadoo was well-built, bald and sported a thick moustache with twirled ends. Avinash put the book aside and rushed to the door. Grabbing Dagadoo's bag, he rummaged through it and found some bananas.

'Where are the apples?' he asked, peering inside the bag.

'Not today,' Dagadoo said apologetically. 'Wait for a few days.'

Avinash was disappointed. 'But I don't like bananas,' he grumbled.

Godavari looked at Dagadoo and then at Avinash. 'Bananas are also tasty,' she said.

Avinash shook his head, looking despairingly at his mother.

'Don't be sad,' she said. 'Wait a few days, and your father will bring you apples.'

Avinash hesitated, then plucked one banana from the bunch and sat on the doorstep to eat it.

'Why are you promising him things you can't afford?' Godavari whispered to Dagadoo as he stood unbuttoning his uniform.

'Apples are expensive,' he said. 'He'll have to wait till I get my salary.'

Avinash ate the banana and as he went down the steps to toss the peel into the gutter flowing nearby, he saw his friend Raja approaching. Raja was tall and thin, and had long hair, some of which fell over his right eye. He had a habit of jerking his head intermittently to swing back his hair. He was wearing black shorts and a faded shirt that had once been a bright red.

'Stop! Don't throw it away—give it to me,' Raja said, stretching out his hand.

He took the banana skin from Avinash and started hungrily scraping its inner side with his lower teeth. In the process, he even ripped off portions of the banana skin.

'I haven't eaten anything since morning,' Raja said after he had finished and tossed the remains of the tattered banana skin into the gutter. 'I'm waiting for my mother to bring something back from the houses she works in.'

Avinash remembered the occasions when he, too, had had to wait for his mother. 'Hunger is horrible,' he said.

'I feel like going on a biting spree—like a rabid dog,' Raja said, baring his teeth and snarling.

'Do you want a full banana?' Avinash asked. 'I wanted to eat apples, but my father bought bananas.'

Raja's face lit up. 'Wow! You're so lucky your father brings you bananas. My father only drinks and beats us,' he said.

'I know,' Avinash nodded, 'People call him bewda, a drunkard.'

When Avinash climbed back up the steps, Godavari was slicing onions and Dagadoo was reading a newspaper.

'I want one more banana,' Avinash said.

Dagadoo smiled at him and buried his head in the newspaper that lay open between his hands.

'It's good that you've finally begun to like bananas,' Godavari said with a grin.

'No, I want to give one to Raja,' he said. Raja had climbed up the steps and was standing behind him.

Godavari looked at Raja. 'Has your mother come back from work?' she asked.

'No,' he replied.

'And your good-for-nothing father?'

'He's not well.'

She cursed under her breath as Avinash plucked a banana and gave it to Raja. 'Poor boy,' she said. 'Raja, wait,' she added. 'Have some cake too.'

'Cake?' Raja asked with a twinkle in his eyes.

Godavari opened her bag and cut the cake with a knife. Avinash got the largest piece, Raja a smaller one. Dagadoo just took a pinch and licked his fingers while Godavari made a tiny mouthful for herself with the crumbs.

Raja was delighted. After eating the cake, he climbed back down the steps, beaming. 'Shall I eat this now or keep it for later?' he asked, looking at the banana.

'You decide,' Avinash said, standing at the doorway.

Raja thought for a while, then peeled the banana and gobbled it up. Then he looked at the skin, folded it up carefully and put it in his pocket. 'I'll eat this later,' he said with a smile and trotted away.

Dagadoo quickly flipped through the newspaper, then folded it and threw it on top of the newspapers piled up in one corner of the house. 'The "Garibi Hatao" slogan is everywhere,' he said, shaking his head. 'Mere words—hollow words.'

Avinash sat on the threshold of the house again.

'Poor Raja,' Godavari said, shaking her head in disappointment. Then, turning to Dagadoo, she added, 'Why don't you make his father mend his ways?'

Dagadoo looked at her. 'I've already tried that several times, but all in vain,' he said. 'Once, he flared up and told me that I should not lecture him as he had paid for his drink from his own pocket and not from mine.'

Godavari cursed under her breath again. 'He's also a migrant from a village like us, but …' she left the sentence halfway. Then she added, 'Look at us. We are also struggling, but we are working honestly and paying attention to our son.'

'Yes. It was so difficult to adjust to city life. Bombay is a city where finding a place to live in is more difficult than finding a means of livelihood,' he said. 'I worked as a coolie and lived with a friend in a slum when we met first. Then I got this job as a watchman, and we saved enough to build this house.'

Godavari looked around the house and then up at the roof. 'Hmm. But it was only possible because you don't drink.'

'That is because I've seen Babasaheb Ambedkar, heard his speeches and read his books,' Dagadoo said. 'This is the crucial difference between me and Raja's father.'

Avinash watched the urban landscape spread out at his feet. The tall residential and commercial buildings in front of the slum had started glittering as darkness fell. They became walls dotted with illuminated squares and rectangles. The streetlights came alive, towering over the streams of vehicles flowing in opposite directions. Colourful neon signboards were lighting up along the carriageways, flashing corporate logos and products. Planes continued to fly overhead intermittently, like huge metal fireflies with glowing lights in different colours. Godavari lit a kerosene lamp. The flame flickered, casting her monstrous shadow on the tin-sheet walls of the house.

In the morning, Avinash left for his school—his main link with the fascinating world outside. It was a huge concrete block built around a playground. The school was swarming with students who would disappear inside every morning and pour out again in the evening. Most were fair-skinned, talkative and perfumed, and they got dropped at the school in cars, bikes and school buses—unlike Avinash and his friends back home.

When he entered the classroom, the students were either fooling around or chatting in groups. A few of his classmates smiled at him, while others ignored him as he passed by.

Atharva, the cleverest student in the class and the darling of all the teachers, was in a huddle with some boys. As Avinash drew closer, he saw him distributing chocolates wrapped in colourful paper from a multicoloured tin.

'My uncle lives in the US,' Atharva told them. 'He brought me these American chocolates.'

'They are yummy, but Swiss chocolates are even better!' someone said.

At the sight of Avinash, Atharva knitted his eyebrows and stared at him sharply with his hazel eyes, prompting Avinash to walk across the classroom towards the bench near a window at the back.

Prasad, with whom Avinash shared the bench, raised his hand and smiled. He was fair and bulky, and was fond of chewing gum. He was also carefree and least interested in competing for higher grades. Sometimes, he would seek Avinash's help and even copy his essays and other homework projects assigned by the teachers. Right then, the bell rang, and the students quickly occupied their seats as the teacher walked in.

Avinash sat through the study periods, jotting down notes as the teachers mechanically scribbled on the blackboard. Occasionally, he would glance at the textbook spread out before him, wondering why his parents were so obsessed with his education, making him struggle to pass the exams. He yawned and waited for the lunch break as the periods changed and different subject teachers took charge one after the other. Prasad sat doodling in his notebook. The lunch break came as a relief. As usual, many students had brought apples and chocolates in their lunch boxes. They formed small groups to eat together and talk. At first, Avinash had tried to mingle with them, but he had ended up a silent spectator. The students usually discussed things like toys, chocolates, movies, songs, vacations, fashion trends, celebrities, festivals and shrines. It was a different world, and he had given up trying to mix with them after being slighted for not knowing anything about the topics that interested them.

The school was an alien territory, enigmatic and repulsive. So was the language of instruction, and understanding the anomalies in the semantics and syntax of English was a perennial struggle.

Once, Raja had asked, 'It must be fun learning English, isn't it? How do you introduce yourself?'

Avinash shook his head. 'It's not fun, Raja, it's quite difficult,' he said. 'But I would say, "I am Avinash," to introduce myself.'

'I?' Raja frowned in confusion. 'But when you say "I", it also means an eye, which is "dola" in Marathi. We see through our eyes.'

Avinash scrunched up his face for a moment, as if in discomfort. 'You're right—the pronunciation of both words is the same,' he said. 'But they are written differently. When I refer to myself, it's spelt with just the letter I and when I refer to my dola, it's spelt e-y-e. There are many such words which sound the same but are written differently and mean different things.'

'You're doomed!' Raja said mischievously and burst into laughter.

For Avinash, English was indeed a funny language, unlike his mother tongue Marathi, in which there were no discrepancies between the written and spoken word.

At school, the 'scholars' who sat on the front benches were all snobbish. They were the darlings of the teachers. Most also attended private coaching classes and promptly answered questions in class. On one occasion, Avinash had raised his hand in class to say that he had not understood what had been explained. The scholars had looked over their shoulders at him contemptuously. The teacher did explain the text again to Avinash's satisfaction, but he had always felt jittery about asking questions again after that.

He felt that attending school was an act of penal servitude that he had been sentenced to by his parents. He used to walk to school in the morning and then wait for liberation that only came in the evening with the long ringing of the bell. The sound would trigger in the students the urge to run home, and it was the only thing which always made them applaud in unison. Avinash would dart home with the jubilation of a prisoner finally set free. It was freedom from being caged in the concrete block, even if it lasted only for what remained of the day. It was not just physical liberty but also mental solace from an alien people and language.

Avinash's home was where he was most comfortable—except when his parents pestered him to study. He would acquiesce, but the sight of his textbooks irked him because they were all old and used, bought on discount. One day, he pulled some textbooks out of his schoolbag and slammed them in front of his parents. 'When will I get *my* textbooks?' he demanded.

'What do you mean?' Godavari frowned. 'These are yours.'

'*Mine?*' he asked, turning the cover of a textbook and reading the name scribbled on the first page in large, uneven letters, 'Madan Laxmichand Shah.'

She nodded. 'That's the name of the student who owned the book when it was new.'

'I want new books,' he said. 'Every year, we only buy old books.'

He flipped through the book to show her the folded pages, the underlined passages and the pictures of historical figures defaced with moustaches, beards, sunglasses or caps with feathers drawn on them.

'Yes, it looks bad,' she nodded. 'Just ignore it.'

'It feels as if someone has blackened my face,' he said.

'All right, next year we'll buy new books,' she said.

He shook his head. 'Last year, you had said the same thing,' he grumbled. 'All my classmates have new books.'

There was a long silence in the room. Dagadoo put aside the newspaper he was reading and cleared his throat. 'Son, it's not the condition of a book that matters, but how well you study it,' he said. 'Don't pity yourself—it will only weaken you.'

'But new books smell so good! And if I get new ones, I can write my name on them instead of carrying books with others' names written on them,' Avinash muttered.

'Remember, despite these old books, you've always passed your examinations every year—that is an achievement for a first-generation learner like you. Now you're in the fourth grade and if you continue to take an interest in your studies, you'll be the first matriculate from our family,' Dagadoo said.

'But sometimes, there are things I don't understand in class,' Avinash said. 'I want somebody to explain them to me.'

Dagadoo and Godavari looked at each other. 'But who can that be?' Godavari asked. 'I'm illiterate. A printed page to me is a parade ground on which an army of tiny chickens has left its footprints.'

Avinash was amused. 'Chicken footprints?' He giggled.

She flipped the bajra roti she was making and smiled back.

'And I don't know English,' Dagadoo said. 'There is nobody in our slum who can guide you. Just ask your teacher.'

'But whenever I ask a question in class, my classmates laugh at me,' he said.

Dagadoo approached Avinash and patted his shoulder. 'Don't feel shy about asking questions, and don't bother about others laughing at you,' he said. 'Ask questions—your teachers will explain things to you. They are paid for it. And remember, teachers like inquisitive pupils.'

'But my classmates laugh at me.'

'Let them. Have you seen Raja?' Dagadoo asked. 'Always remember, things could've been worse for you.'

Avinash thought about it for a moment. Perhaps his father was right. There were people less fortunate than him. It was a sobering thought. All his friends in the slum were in Marathi-medium schools, making him something of a celebrity. Sometimes they would ask him to translate Marathi words into English out of curiosity, making him struggle for the right word.

Since the neighbourhood was predominantly made up of first-generation illiterate or semi-literate Buddhist migrants from Maharashtra's villages, many of their neighbours used to approach Dagadoo to write or read letters in Marathi. All of them were either part-time workers or labourers in factories or worked in various government departments. They belonged to communities that were formerly considered untouchable, mainly Mahars, and had migrated to the city to escape caste oppression in villages and converted to Buddhism under the leadership of Dr B.R. Ambedkar. While reservation in education and government employment had opened up opportunities for a dignified livelihood, some people, like Raja's father, had taken to alcohol at the cost of the well-being of their families.

When Avinash got enrolled in the English-medium school, some of their neighbours were amused by Dagadoo's courage, while one tried to deter him from this, considering the expenses. However, Dagadoo had remained firm and said that he wanted the next generation to take a leap into mainstream society.

But there were a lot of people, like his classmates, who were more fortunate than Avinash, and this thought tormented him. 'Yes, but look at my classmates.'

His father smiled. 'Son, there will always be some people in a better condition and some in a worse condition than you,' he said. 'Make the best use of whatever you have instead of worrying about what you don't.'

Avinash looked at his father. 'What do I have?' he asked. 'I have *nothing*.'

Dagadoo smiled. 'You're a healthy boy,' he said. 'You have parents to care for you, a house to live in and the opportunity to go to an English-medium school. Don't waste your time and energy complaining.'

Unconvinced, Avinash stared at his father, trying to come to terms with his plight. Soon, he got busy with his homework. He found himself at a dead end when he came across the word 'stationary'. The pronunciation of the word was the same as that of the word 'stationery', but both words meant different things and were spelt differently. He wanted to overcome the confusion.

He wrote the two words down, one below the other, in his rough notebook, trying to think of some way to match the meaning with the letters, to make each word easy to remember. He found only a one-letter difference between the two: the 'a' in the former was 'e' in the latter. After some time, he came up with a formula to remember the difference. The letter 'e' was also used to spell the word 'pencil', a writing instrument, and 'stationery' meant writing material. Thus, it was easy to distinguish 'stationery' from 'stationary'. Suddenly, he felt a deep sense of accomplishment. It was a baby step towards learning on his own, but it felt like light at the end of a long tunnel engulfed in a darkness that he had thought would last forever.

It was raining outside, and the sound of the downpour had blended with the murmur of distant traffic. The class was silent, except for the teacher's voice, which rose and fell lyrically as she interpreted a poem. She was walking between the rows of benches, a textbook open in her hand. She read a line, took a deep breath and smiled. Then she paused and looked out of the window before explaining the metaphors in the poem.

'This is the hallmark of a good poet,' she said. 'Look at how he describes the rain as "silky blue threads flowing from the sky".'

The scholars sitting on the front benches nodded wisely. As if waiting for their approval, the teacher smiled and made a gesture with her free hand to show the invisible threads of silk flowing from the ceiling of the classroom to the floor.

Avinash was looking out, watching the rain beating against the windowsill. As the downpour got heavier, his heart skipped a beat thinking about his house on the slope of the hill. A heavy downpour usually led to swollen streams of water gushing downhill, often damaging the huts, even if partially.

He closed his eyes and prayed for the rain to stop. He was lost in these thoughts until Prasad nudged him. When Avinash opened his eyes, he found that there was pin-drop silence in the class. The teacher, too, had stopped speaking. He turned to find the entire class staring at him like a creature with a hundred eyes, poised to pounce.

'What's happening?' the teacher's voice tore through the silence. 'Stand up.'

He rose to his feet. 'Nothing, ma'am,' he said.

'Were you sleeping in the class?'

'No, ma'am.'

'Don't lie,' she shouted, walking towards him.

'No, ma'am, I'm not lying.'

She came to his bench and stood there with her hands on her hips. 'The entire class saw that your eyes were closed,' she said. The scholars on the front benches nodded.

'I was …' he began, but stopped, unsure of whether he should reveal the truth or not.

'Yes?' the teacher asked, raising her eyebrows. 'Don't tell me that you were meditating.' She turned around, smiling at the class. Some of the students giggled.

'No, I was not meditating,' Avinash said. 'I wanted the rain to stop.'

A murmur rose up in the class and the teacher frowned. 'Why?' she asked, taking a step towards him. 'You don't like the rain?'

Avinash was now able to smell her perfume. 'I was wishing the rain away,' he said.

There was a burst of laughter in the class. 'Oh my God!' the teacher exclaimed after the laughter subsided. 'We're reading a beautiful poem on rain and this boy is …' She left the sentence midway and shook her head. 'Why are you wishing away the rain?'

'He's like Little Johnny from the nursery rhyme, ma'am. Like Johnny, he wants the rain to go away so that he can play,' one of the scholars from the front row said, triggering a fresh round of laughter.

'Is that right?' she asked, trying to stifle her laughter.

'No,' Avinash said.

'Then what is it?'

He looked at her and then out of the window.

'Yes?' she asked, bending forward.

'I'm worried that the heavy rains might damage my house,' he said finally.

She thought for a while. 'Oh! Where is your house?' she asked finally.

'In Bhimnagar,' he said. 'On the slope of a hill.'

The teacher looked stunned. 'Oh! Really?' she asked, taking a step backwards.

'Yes,' he said.

Another murmur rippled through the class. 'Quiet!' the teacher shouted, walking back towards her table.

Avinash looked out of the window again. The downpour had thankfully weakened to a drizzle.

'Sit down and pay attention now,' the teacher said, looking at Avinash before returning to the poem.

Avinash tried to imagine silky blue threads flowing from the sky and cascading down the hill, forming beautiful streams around the houses in the slum. What flashed through his mind, however, was muddy water ferociously gushing downhill in the narrow gutters between the houses, damaging them while cutting past the corners.

The bell rang, triggering the usual commotion in the classroom. The rain had stopped by then, and the teacher was the first to leave the class, followed by the students jostling with one another to get out as it was the last period of the day.

Avinash rushed home, worried about the extent of damage he'd find. When he reached the slum, there was sludge all over the road, with large stones placed at various spots for people to walk on. Plastic pots and buckets were lined up as usual in front of a dry tap. Some boys were walking around barefoot in ankle-deep muck. They had tied threads to the tails of dragonflies and were flying them like kites. A few others were playing the most popular monsoon game of throwing a thin foot-long iron rod into the sludge. Usually, the broken rib of an umbrella was used. If it stood erect after piercing the ground, the player won a point. He would pick up the rod, move a few steps ahead to find a proper spot and then throw it again. If it didn't remain standing, he was out, and then the next player would have his turn.

Avinash approached them, stepping carefully through the sludge. One of boys playing was Sudhir; he was the same age as Avinash, but was taller and sturdier.

'Want to play?' Sudhir asked as he threw the rod into the mud. It pierced the sludge like an arrow and stayed erect.

'No, not now.'

Sudhir picked up the rod, looked around and stopped. 'Your mother is on her way,' he whispered.

Avinash turned and saw Godavari trudging home. He went to her and took the cloth bag she was carrying. As they turned into one of the gullies and started ascending the stones that served as steps leading up to their house on the hill, there came the familiar whiff of alcohol. Two residents of the slum were sitting cross-legged on a mat under the extended roof of a house, which was also the local liquor den patronized by the slum's residents and their guests. A couple of policemen in plainclothes also visited it intermittently.

Zende, the owner of the liquor den, was a sturdy, middle-aged man of average height, with curly hair, a thick moustache, large eyes and a paunch. He was a semi-literate migrant from Konkan, who had been unable to find a stable job for years. After doing some odd jobs, he came in contact with a few local goons and became a retail distributor of illicit liquor. He lived with his wife, who sometimes ran the shop in his absence. The local residents were either his customers or they tolerated him because of his friendly nature.

As Avinash and his mother made their way past the liquor den, they saw Zende appear at the door with two aluminium glasses filled with liquor. He was wearing a striped T-shirt in bright red and yellow with the lower end hanging over his belly. A chequered blue-and-black lungi was tied around his waist. He handed the glasses over to the two men. One of them dipped his finger in the glass and sprinkled some drops of alcohol around ritually. He gulped down the liquor quickly, his eyes closed, his face twitching. Then he quickly picked up a pinch of salt from the aluminium plate kept nearby and licked it. His friend, who was watching him with a smile, followed suit. Then the duo stared blankly at the floor, waiting for the alcohol to swamp them. They knew they could sit there and wait until the place became crowded and they would have to make room for new customers.

When Avinash and Godavari reached home, they found that some of the flat stones that served as stairs to the door had come loose. Avinash balanced himself on the stones and reached the door while Godavari examined the damage. The house with its tin-sheet walls, like many others in the neighbourhood, was in the fourth and last row on the hill slope. Through the narrow gully that separated their house from the neighbour's, rainwater had gushed down the hill in full force and turned left as the improperly aligned houses in the lower row blocked its way for a few feet. In the process of rushing down, the rainwater had brushed past the corner of their house, laying bare some of the stones at the bottom of the crude staircase.

Godavari got busy collecting soft mud, small stones and pieces of wood and metal from the sludge around. Then, looking at the gaps between the stones, she arranged the stones in place like the pieces of a jigsaw puzzle and stuffed the material into the crevices to stabilize the stones before using balls of mud to seal the gaps.

Seeing his mother make the mud paste, Avinash bent down to do the same. 'Don't spoil your uniform!' Godavari shouted.

Avinash went inside and quickly changed into an old shirt and a pair of shorts. Then he came out and plunged his hands into the mud to knead it into soft balls.

'Will this survive the heavy rains?' he asked.

Godavari looked at him, her face sullen. 'I don't know—probably not,' she said. 'But what else can we do?'

'We face this problem every monsoon. Can't we fix it permanently?' he asked.

'Yes,' she said. 'If we use cement instead of mud.'

'Then why don't we?'

She sighed. 'Grow up fast and earn enough money for us to do it,' she said.

'Yes,' he said. 'When I grow up, I'll earn lots of money to build our house with bricks and cement. We'll replace the tin-sheet walls with concrete ones.'

Godavari smiled and looked at him with a hundred dreams in her eyes. 'But first, we need to replace the existing tin-sheets that have rusted,' she said, staring at the house. Then she plunged her hands into the mud again.

Avinash looked at the house for a moment and then began making tiny animal models out of the mud balls. 'Don't play with the mud,' his mother said. 'I have to finish this and then cook before going down the hill to fetch water.'

A few days later, the rain finally stopped. Avinash heaved a sigh of relief as the sun shone brightly, drying up the muck and hardening the repairs they had made to the house. At school, there was a flurry of activity in his class as the students struggled with a painting assignment. The art teacher, Raghunath Panvelkar, was moving around the classroom, his hands behind his back, glancing at their creations. Panvelkar was a short, middle-aged man with a thin moustache, a receding hairline and a bulging paunch. Whenever he demonstrated his art, the blank paper in front of him came alive instantly with either an amazing landscape, a portrait, an image of an animal, a bird or whatever he wanted it to be. Sometimes, he would start painting straightaway, without doing any sketching beforehand. All the students watched him in awe and tried to imitate him, usually with disastrous results.

Avinash had nearly completed the landscape he was drawing and was giving it some final touches when he suddenly realized that Panvelkar was standing near him.

'Good,' Panvelkar said, taking Avinash's drawing book in his hands and holding it high up for the class to see. 'Attention, everyone. Look at this.'

For a moment, all the activity in the classroom paused as everyone looked up at the painting. Avinash stood up and, unused to being the centre of attention, he found the classroom's eyes on him and his creation unnerving. There were exclamations like 'Wow!' and 'Ooh!' from some of the students. The scholars on the front benches had turned around and were looking at the painting with their eyes wide open.

'While painting a landscape, most of you typically draw triangular mountains, with the sun rising behind them, a river, a couple of clouds and birds flying,' Panvelkar said. 'But look at what Avinash has painted. There are the usual things that you all draw, but with a difference. There is no sun in the painting, but the colour scheme and the shadows indicate that it's there, somewhere in the east, beyond the painting's frame.' He patted Avinash, put the drawing book back on the desk and walked ahead.

After the class, many of the students approached Avinash, asking him to help them; one of them was Atharva.

'How come you paint so well?' he asked.

'I don't know,' Avinash replied. 'I just like to paint.'

'Will you help me?'

'Yes, sure.'

'After school, let's go to my house—I live quite close by.'

Avinash thought for a moment. 'Not today,' he said. 'I'll come with you tomorrow, after informing my mother.'

'All right,' Atharva said, walking back to his seat.

The next day, after school ended, Avinash walked with Atharva to his house. It was located in a multi-storeyed residential complex near the school. A watchman was sitting inside a cabin at the gate. Once they entered the building, Atharva pressed the doorbell of a flat on the ground floor. Avinash noted that there were red finger marks and a swastika drawn on the door and the wall. A small doll dressed in black clothes was hanging upside down from a nail on the doorframe. A moment later, Atharva's mother opened the door. An obese woman, she was fair-skinned and hazel-eyed like him. She was wearing a lavender nightgown with a white floral pattern on it. Atharva rushed in and threw his schoolbag on a couch.

Avinash removed his shoes before entering the house. It was a spacious apartment with the kind of furniture, curtains and objects that he had only seen behind the glass walls of showrooms along the road home. The garlanded idol of a deity, with incense sticks and flowers at its feet, faced the door. A showcase on another wall held several marble, crystal, glass, brass and porcelain art objects.

Atharva's mother turned around and went into the kitchen after looking at Avinash curiously, and Atharva followed her. Avinash could hear the clinking of utensils and the sound of water being poured into a glass. Atharva appeared with a glass of water a second later, and Avinash finished it. He put the glass on the table, and Atharva took it back inside.

'Who is he?' Avinash heard Atharva's mother ask.

'His name is Avinash,' Atharva replied. 'He's my classmate.'

'Avinash? Avinash who?'

'Avinash Gaikwad.'

'Gaikwad?' his mother repeated.

Then there was a pause, after which Atharva's mother said, 'Keep that glass aside. It will have to be washed separately. Why have you brought him home?'

'Err ... he's going to teach me painting.'

There was a moment of silence, and then some more whispering. A minute later, Atharva came out of the kitchen. 'Let's go to my room,' he said, picking up his schoolbag.

Avinash followed him to a room painted in a different colour. There was a study table with a lamp, two chairs, a cot and a cupboard inside the room. There were colourful pictures of cartoon characters painted on one wall. A photograph of Atharva in a decorative frame stood on the table, and a cricket bat and a few balls were lying in a corner. There was also a small bookshelf on one of the walls.

'Wow!' Avinash exclaimed. 'You have a separate room for yourself?'

'Yes. You don't?'

'No.'

'Then ask your father to buy a larger house,' Atharva said indifferently.

Avinash tried to think of an answer, but nothing came to mind. He pictured the rusted tin-sheet walls of his house which didn't even have a water connection, a toilet and electricity, and found himself at a loss for words. He approached the bookshelf, where schoolbooks, storybooks and comics were neatly arranged. 'May I see your books?' he asked.

Atharva nodded. Avinash opened a couple of books and smelled them, keeping his closed eyes. He browsed through some of them and then put them back on the shelf.

'You have to teach me how to draw like you,' Atharva said, opening his schoolbag. Avinash nodded and they spent nearly an hour sketching and painting. Atharva was an obedient student, asking questions and following instructions. After they finished, Avinash went to the bathroom to wash his hands. As he watched his reflection in the mirror on the wall, he let himself fully feel the sensation of running water on his hands. After wiping his hands with his handkerchief, Avinash returned to the room and stood in front of the bookshelf again.

'I can lend you a book or two if you want,' Atharva said. 'But you must return them within a week.'

Avinash's face lit up. 'Oh, really? I'd like to borrow them then,' he said.

Atharva handed over a storybook and a comic, which Avinash slid into his satchel.

On his journey back home, the images of Atharva's house kept coming back to Avinash's mind. It was a dream house, seemingly existing in some other dimension and entirely out of his world.

When he reached home, Godavari was cooking and Dagadoo was sleeping as he was on night duty that day.

'What took you so long?' she asked. 'Is your friend's house far away?'

'No, it's near our school,' Avinash said, throwing his schoolbag down and unbuttoning his uniform.

Their voices woke Dagadoo up, and he opened his eyes as Avinash said, 'He lives in a big concrete house in a big building and has a separate room all to himself.' He was sitting on the threshold of the house, dangling his feet on the stairs below, as his parents looked at each other.

'Have you realized that while your friend has so many things, he still had to call you to learn something?' Dagadoo asked. 'That means you're better at certain things than he is.'

Avinash allowed the idea to swirl through his mind. It was a nice thought, something that made him feel good. There was indeed something in him which made him better than others.

In a few days, he finished reading the books he had borrowed from Atharva and returned them. He read the storybook with curiosity and got lost in its imaginary world of fairies, angels and demons. The comic book, on the other hand, left less room for imagination as it graphically illustrated the travails of a hero with superhuman powers which made him invincible. The characters and events in both the books amused Avinash. But ultimately, he found that the stories of heroes combating monsters, aliens and ferocious creatures were cut off from the realities of his world. Nevertheless, the books were entertaining and made him familiar with some new words, which he wrote down in a small notebook where he kept a record of newly learnt words.

CHAPTER 2

When the Giraffe brand compass box was launched in the market, it became an instant craze among students. Within a week, everyone in Avinash's class had one—except him. One evening, when he had accompanied Godavari to the market, he saw the compass box at a stationery shop. He told her about it, and she hesitantly inquired about its price. The shopkeeper promptly presented one of the compass boxes at the counter and mentioned its price.

'Oh, we'll buy it later,' she said, handing it back. Avinash knew the reason behind her answer and kept quiet.

At school the next day, Panvelkar announced that he would conduct a special coaching class after school hours to prepare deserving students for the elementary and intermediate grade drawing examinations conducted by the state government. A few interested students raised their hands. Avinash wanted to take the class as well, but he did not raise his hand—signing up for the special class meant paying an extra fee.

He avoided looking at Panvelkar and kept doodling in his notebook with a pencil stub, desperately wishing for some magic that would make him disappear from his teacher's sight.

'What about you?' he heard Panvelkar ask, but he did not look up. There was silence in the class.

'Avinash, I'm asking you,' Panvelkar said.

Prasad nudged him, and Avinash's heart missed a beat. He stood up and looked around. The entire class was agog over the conversation that was unfolding.

'Not interested?' Panvelkar asked. Avinash avoided making eye contact with his teacher and didn't say anything. 'You will pick up very fast,' Panvelkar said. 'I want students like you.'

'I'll ask my parents,' Avinash mumbled, hanging his head.

Panvelkar looked at him, bewildered. 'All right,' he said. 'Let me know.'

That evening, when Avinash brought up the topic at home, Godavari got irritated. 'Where will the money come from? You think it grows on trees?' she shouted.

Without saying another word, he went and sat on the threshold of the house, looking at the fascinating spectacle of the city spread out below, vibrant as ever.

A few days later, while walking in the school corridor during recess, Avinash spotted Panvelkar coming down the corridor from the opposite direction. To avoid him, he started walking behind some students. Keeping his head down as he walked, Avinash hoped that Panvelkar had not seen him, but in vain.

'Avinash,' he heard Panvelkar's voice and stopped. 'Have you told your parents about the drawing class?'

'Err ... yes, sir,' he said. 'But they said there was no need to join it.'

'Why? What's the problem?' Panvelkar asked.

'They are not interested.'

Panvelkar looked at him for a while. 'Are *you* interested?'

'I am, but ...'

'But?'

'They say we can't afford it.'

'Oh. Ask your mother or father to see me, and you start coming to the extra class from today,' Panvelkar said.

Avinash nodded. He wasn't sure how his parents would react, but he hoped that Panvelkar would convince them to let him join the class.

The temptation of playing with colours was irresistible. So, that day, he stayed back after classes and went to the art classroom.

Without a word, Panvelkar opened a cupboard and provided him with pencils, colours, brushes and paper. Then he started instructing all the students in the class, and Avinash soon got lost in his favourite subject.

Reaching home late in the evening, he found Godavari busy cooking and his father away on duty. She greeted him with a glare. 'Why are you so late?' she demanded.

When he told her about what had happened, she calmed down and after a long pause said, 'Your education is becoming more and more expensive by the day.'

The next day, when Avinash and the other students were in the art class, Dagadoo appeared at the door of the classroom. He was dressed in his watchman's uniform. Avinash went to Panvelkar and told him that his father had come to meet him. Panvelkar asked him to continue with his work and went to talk to Dagadoo. The students in the class looked at one another, their eyebrows raised in curiosity.

'That's my father,' Avinash said.

'Your father is a watchman?' Atharva asked.

'Yes,' Avinash replied. Atharva shrugged, while some of the more amused students giggled.

After a brief whispered conversation, Dagadoo folded his hands, smiled and left.

'Your father has agreed to let you attend this class,' Panvelkar told Avinash when he came back in. 'You can continue now.'

When Avinash reached home that evening, Dagadoo told him that Panvelkar had waived the fee for him. It came as a beautiful surprise, and from that day onwards, Avinash started finding the school less repulsive. He would wait eagerly for the regular classes to conclude so that he could rush to the art classroom.

A month later, Panvelkar announced that an inter-school painting competition had been organized. He selected Avinash and three others, including Atharva, from the entire school to participate in it. When Avinash hesitated, Panvelkar called him closer and whispered that he would also provide the necessary drawing material for the competition, which was in two weeks' time. The competition venue was the spacious hall of another school nearby.

On the day of the competition, as he was nearing the entrance, Avinash saw Atharva approaching. They smiled and wished each other luck as they walked in together.

'I had gone to a temple today to offer special prayers for my success,' Atharva said, pointing at the tilak, the holy mark, on his forehead. 'You didn't go?'

Avinash shook his head. 'We follow Buddhism, and there is no god in Buddhism,' he said as Atharva cast him a scornful glance.

Suddenly, a cat crossed their path, startling Atharva, who halted and retraced a few paces, muttering something inaudibly.

'What happened?' Avinash asked.

'Didn't you see the cat crossing our path?'

'So what?'

'That's a bad omen! I don't think either of us will win a prize today.'

Avinash scoffed. 'I don't believe in superstitions,' he said.

'You will, when we don't win any prizes,' said Atharva confidently.

✿

A little later, the competition began once the topic was announced, and the contestants became busy with their artwork. After the competition got over, Atharva was anxious and sweating profusely. 'Do you think we'll win the prize?' he asked Avinash as they came out of the hall.

'I don't know—there were some students better than me and some worse,' Avinash said. 'Participating in the event was a big thing for me, and that's what I enjoyed.'

Atharva sighed. 'I hope my prayers are answered,' he said. 'Aren't you afraid that your parents will shout at you if you don't win a prize?'

'No.'

'Really? How come?'

Avinash smiled. 'I'm the first person in my family to go to school and learn. Even if I lose, my parents won't mind, and I'll try to do better in the future. If I win, it's simply a bonus.'

'You're so lucky! I have to get at least a consolation prize, or my parents will yell at me,' he said.

'Oh! Really?'

Atharva nodded his head. 'They want me to top in everything,' he said. 'They don't understand that I can't be good at everything.'

'Don't worry, they'll understand,' Avinash said. 'They are educated.'

Atharva didn't reply and went home with a gloomy face.

At home, Avinash found Godavari cutting vegetables. Dagadoo and two men from the neighbourhood were drafting a letter to the civic authorities about some issues in the locality.

'How was the competition?' Godavari asked.

'I enjoyed it.'

'Who won?'

'I don't know,' Avinash said. 'The result will be announced in a few days.'

She folded her hands, looked up at the roof and said, 'He will bless you.'

Dagadoo looked up and then stared at Godavari. 'There is nobody up there,' he said. 'Nobody is going to descend from the sky and perform miracles. It's all about sincerity, hard work and skill.' Then he turned to Avinash. 'Don't be disheartened if you don't win a prize,' he said. 'At least you got an opportunity to show your talent. Many talented people don't even get that.'

As usual, there were hundreds of students in uniform walking towards the school, some in groups and some with a friend or two, but Avinash walked alone.

He entered his classroom and was about to sit down when everyone started clapping around him. Someone dressed in a colourful attire was at the door, surrounded by a few students. Avinash got up for a better view. It was Prasad—he was wearing a bright red shirt, a white jacket, a pair of white trousers and white shoes instead of the usual school uniform.

The bell rang, and silence fell as the teacher walked in. She called Prasad to the front of the class and all of them wished him a happy birthday. He was full of smiles and went around distributing chocolates to every student. When he finished and took his seat, he gave Avinash one more chocolate.

'You've already given me one,' Avinash said, opening his palm to show him the chocolate.

'Keep this too,' Prasad said. 'We share the same bench and are good friends.'

Avinash smiled at his bounty. He looked at the chocolates wrapped in silver foil with deep blue checks. He had seen such chocolates only in shops.

'Remember to give me an extra chocolate on your birthday too,' Prasad whispered.

Avinash's heart stuttered. Distributing such chocolates was an expensive affair. He couldn't recall ever having celebrated his birthday in school, but his parents would celebrate it at home. Suddenly, he remembered that he was born in May, when the school was closed for summer vacation, and heaved a sigh of relief.

He held both chocolates out to Prasad. 'I can't take these,' he said, 'because I won't be able to return the favour.'

Prasad was puzzled. 'Why not?' he asked.

'My birthday is in May, during the vacations.'

'Oh,' Prasad said, and then added after a pause, 'No problem. At least take one.'

Avinash nodded and unwrapped one chocolate to relish it. The teacher had instructed the students to throw the wrappers in the dustbin behind the classroom door, but he didn't feel like throwing away the glistening wrapper. After flattening the wrinkles by running his thumbnail over them, he put the wrapper inside his book—it still had a bit of the chocolatey aroma left.

That day, a pleasant surprise awaited him at home. His aunt Savitri had come to visit, and like every other time, she had brought biscuits and sweets for him. As he entered the house, she kissed him on the cheeks and ran her fingers through his hair while his mother watched happily and Dagadoo sat reading the newspaper. She made Avinash sit beside her and pulled out packets of biscuits and sweets from her bag. 'Next time, I'll bring you chocolates,' Savitri said.

'Will you bring a chocolate like this?' Avinash asked, opening his book and showing her the chocolate foil.

Godavari became restless and irritated. 'Aren't you ashamed of yourself?' she asked. 'She has already brought you so much.'

'Don't scold him,' Savitri said. 'Next time, I'll bring this for him.'

'Don't spend so much,' Godavari said.

Savitri looked at her sister. 'Don't worry,' she said. 'He deserves it. He goes to school and is not illiterate like us.'

Avinash liked being pampered by his aunt. Somehow, he found her to be more generous than his parents. She was always good to him and never got angry. His parents were good too, but they were very rigid about his schooling, forcing it down his throat like a bitter pill.

'So, what did you learn at school today?' Savitri asked him.

He immediately thought about a lesson the English teacher had read from the textbook. It was about children in Canada enjoying snowfall after their school closed down early. Avinash had tried hard to imagine snow. Was it in the form of a powder, flakes or frozen droplets? He had been relieved that it did not snow in his slum, or else it would've piled up on the hill and the roofs of their fragile houses, and that would've been quite disastrous.

'Have you seen snow?' he asked after narrating the story.

Both the sisters looked at each other. 'No,' they said in unison.

'Even our forefathers never saw snow,' Dagadoo said, folding the newspaper.

'I want to throw snowballs and make a snowman,' Avinash said.

'Cold places are far away, and we can't afford to visit a foreign country or even the Himalayas,' Dagadoo said. 'When you grow up and earn enough money, we can all visit such a place. Till then, use your imagination to think about what it would've been like.'

Avinash was disappointed. 'But some of my classmates have visited such places,' he said.

'There's no need to be sad. See, most people living in cold regions don't know what a desert is, and those living in deserts have no idea about snowfall,' Dagadoo said. 'We have deserts as well as cold regions in our country, but there are millions of people who've never seen the sea, just as we've never seen snow fall or been to a desert.'

'If there is so much to see in our country, why are they shutting us up in the classroom?'

'It seems like a good idea that all students should be exposed to diverse regions and cultures instead of learning only inside classrooms,' Dagadoo said. 'But this is wishful thinking. Who will organize it and bear all the expenses?'

Avinash felt hopeless and condemned to living in a small and claustrophobic world. First, there was the natural world which was so vast, diverse and difficult to understand. And then there was the man-made world with its compartmentalized life. There were so many unknown things about both the worlds, so much that was beyond his control. He felt lost and confused.

'Have you ever seen a village?' Savitri asked him.

'No, I've only seen pictures of villages.'

'Would you like to visit one?'

'Yes, but who will take me to a village?' he asked.

Godavari laughed. 'We will—next weekend!' she said.

'Do we have a village?' he asked, triggering a round of laughter in the house.

'Where do you think we came from?' Savitri asked when the laughter subsided. 'Our ancestors lived in villages, and many of our relatives still do. We migrated to this city in search of work.'

'But how come I've never been to our village?' he asked.

'Because your mother is jittery about your health after having lost two kids before you were born,' Savitri said. 'She had visited the village when you were just a year old, but she cut short her stay when you fell sick. She is overprotective of you.'

Godavari looked at Savitri and then at Avinash. 'Now we are finally going to the village, but you will have to listen to everything I say,' she said. 'No wandering around in the sun or eating anything and everything like the village boys do.'

Avinash jumped with joy. He would at least be able to see an actual rural landscape with the greenery of real fields.

They made the overnight journey to their village in the crowded general compartment of a low-fare passenger train that halted at all stations. Avinash was looking forward to seeing beautiful landscapes through the window, but it was dark outside. All he could see were the silhouettes of buildings, mountains, trees and power transmission towers that passed by rapidly as the train clanked ahead. Ultimately, however, he lost interest and slept atop the newspapers his father had spread on the floor of the compartment while others dozed on their seats.

At daybreak, he woke up to bright sunlight and the cries of tea vendors on the platform where the train had stopped.

'Get up,' Godavari said. 'We're almost there. We have to get off at the next station.'

Avinash sat at the window, looking out as the train pulled away from the station. The rural landscape had come alive in a variety of colours. The clear blue sky stretched over fields that spread out in rectangles, squares and quadrilaterals of various sizes in myriad tones of green. There were trees standing tall along the boundaries of the fields.

At the next station, they got off the train and walked towards the bus stand. It was swarming with people who were milling around the red buses parked neatly in the bus bays. The place was dirty, with litter all around. Stray dogs and pigs were rummaging through a pile of garbage in one corner of the compound. Dagadoo spotted the right bus and they jostled their way in. The bus was crowded with village folk—the women wore colourful saris, while the dominant colour of the men's apparel was white. Most of the men also sported either a white Gandhi cap or a turban. The bus was rickety and the ride bumpy. After about an hour, Avinash and his parents alighted at a deserted intersection. They took a left and began walking on a narrow road, with patches of the asphalt missing and the gravel beneath lying exposed.

Avinash was awestruck by the distinct smell of the countryside and the vastness of the space all around. There were huge trees along both sides of the road. Their branches spread overhead, forming a canopy and offering a cool, soothing atmosphere to those passing underneath. Beyond the trees were lush green fields of standing crops with scarecrows made of inverted earthen pots propped up at regular intervals; some had turbans wrapped around their heads, with the fabric fluttering in the breeze. A few scattered houses and some livestock were also visible.

An absolute silence spread out all around them. It was so overbearing that Avinash felt he had gone deaf. The tranquillity was only intermittently punctuated by the chirping of birds, the buzzing of flies and the distant cries of farmers. It was a totally different but fascinating world, and Avinash felt much closer to nature here than he did in the city. He was so impressed that he wished he could disintegrate into tiny particles and move freely amongst the trees and the fields, rustling the leaves and the crops.

After walking for about half an hour, the spire of a temple became visible. They also spotted a couple of houses nestled amongst some trees. A dirt track branched out just before the village came into full view and they took the diversion. The track snaked around the trees and led to a cluster of thatched huts. Two dogs started barking as soon as they saw them, and a group of boys playing marbles under a tree stopped and looked up at them. A middle-aged man wearing a white dhoti and a white sleeveless cotton vest came out of a hut and quietened the dogs. Then he turned and rushed towards them, smiling and yelling, 'Dagadoo has come home!'

'That's my cousin, Soma,' Dagadoo told Avinash. 'You can call him Tatya.' Soma had a dark complexion, was well-built and hairy, and had a thick moustache. At his behest, two boys came forward and took their baggage from them.

A pair of brown oxen, tied to a wooden stump under a tree, turned their heads. They flicked their ears and looked at the visitors, ruminating all the time. A strong smell of cow dung and urine hung in the air. There were also four goats and a few chickens moving around.

Soon, several people came out of the huts and greeted them. Soma ushered them to a house where a woman served them water in aluminium glasses.

'This is Narmada, your aunt, Soma's wife,' Dagadoo said.

Avinash drank the water, but it tasted different from the water back home. He didn't like it. When his face twitched, his father said, 'The water is drawn from a well here—it will taste different.'

Soma then took them to a wrinkled old woman sitting on a cot. She smiled when she saw them. Dagadoo and Godavari touched her feet reverently, and Avinash followed suit. The old woman kissed both his cheeks.

'This is your grandmother, my aunt, Jiji,' Dagadoo said.

Soma called one of the boys who had carried their bags, 'Khandoo, come meet your cousin.'

Khandoo was short and sturdy. He was wearing loose khaki shorts and an oversized white shirt with the sleeves rolled up. As everyone settled down, Dagadoo became nostalgic about the time he'd spent in the village. Khandoo came and took Avinash by the arm and led him out of the house. Some other boys joined them as well, and the whole group walked towards a clearing near the hut.

'There is a pathway near that mango tree that is the shortest route to the village,' Khandoo said, pointing to some trees ahead.

Avinash looked at the trees, but he couldn't identify the mango tree. 'Where is the mango tree?' he asked.

All the boys looked at him in shock. 'There, look,' they pointed. 'It is next to the babul tree. Come!'

Avinash was still bewildered as they all approached the tree. Khandoo jumped up and grabbed a low-hanging branch. 'Look at its leaves!' he said to Avinash.

It was then that Avinash discovered just how little he knew about trees. He remembered drawing the leaves of neem, peepal and tamarind trees in the art class, but there were so many species of trees he was still oblivious to.

They walked further and came across a huge banyan tree. The boys climbed it like monkeys and swayed from the low-hanging vines, some of which were almost touching the ground. Some branches had even entered the soil and grown as parallel trunks, albeit of a smaller girth.

'Come on, climb up!' Khandoo invited Avinash.

Avinash tried to, but he couldn't get a leg up. 'I can't,' he said. Then, with some success, he managed to hold on to a low-hanging vine and swayed back and forth. The boys burst into laughter. Khandoo then climbed down one of the vines, swung like a pendulum for some time and then let it go, landing on the ground with a smile.

'Have you seen a well before?' he asked. When Avinash shook his head, he called the other boys, and they proceeded towards a well nearby. Avinash approached the circumference of the well cautiously and peered in. About thirty feet below was a glassy circle of water, half covered with fallen leaves, reflecting the sky. Like a hibernating creature that had opened an eye to stare at them, the still water had a greenish tint. A few frogs were leaping around, forming dissolving circles on the surface of the water. There was a ramp on one side of the well with pulleys installed for bulls to draw the water up.

'Come, let's go sit on the paar,' Khandoo said, pointing to a waist-high parapet built around the trunk of a neem tree near the house. As they climbed the paar, Avinash could see the roofs of some houses in the distance, with the temple spire towering above them. There was the occasional movement of livestock and villagers, while the temple bell tolled intermittently.

Avinash found the arrangement rather strange. 'Why do you live outside the village?' he asked.

Khandoo shrugged. 'We've always lived on the outskirts.'

At once, Avinash realized that back home, he too lived on the outskirts, watching the vibrant city from the threshold of his house in the slum.

'We are natives of this village,' Khandoo said. 'Our ancestors have always lived here, on the outskirts.'

'But why didn't they live in the village?'

'It has always been like this.'

Avinash was not convinced and felt that something was missing in this explanation.

'Forget about the village. Tell us about Bombay,' Khandoo said as the others nodded.

Suddenly, Avinash found himself representing a city about which he actually knew very little. He had not even seen the entire city. He fell silent as he tried to think of an answer.

'Have you seen aeroplanes?' Khandoo asked.

'Yes. They fly over our house all the time,' Avinash replied.

'Wow! And the city must be full of tall buildings everywhere,' Khandoo said, beaming. 'Do you live in a tall building?'

Avinash shook his head. 'No,' he said. 'In fact, my house is smaller than yours. We live in a slum on a hill.'

'Oh,' Khandoo pursed his lips. 'But I've heard that anyone can earn a lot of money in the city.' The others nodded.

'Yes, but it needs a lot of time and effort if you are poor,' Avinash said. 'It's different for those whose families have wealth.'

There was a pause, after which Khandoo asked, 'But how come their families are already rich?'

The boys came up with several explanations, ranging from people owning huge land holdings, businesses and lucrative jobs to engaging in unlawful activities.

'Some people are born rich,' Khandoo said. 'See the sarpanch of our village, Ramrao Patil—his family owns more land than anyone else in the village. He also heads the village panchayat, and his father was the sarpanch before him.'

'But how was his father able to buy so much land?' Avinash asked.

'He didn't buy it. The land belonged to his grandfather—he inherited it.'

'How did his grandfather have so much land?'

'I don't know. I guess he inherited it from his ancestors.'

'But then how did their forefathers have so much money?'

'I don't know. They must have been wealthy already?'

'How?'

'Their forefathers must have earned a huge amount of money.'

'How?'

'I don't know!'

'Why couldn't our forefathers do it?'

A silence fell over the group, interrupted only by the rustling of leaves as the branches of the trees swayed in the breeze. Avinash yearned for a satisfactory explanation.

'Have you seen the sea?' Khandoo asked, breaking Avinash's chain of thoughts.

'Yes, I have.'

'When? How big is it?'

'I saw it when I visited Chaityabhoomi. The sea is very vast ... it stretched as far and wide as the eye could see,' Avinash said, recollecting his visit to Chaityabhoomi with his father.

A sudden gust of wind rustled the leaves. He looked around and saw that the boys were all looking at him expectantly.

'I've heard of people visiting Chaityabhoomi,' Khandoo said. 'It's like an annual pilgrimage.'

'But it's a different kind of pilgrimage,' Avinash said. 'Most people who visit Chaityabhoomi carry home books, not sweets or blessings, as prasad.'

As the boys tried to make sense of what Avinash had said, he got lost in reliving the visit.

It was 6 December, Babasaheb Ambedkar's death anniversary. Tens of thousands of people were walking towards Chaityabhoomi, his final resting place in Dadar, on the coast of Bombay. Several roads had been closed to traffic to facilitate the never-ending stream of visitors. Hawkers were selling pictures, calendars and books about the thoughts and ideas of the Buddha, Babasaheb, Jyotiba Phule, Savitribai Phule, Chhatrapati Shahu Maharaj and other social reformers. Men and women of all ages, from different parts of the country, were waiting in a long queue to pay their respects. When the stupa came in full view, Dagadoo stopped, folded his hands and bowed.

'Are we not going inside?' Avinash asked.

'No, not today.'

Avinash wondered why his father had brought him so far if they were not even going inside.

'I want you to become a practising Ambedkarite, not a worshipping one,' Dagadoo said.

Avinash tried to grasp the meaning of what his father had said but could not.

'But I want to go inside,' he said.

'Not now,' Dagadoo said. 'We'll visit again someday. Today,

let those coming from far-off places visit it—let's not lengthen the queue. Come, we'll go this way.' Taking Avinash's arm, Dagadoo began walking towards the seashore.

Avinash was overwhelmed by the vastness of the sea stretching out in front of him. The breeze and the sound of the waves captivated him, and he felt like a speck in the swelling crowd of humanity on the beach. He was at the edge of the man-made world, overlooking the magnificence of nature. Enchanted by the sight, he did not hear his father speaking to him until Dagadoo nudged him.

'Come, let's go,' Dagadoo said. 'I'll show you something very important. Something more important than offering Babasaheb these floral tributes.'

A few minutes later, they entered Shivaji Park. It was teeming with people and there were hundreds of stalls filled with books written by various social reformers. Besides, various government agencies, social organizations and government employees' associations were providing information and free guidance about welfare schemes, educational courses and employment opportunities. Free medical check-ups and meals were also being provided to the public.

While moving through the crowd, Dagadoo stopped frequently as he came across familiar faces. He would greet the people with a 'Jai Bhim', and then a brief chat would follow. He would also stop at bookstalls and browse through the books on display before moving ahead. At one stall, Dagadoo bought two books for himself and a booklet for Avinash. 'This is for you,' he said. 'I want you to start reading about Babasaheb, and also what he wrote. It will give you a proper perspective and make you a true Ambedkarite, which means being neither a communist nor a religious fanatic.'

Avinash looked at his father blankly, trying to understand what he meant. He felt overwhelmed by the sea of countless books that all seemed to want to tell him something. He looked at the booklet in his hand, a brief biography of Babasaheb. It struck him then that it was different from the books he had borrowed from Atharva.

CHAPTER 3

While the boys were busy talking, the discussion inside Soma's house continued, peppered with occasional bouts of laughter. Later, it spilled out of the house, with the women talking to one another as they left to offer their prayers to a deity. Godavari was carrying a coconut, some prayer material and a vessel filled with water. Jiji was walking very slowly, dressed in her nine-yard sari, taking small steps. Soma was walking beside her.

'Boys, come with us,' Godavari hollered. They immediately joined the women and everyone set off towards a huge neem tree. A winding pathway led to a half-buried black, round stone under the tree. Avinash saw that the stone was smeared with vermillion. Coconut shells and half-burnt incense sticks lay around it, and a small brass bell hung from a branch of the tree.

Khandoo poured water on the stone and applied some fresh vermillion powder over it. Then, he smeared the foreheads of all those present with the same colour. The boys were told to light a few incense sticks, which was a tough task in the breeze. After wasting several matchsticks, they finally managed it by cupping their hands around the flickering flame. There was a whiff of aromatic smoke as the incense sticks were stuck in the mud in front of the deity. The boys then rang the bell, taking turns to do so.

Godavari asked Avinash to break one of the coconuts on a nearby stone and then offer it to the deity. He managed it only after several unsuccessful attempts, which triggered a round of laughter in the group. The coconut water was sprinkled on the deity, after which everyone folded their hands and bowed. Then the kernel was broken into pieces and distributed among those present.

As they sat under the tree munching the coconut pieces, Avinash noticed that Dagadoo was not there.

'Tatya, where is my father?' he asked Soma.

'He did not come,' Soma said, shaking his head. 'He has gone to the neighbouring village to meet his friends.'

'He deliberately left for the other village to avoid coming here with us,' Jiji said.

'He has never come here with us,' Soma replied. 'He doesn't believe in gods and rituals.'

'He has always been like that,' Jiji added. 'Always arguing and questioning the things we've been doing for generations.'

'Don't get angry,' Soma said. 'He has given up on these things.'

Then, Jiji called Avinash and made him sit beside her. 'Do you know who raised your father?'

'How would he know?' Godavari asked. 'We've not told him anything.'

'Why not?' Jiji snapped. 'He should know these things. He should know where his roots are. Otherwise, he will move around like a rootless person and become vulnerable in this evil world. Knowledge about his roots will link him with his family, relatives and community, giving him a sense of belonging, unlike an orphan child.'

Turning to Avinash, she said, 'Your father lost his mother when he was three years old, and his father when he was five—we brought him up.'

Soma nodded. 'When we were teenagers, he used to accompany my father, Kondiba, on his duties around the village, like patrolling the village boundary at night or skinning dead cattle,' he said. 'We were untouchables, totally at the mercy of the villagers.'

Jiji nodded. 'We would feast when a bull or a cow died because we'd get summoned to dispose the carcass. We used to skin it and eat beef to our heart's content,' she said. 'Then, we would clean the bowels, cut them into small pieces, add salt and dry them before storing them in earthen pots. During difficult days, when we didn't have much to eat, we would boil these pieces to fill our bellies.'

Avinash was speechless as he tried to come to terms with the stark realities of his lineage. He had never known anything about the grim truths of his father's life outside of the city.

'We would've languished in poverty, illiteracy and indignity forever, but Babasaheb's movement changed our situation,' Soma said.

'And Dagadoo got caught up in the movement,' Jiji said. 'He used to go around the villages, asking our people to stop skinning dead cattle, eating beef and running errands for the upper castes. He asked them to stop believing in superstitions and rituals, and respond, instead, to Babasaheb's call to move to the cities for education and employment—to escape caste.' Then she paused and looked around.

'But why did our people not do something else and earn money?' Avinash asked.

'We were not paid for the work we did as village servants,' Soma said. 'It was our traditional duty.'

'What if someone refused?'

'Any person who refused was beaten up and ostracized,' Soma explained. 'There was no other way but to fall in line.'

'But my father says that the Constitution takes care of all people—'

Soma and the others burst out into laughter before Avinash could even complete his sentence.

'Son, there was no Constitution in those days,' Soma said. 'The Constitution came into being only in 1950. The ancient traditions were so oppressive that they deprived our people, as well as women of all castes, of education, employment opportunities, the freedom to pursue economic activities of their choice, and social status.'

Avinash found it unbelievable. 'Why didn't our people unite and oppose it?'

'It is very easy for you to say this,' Soma said. 'But the system was run by orthodox priests and wealthy upper-caste people citing some holy texts that vertically divided society into castes and sub-castes, besides branding all women as inferior to men. Specific upper castes were granted the privileges of priesthood, scholarship and business.'

Avinash was stunned. 'Is that why our people remained poor and illiterate?' he asked.

'Yes. Without the efforts of social reformers like Mahatma Phule, Savitribai Phule, Chhatrapati Shahu Maharaj and Babasaheb Ambedkar, we would've continued to suffer endlessly.'

Avinash pondered over the revelations.

There was a lull in the conversation before Jiji continued, 'We tried to stop your father when he decided to migrate to Bombay. But he was adamant. He moved and got employed as a watchman. After that, his visits to the village became less frequent. Later, he embraced Buddhism at the conversion ceremony Babasaheb organized in Nagpur.'

'After his conversion, Dagadoo vowed not to touch liquor or worship any god,' Soma said.

'Do you mean he used to drink earlier?' Avinash asked with surprise, looking at his mother, who nodded in response. 'I've never seen him drink.'

Soma laughed. 'He used to drink, but he gave it up and has kept his word,' he said.

Learning the truth about his father's life and his own ancestry set Avinash thinking. He began to understand why Dagadoo was so passionate about his education. Suddenly, he felt burdened with a heavy responsibility. He also felt ashamed about having compared himself with his classmates. They had inherited all their privileges by virtue of their birth, while he had inherited poverty, illiteracy and social stigma.

'The traditions have long been biased against us,' Narmada said. 'Of course, now our children can get an education and find jobs. The Constitution has provided a shelter for us.'

'So have we given up our old way of life entirely?'

'Well, the Constitution brought in a silent, bloodless revolution. No more village duties. We are leaving our old ways behind, forever. We've also stopped worshipping gods after converting to Buddhism.'

'But we still live on the outskirts of the village.'

'Yes, son. We've always lived on the outskirts of the village. This cluster of houses used to be called "Maharwada" in the past, meaning a settlement of Mahars, but now we call it "Rajwada".'

'But it's still outside the village. When can we shift inside?'

Soma shook his head. '*We* have changed, but not the society we live in. I don't know when it will happen or whether it will happen at all,' he said. 'Even if we earn lots of money or get access to higher education today, I don't think we can buy or construct a house in the heart of the village.'

There was silence.

'You said we've stopped worshipping gods,' Avinash said. 'But then how come we are still worshipping this traditional deity here?'

'Yes, we've stopped worshipping gods.' Soma stole a glance at Jiji and smiled sheepishly. Then, in a low voice, he murmured, 'But my mother belongs to an older generation, and it's impossible to make her change her beliefs at this age. So, I have to pretend that I still believe in all this because I don't want to hurt her feelings.'

Jiji moved forward and patted Avinash. 'You go to school, isn't it?' she asked, and he nodded. 'Good. Become a big man,' she said. 'But don't forget where you come from and always help the oppressed.'

In the evening, members of the families living in the Rajwada returned home after working in the fields all day and went about their evening chores. The women started cooking dinner and there were more rounds of nostalgic discussion as everyone sat together in front of Soma's house.

By the time Dagadoo returned a little later in the evening , none of the men were in sight. 'Where are the men?' he asked.

'They are drinking and chatting there,' Khandoo said, pointing to a house that belonged to Soma's distant cousin. Dagadoo shook his head.

When dinner was ready, the men came staggering out of the house and sat cross-legged on the floor inside Soma's house; Dagadoo joined them.

'We are celebrating your return, and you don't even keep us company,' Soma complained. Some of the other men nodded in support.

At first, Dagadoo ignored them, but ultimately, he got irritated. 'We'll talk in the morning. You are all drunk now,' he snapped.

'Who? Me?' Soma asked, shaking his head. 'I can still drink an entire bottle without losing my balance. I'm strong.' He raised his right arm and flexed his biceps. 'I'm a child of Bhim. Jai Bhim!'

'Is this something to be proud of?' Dagadoo asked. 'You're insulting Babasaheb, who was a teetotaller.'

Soma folded his hands. 'I mean no offence to anyone,' he said, grinning. 'I'm just having a little fun.' The others followed suit, folding their hands and mumbling inaudibly.

The entire family had dinner, after which Soma and the other men went to sleep. The kids were asleep as well, but Avinash couldn't sleep. What he had heard from Jiji and Soma earlier in the afternoon was haunting him. He crept up to where his father sat discussing family matters with the women, and pulled at his sleeve to get his attention. When his father finally looked at him, the boy asked him whether what he had heard was true.

Dagadoo stared at him blankly for a moment, and then he sighed. 'Now you know why I'm always so anxious about your education and behaviour,' he said as Avinash nodded.

'You are the hero of your life—just like a comic-book hero who fights aliens from space and villains among men with his superpowers,' Dagadoo said. 'But the difference is that you don't need superpowers or violence. Overcome your hurdles peacefully, with honesty and hard work—the Constitution will protect you.'

In that moment, all the pieces of the jigsaw puzzle began to fall into place in Avinash's mind.

At dawn, Avinash woke up to the noisy chatter of his parents, uncle and aunt. Godavari tugged at the bedsheet he had snuggled in. 'Come on, get ready quickly!' she said excitedly. 'My brother is coming to take us to a wedding. We must go!'

Avinash wanted to go back to sleep, but she pulled his hand and made him sit up.

'I don't want to go,' he said. 'Khandoo is going to teach me how to climb trees.'

'No, you're coming with us,' she said. 'Get ready now.'

Just then, he heard the dogs barking outside. Still yawning with sleep, he went out of the house. Dagadoo and Soma were standing under a neem tree, and a bullock cart drawn by a pair of white oxen was approaching them. The horns of the bulls were painted a bright red, and the bells tied around their necks were tinkling. A tall, hefty man in a white kurta, dhoti and turban was the lone person in the cart, and he pulled the reins on reaching the neem tree.

'Jai Bhim,' he said with a smile and jumped down as Dagadoo and Soma returned the greeting. Godavari had also come out of the house, and she stood there beaming. The man turned and handed her some cloth bags with a smile. Then, he released the oxen from the yoke and patted them before tying them to a wooden stump nearby.

'Give them some water,' he said to Khandoo, and Khandoo came running up with two buckets of water and put them in front of the bullocks. As they started drinking thirstily, he scattered a bundle of grass in front of them.

Godavari brought a glass of water for the man, who removed his turban before gulping it down quickly. Then, he wiped his mouth with the back of his hand and looked at Avinash from head to toe. 'He was just a small child when I saw him years ago,' he said. 'He has grown up, but he's so thin. It seems like you don't feed him properly.'

'He has always been like this,' she said.

'Then let him stay with me for some months,' he said. 'I'll make him robust like me.'

Godavari turned to Avinash. 'This is my brother,' she said. 'You can call him Pandu mama. We are going with him to attend a wedding today.'

Soon, the men sat under the tree and started chatting. After breakfast, Avinash, his parents and Soma embarked on their journey in Pandu's bullock cart.

'Have you travelled in a bullock cart before?' Pandu asked Avinash.

'No,' he replied.

'All right, today I'll teach you how to drive it.'

Pandu handed over the reins of the cart and showed Avinash how to start, stop and change direction by using them to control the bulls. Avinash was thrilled with the power of having the two bullocks at his disposal. He tugged at the reins and the bulls started walking. He could see their backs, humps, horns, the yoke and the road ahead. However, the fun didn't last long because Pandu handed him a whip and asked him to hit the bullocks to get them to increase their speed.

Avinash looked at the whip and then at Pandu. 'No, I can't,' he said. 'It will hurt them.'

Pandu burst into laughter and, taking the whip back from Avinash, started whipping the bulls, who immediately accelerated their walk to a trot. 'This is how you drive a bullock cart,' he said, cracking the whip again.

'Pandu, don't force him to do anything,' Dagadoo intervened, gesturing to Avinash to get into the back and sit with him. Pandu whipped the bullocks again, and they started galloping, making the ride bumpier. He looked over his shoulder at Avinash and laughed. 'You're a useless boy,' he said. 'You need to use force to control animals and human beings who behave like animals.'

After about an hour on the asphalt road, they took a dirt track with trees lined along both sides, and the temperature immediately dropped several degrees. Soon, they could see some houses and a temple nestled among a grove of trees in the distance. They bypassed the village and turned onto a narrow track. The air was now filled with the sound of a sambal—a pair of tabla-like drums tied around the waist and beaten with curved wands—being played. As they continued down the track, they came upon a clearing where a pandal had been erected in front of some houses. A group of youngsters and some children were dancing near the pandal. Some men and women, dressed in their ceremonial finest, were sitting under the shade of the pandal. A few bicycles and bullock carts were parked under some trees, and Pandu pulled up his bullock cart beside them. As they all got down, Dagadoo and his family were welcomed by a group of women who applied turmeric powder and kumkum on their foreheads. Godavari was gifted a sari, while Dagadoo and Soma were honoured with turbans.

Godavari then took Avinash around, introducing him to her relatives. He was immediately surrounded by people he didn't know. They were all smiling and touching him. An old woman hugged him and planted kisses on his cheeks. 'She's my mother, your grandmother,' Godavari said.

Avinash looked at his grandmother's heavily wrinkled face, and was immediately drawn to her sparkling eyes.

Savitri, who had been sitting among the women, approached them now. Smiling widely, she hugged and kissed him. Avinash was introduced to so many new people that he soon lost track of their names, their faces and his relationship with them. Most of the men were dressed in the traditional white clothes worn in the villages while the women wore colourful saris. Some of the men were already stinking of liquor. As the temperature continued to soar, some impatient relatives began to ask the bride's father to start the wedding ceremony.

About half an hour later, a young man dressed in ceremonial finery arrived on a bicycle. He went straight to the bride's father and whispered something to him. Immediately, the bride's father appeared visibly upset. To the inquisitive people around him, he said, 'The person who was supposed to conduct the wedding ceremony won't be able to come.' At this pronouncement, more people gathered around him, murmuring with concern.

One of the men showed Avinash the wedding card and then pointed at his wristwatch. 'Look, it's nearly 1 p.m., and the guests are all hungry,' he said.

Avinash read the wedding card in the man's hand and saw that the wedding had been scheduled for 11.30 a.m. He also noticed something peculiar—every male name on the card had the word 'ayushman' written before it, while every female name had the word 'ayushmati'. He was curious about the nomenclature and decided to ask his father about it later.

The bride's father called Dagadoo, and they huddled together, away from the crowd, whispering and gesticulating. Minutes later, Dagadoo walked up to the dais inside the pandal and called for the crowd's attention. He then announced that he would be conducting the wedding ceremony.

The band stopped playing, and the bride and the groom, both wearing white, came out before the gathering. They stood on either side of a table on which idols of Buddha and Babasaheb had been placed. Godavari pointed to the bride and whispered in Avinash's ear, 'She's my cousin's daughter.'

Dagadoo instructed the bride and the groom to light candles and offer flowers to the idols. Then he recited the Buddhist Trisharan-Panchsheel prayer, followed by the 'Astha Gatha'. The couple garlanded each other, formalizing the marriage, and people showered them with flower petals. The band began to play again, prompting a few young men and a handful of boys to break into a jig. With the ceremony now over, some people rushed to hand their gifts—mainly utensils and other household items—to the newly-wed couple, while others sat on the ground for lunch. The meal was made up of sweet lapshi, spicy sprouted moong and rice served on patravali dishes, which were made of leaves stitched together with thin shoots.

All this while, Avinash had been stunned as he had never seen his father conduct a wedding ceremony before. 'You conduct wedding ceremonies as well?' he asked when Dagadoo came out of the pandal.

Dagadoo smiled. 'The boudhacharya couldn't come, so someone else had to do it.'

'Boudhacharya? Who is that?'

'Boudhacharya are common people like us who can recite Buddhist principles. They are not monks; they don't earn their livelihood by performing rituals, and are, instead, expected to do it as a free social service.'

'But you are neither a monk nor a boudhacharya.'

'That's true, but in such a situation, anyone can fill in.'

Avinash was amused. 'The ceremony was so short, wasn't it? Everything was over within minutes!'

'In Buddhism, there are no lengthy or meticulous rituals that must be performed by priests from a particular caste at a predetermined auspicious moment. In our community, anyone can solemnize a wedding if required.'

Avinash found that interesting. 'But the ceremony was delayed by almost two hours. That was a little unpleasant,' he said.

'Yes, while it's a good thing that we've given up performing rituals at a precise muhurat or auspicious moment, the problem is that we've ignored the importance of time,' Dagadoo said. 'Most of our ceremonies are never conducted on time, making us a laughing stock in the eyes of other communities. It's a peculiarity we've failed to address.'

Suddenly, Avinash remembered the invitation card. 'I read the wedding card, which referred to people as "ayushman" or "ayushmati". What does that mean?' he asked.

Dagadoo smiled. 'As a collective effort to cleanse the Marathi language of its religious, caste and gender biases, we've formulated alternate words,' he explained. 'A man is called "ayushman", which means one who has life or one who is alive, instead of the traditional "shri". Similarly, a woman is called "ayushmati", meaning one who has life, irrespective of her marital status. Otherwise, a married woman is traditionally addressed as "saubhagyawati" or "bhagyawaan", which means one who is lucky enough to have a husband.'

'But are these new words being used widely?'

'They are used within our community, but they are yet to be widely accepted by others. We have, however, made a beginning.

'Oh, really?'

'Yes. There are other alternate words that we use as well,' Dagadoo said. 'Like "smriti-shesh" for the dead, which means one who remains only in memory, instead of "swargawasi", which means one who resides in heaven. We also use "rashtra adyaksh", meaning head of the nation, instead of "rashtrapati", which traditionally means president, to eliminate "pati", meaning husband or master, from the word.'

Avinash was curious. 'But why do we need to do this?' he asked.

'Because we don't believe in the concepts of god, heaven, hell or male dominance,' Dagadoo explained. 'Buddhism doesn't believe in any supernatural beings or miracles or paradise, but in making this world a better place for all living beings through the principles of equality, liberty, compassion and non-violence—much like the principles included in the Indian Constitution.'

Avinash found these ideas exciting. It was like being a part of a movement that was still alive.

Dagadoo and his family returned from the wedding and stayed overnight at Pandu's house. The next day, they returned to the city.

CHAPTER 4

Back at school the next day, Avinash sensed that something had changed after his visit to the village. The school—with its building, classrooms, teachers, staff and students—was the same, but deep within him a metamorphosis was beginning to take place. He began to look at the school with a different perspective, realizing that he was as much a student as anyone else, albeit with a different background, and that he had to make the most of it.

During the first period, a peon came into the class with a note. The teacher read it and looked at Avinash. 'The principal has called you to his office immediately,' she said.

Avinash felt his stomach churn because he knew his school fees was overdue. Mentally preparing himself for a reprimand, he walked slowly behind the peon to the principal's cabin, his heart pounding rapidly. He knocked on the door, pushed it open a bit with a trembling hand and asked, 'May I come in, sir?'

'Yes, come in,' the principal replied from within.

As he opened the door wider, he saw Panvelkar sitting inside with his back to the door. This eased his tension a little. The principal was also smiling broadly—he didn't seem to be angry. Avinash relaxed a bit and looked around the room.

He had visited the office with his father years ago, and nothing had changed since then. The portraits on the wall, the bookshelf with all the files, the cupboard, the trophies, the huge wooden table with the plastic globe on it, the chairs—everything was in the same position.

'Congratulations, Avinash! You've won a prize in the inter-school painting competition!' the principal exclaimed.

The news was a surprise, a whiff of fresh air. Panvelkar got up and patted him on the back. Congratulations!' he said. 'We'll attend the prize distribution ceremony next week.'

Avinash thanked them and left the cabin beaming. Back in the classroom, when Prasad asked him why he had been summoned, he broke the news to him.

'Wow!' Prasad exclaimed and raised his hand to draw the teacher's attention. When she looked at him, he told her about Avinash winning the prize.

'That's good news,' the teacher said. 'Congratulations, Avinash!' He stood up and the entire class applauded him.

Soon, the news of Avinash winning the prize was put up on the noticeboard in the main entrance lobby of the school building. As word spread, he became a celebrity of sorts. Students he didn't know turned to look at him or point him out to others. But the bigger surprise was to come a week later.

At a ceremony held in the playground of the school where the competition had taken place, all the prizewinners were felicitated. A box wrapped in glittering paper was gifted to each one of them. When his name was announced, Avinash climbed up the dais and bowed to all the students and teachers from several schools assembled there. After collecting his prize, he went up to the microphone and said, 'Thank you! Jai Bhim!' before descending from the podium.

After the programme was over, he was surrounded by his classmates. 'What did you say on the dais?' Prasad asked.

'Jai Bhim,' Avinash replied.

'Bhim?'

'Bhimrao Ambedkar.'

There was a pause and then Atharva said, 'Oh! I know—the god of the slum dwellers.'

'I live in a slum, yes, but not out of choice,' Avinash said curtly. 'And he is not our god, but our liberator.'

Atharva shrugged and looked at the prize. 'What's inside the box?' he asked.

'I don't know,' Avinash said. 'I'll open it at home.'

'No, no,' Prasad protested. 'Open it here so all of us can see what you've won.'

After much hesitation, Avinash opened the box and jumped with joy because inside was a Giraffe brand mathematical instruments box, a dozen bottles of watercolour paint, some brushes, pencils, erasers, sharpeners and a drawing book.

'Great! Now you also have a Giraffe compass box,' Prasad said, patting his back.

Atharva chuckled. 'What's the big deal? We already have these things,' he said, shaking his head. 'I thought you might have gotten something that we don't have.'

'Boys, you must congratulate Avinash for making the school proud,' Panvelkar intervened. He had been standing nearby and listening to the boys talk. 'Don't forget that while you may already have these things, they were given to you by your parents, but Avinash has earned them through his talent.'

The boys congratulated him, some with sullen faces. Atharva offered Avinash a limp handshake, muttering, 'My parents will curse me for not getting any prize.'

'Do you remember the cat which had crossed our path on the day of the competition?' Avinash asked.

'Yes,' Atharva said. 'It was a bad omen.'

'For you, not for me. You believe in superstitions, but I don't. The same cat had also crossed my path, but I've won a prize.'

Atharva narrowed his eyes, trying to think of an answer but unable to find one. In the meanwhile, Avinash put the box in his schoolbag and headed home, brimming with joy.

When he told his parents about his achievement, their faces lit up. Godavari held him close and ruffled his hair. Dagadoo smiled, his eyes glittering.

Avinash opened the box to show them its contents. Godavari's eyes welled up at the sight of the compass box. 'This is what you've wanted for a long time, isn't it?' she asked.

'Yes,' Avinash said, waving the box as if it were a trophy.

She folded her hands, closed her eyes and muttered, 'This is God's blessing.'

'He got this because of his talent and the opportunity to display it,' Dagadoo said. 'Let him build his confidence on his own merit instead of looking out for external reasons.'

Godavari looked at Avinash who was deeply engrossed in exploring his newfound treasure. Then she turned to Dagadoo and whispered, 'But he needs to believe in some supernatural being, otherwise he might become uncontrollable. He needs to fear something very powerful so that he behaves properly and also has the confidence to face difficult situations.'

Dagadoo laughed. 'Don't worry. Beliefs do have the potential to aid morality and provide strength in adverse situations. But they can also lead to blind faith, intolerance and fanaticism. An atheist is not necessarily a monster if he's ethical,' he said. 'And instead of fearing an invisible entity, he can fear the Constitution, which will protect him if he's in the right and also punish him if he goes wrong.'

Science was a fascinating subject and Avinash liked it because it helped him understand the world better. Also, his marks in the subject were excellent. The science teacher, Krishnakant Chaturvedi, was an expert and could blurt out formulae, conduct experiments and balance chemical equations in the blink of an eye. He always had the required information on his fingertips.

So, when he announced the formation of a science club at school, Avinash promptly volunteered to join it. The club was to have a separate space for science buffs to interact, conduct experiments and read books in. Chaturvedi selected him, along with

Atharva, and instructed them to prepare diagrams on large sheets of paper to display on the walls of the science room. For a week after that, Avinash and Atharva, along with four other students, stayed back after school to prepare the diagrams.

A couple of days before the inauguration of the club, during the science period, Chaturvedi asked those joining the club to raise their hands. About ten students, including Avinash, did. Chaturvedi counted them and glanced down at the list of names in his hand. Then he looked at Avinash.

'You're the only one who has not paid the membership fee yet,' he said.

Avinash stood up. He had brought up the matter with his parents. Godavari had bluntly refused, asking him not to join the club at all, while Dagadoo had asked him to wait for a couple of days.

'I will pay, sir,' Avinash said, avoiding his teacher's gaze. The entire classroom was looking at him, making him wish he had the power to vanish into thin air. He hung his head and waited. The silence in the classroom was punctuated by the sound of Chaturvedi's footsteps as he walked towards him.

'When are you going to pay?' Chaturvedi shouted.

Avinash lifted his head, but he didn't have an answer.

'When you are asked to do something, you must do it!' Chaturvedi shouted again. 'But you don't because you are irresponsible.'

There was a moment of pin-drop silence, and then, before Avinash could say something, Chaturvedi slapped him. The sound cracked open the silence in the classroom like a streak of lightning, and Avinash felt as if his cheek was on fire.

'Sit down,' Chaturvedi shouted again and walked back towards the blackboard. 'Only those who've paid the membership fee will be permitted to attend the inaugural programme and enter the club room,' he declared. Then he collected himself and returned to the textbook.

Avinash sat down quietly, looking at the textbook open in front of him. He could hear Chaturvedi's voice in the background but could not grasp what was being taught. He had lost the nerve to look at his teacher and wanted to run home. A strong urge to look out of the window gripped him, but he knew it was risky. If Chaturvedi noticed him staring outside, there was the strongest possibility of him receiving another slap, or something even worse—like being driven out of the class. He wished the bell would ring immediately and end the science period. When it finally did, he heaved a sigh of relief.

'He's so short-tempered! There was no need to slap you!' Prasad exclaimed after the teacher left the room. 'And he should've at least allowed you to attend the inauguration because you made the diagrams for the walls.'

Avinash forced a smile. 'It's not a problem,' he said. 'But tell me, why didn't you join the science club?'

Prasad shook his head. 'I'm not interested,' he said. 'What will I gain from it? Ultimately, I have to handle my father's business. The only thing that matters is making money. My schooling is just for the sake of being able to say that I'm educated.'

'But don't you want to do something of your own? Something which will bring out your talents, help you develop a distinct identity?'

'No need,' Prasad giggled. 'Our family has traditionally been in business, and we are proud of it. My life is set. Why should I go into uncharted territory?' he asked. 'The only thing expected from me is to find newer methods to make more money.'

Avinash smiled. 'I have no such family tradition—I have to start from scratch.'

'You are doomed then.'

Avinash thought for a while. 'Not exactly. In fact, I'm free to do whatever I like, in unknown territories. There's no family pressure over me,' he said.

'But it will be very difficult.'

'Yes, it may be,' Avinash said. 'But my father says difficulties are opportunities to prove our worth.'

Prasad shrugged. 'Best of luck,' he said.

As he made his way home in the evening, Avinash wanted to tell his parents about what had happened in Chaturvedi's class. But when he reached home, he changed his mind. His parents were in a good mood, and he didn't want to cause them any anguish.

A few days later, the science club was inaugurated as scheduled, with the teachers and the student members in attendance. Avinash stayed away, but when he went to school the next day, he was surrounded by some of his classmates who were in the club.

'We missed you,' Atharva said. 'We saw your diagrams prominently displayed on the walls.'

Avinash just smiled in response.

For a few days after that, he went on a painting spree at home. He pasted his artwork on the tin-sheet walls to cover up the holes, and the ambience of his home improved a bit.

For several years, Avinash continued to focus on his studies despite being subjected to many demoralizing incidents. He cleared the elementary and intermediate grade drawing examinations conducted by the state government. His parents were happy and Dagadoo got the certificates framed in order to display them in the house. But one thing always simmered at the back of Avinash's mind—he needed to contribute to the family's income. There was little that he could do as a student who had to attend school for the whole day. Nevertheless, he wanted to do something.

One day, while descending the hill, Avinash saw Raja coming out of Zende's den with a tumbler full of liquor for his father. After exchanging pleasantries, he told Raja that he was looking for work.

'You can join me if you are ready to paint walls,' Raja said. 'I'm assisting a painter for a few days.'

'But I can't miss school.'

'That's not a problem; he does the work at night.'

Avinash's parents initially refused to give him permission to go with Raja, but he insisted and, ultimately, they relented. That night, Avinash accompanied Raja to a site outside the local train station where a tall, bearded man wearing a kurta-pyjama and sporting long hair was sitting on the pavement and smoking a beedi. A couple of buckets and some painting materials were lying next to him. Raja introduced Avinash to the painter, Gopal.

Gopal looked at Avinash from head to toe and smiled. 'Ready to work late at night?'

'Yes,' Avinash replied.

After a brief conversation, the work began. The wall was first cleared of dirt and handbills. Gopal asked the boys to apply a coat of white paint on the wall with broad brushes. Avinash found it exciting at first, but after a while his arm began to ache, and the work became monotonous.

As the hours crawled by, the traffic on the road lessened and with it, the noise and smoke. Shops closed down, reducing the amount of light along the road. Hawkers wound up for the day, revealing the actual width of the road, which otherwise remained hidden during the day due to their encroachment. Whenever a local train arrived, people hurried out of the station and disappeared into the surrounding lanes within a minute or two.

As midnight approached, Avinash began to feel drowsy. An hour later, they stopped work. Gopal took away the painting material and left while Avinash and Raja headed home. The roads were deserted except for late-night workers hurrying home. A few stray dogs were barking at an alcoholic staggering on the pavement. The man was mumbling angrily and making gestures with his hands at someone only he could see. When Avinash reached home, his father had already left for his night duty, but his mother was still awake.

'How was the work?' she asked. 'If it's too exhausting, don't do it.'

He shook his head. 'No, it's all right,' he said, washing his hands and face. After drinking a glass of water, he lay down and closed his eyes. When he opened them again after what seemed like a moment, it was already morning and Godavari was waking him up for school. The entire cycle continued for about a week before the stretch of boundary wall they had been whitewashing dried up and Gopal started painting huge letters on it. Avinash watched Gopal work with awe. The man handled the curvature of large alphabets and the angle of the shaded areas around them in such a manner that it gave the alphabets a three-dimensional look. He had total control over his brush, moving with speed and accuracy even while creating intricate lines—just like Panvelkar.

Once the outline of the public service message about keeping the city clean was complete, Gopal asked the boys to fill in the colour. He observed them for a while and then approached Avinash. 'You have good control over your hand.'

Avinash smiled. 'I don't know about that,' he said, 'but I like to paint.'

Gopal patted him. When Raja messed up the curve of a letter by overshooting the outline, Gopal got annoyed as he had to repair it. 'Raja, let Avinash handle the boundaries of the curves and the corners,' he said, and Raja nodded.

For Avinash, this part of the work was fun, and he enjoyed it so much that he felt no fatigue in remaining awake till the wee hours. A couple of nights later, they were done with the painting, and Gopal walked the stretch of the wall, examining his artwork and smoking a bidi. 'Good job, boys,' he said, the words mingling with the bidi smoke coming out of his mouth. Then he crossed the road and walked over to the footpath on the opposite side to look at the wall from a distance.

After a while, he sucked at the bidi stub repeatedly and tossed it into the gutter. Then, he clapped his hands. 'All right, boys, let's celebrate,' he said with a smile.

'Celebrate?' Avinash asked, looking around. As usual, most of the shops had closed for the day by then and they could hear the sound of shutters being drawn.

'Come with me,' Gopal said. They collected the painting material and walked for some distance before turning into a lane lined with closed shops on both sides. At a distance, some people could be seen standing near a narrow passage between two shops. A naked electric bulb hung between the shops. At the entrance to the passage, a man was standing behind a folding table with a tray of boiled eggs and a small plastic container with salt and pepper kept on it.

'Wait here,' Gopal told the boys as he vanished into the lane. The smell of liquor hung in the air, and after some time, Gopal emerged from the lane with a broad smile on his face. He had bought boiled eggs for all of them. They ate the eggs quickly, and, on their way back, they stopped at the railway station to drink water.

'When will we get paid?' Raja asked, wiping his mouth with the back of his hand.

Gopal lit a bidi, took a long drag and let the smoke waft out of his nostrils. 'I don't know,' he said. 'But don't worry—I'll come to your house as soon as I get paid.'

That night, Avinash could not sleep for hours after returning home. He kept thinking about what else he could do, apart from painting walls, to earn some money.

Several weeks later, Gopal appeared at Avinash's home when he was doing his homework. Godavari was cooking and Dagadoo was away on duty.

'Today is your lucky day,' Gopal said, pulling out some notes from his pocket. 'This is your payment for painting the wall.'

'Give the money to my mother,' Avinash said. Godavari washed her hands, wiped them with the pallu of her sari and accepted the money with a smile on her face.

'I'll make some tea for you,' she said, folding the notes and putting them behind a photo frame.

'No, sister. I'm in a hurry,' Gopal said.

'Do you have any work available now?' Avinash asked.

Gopal shook his head. 'Not at the moment, but I'll let you know when I do,' he said as he descended the stairs.

And he did, a few months later. There was another wall to be painted at a new location, and both Avinash and Raja were glad to assist him.

Avinash continued to paint well at school. Panvelkar was happy with his progress and displayed some of his paintings, along with those of others, on the walls of the art classroom. Avinash was filled with pride every time he saw his paintings adoring the walls of the classroom. While painting landscapes, however, he longed to visit the village again and be closer to nature—to see it, smell it, hear it and feel it.

One day, Godavari told him that Pandu had invited them and Soma's family to visit the annual fair in a village. Dagadoo said he had better things to do, but Avinash thought it was a windfall.

A couple of days later, Avinash and Godavari left for the village. When they reached, they found that Savitri was already there. Soma and his family joined them soon. Early the next day, they began their journey. As the sky behind the hills on the horizon lit up gently, the darkness began to wither away. The silhouettes of the trees along the track lightened, revealing the colours of the leaves and the flowers. Insects and birds flew around, buzzing and chirping as they went about their morning errands. A fresh day in the countryside, in all its splendid colours, sounds and aromas, had dawned.

Pandu was humming a folksong as he drove the bullock cart to the shrine. Avinash, Godavari, Soma and several others were seated behind him, while Savitri and some more women were following them in another bullock cart. The women were talking about mundane matters, while Avinash was observing the natural world waking up. When Pandu cracked the whip, the bullocks broke into a trot, the tinkling of the bells around their necks growing louder. But after a while, they lost momentum. Annoyed with their leisurely pace, Pandu abused them loudly and reached out to twist their tails, making them run.

A couple of hours later, they turned onto a patchy road, making the journey bumpier than before. The sun had now risen, and the temperature was gradually increasing.

An hour later, they spotted a flag on the spire of a huge temple a little ahead. The sound of clanging bells and music played by rustic sambal bands filled the air. There were suddenly many more bullock carts on the road to the shrine. Besides, jeeps and small trucks roared past intermittently, raising clouds of dust.

As they got closer, they saw that tents had been pitched along both sides of the road. Flowers, garlands, prayer material, charms, pendants, foodstuff, toys, idols and photographs of deities were on sale. There were also goats tied outside some of the tents. Nearby, men stood with their bullocks around a watering hole. A short distance away from this watering hole, there were people drawing water from a well. Pandu pulled the reins of his bullock cart and halted under a tree for some respite from the heat. The other bullock cart followed suit. The occupants of both the carts jumped down, and the bullocks were released from the yokes. They were first taken to the watering hole, and then brought back to be tied under the tree. From the several bundles of grass tied underneath the carts, a few were pulled out and strewn in front of the oxen. The women spread a couple of mats under the tree and sat down, drinking water from the pots they had brought along. Avinash and Khandoo started chatting, while Soma and Pandu left with a couple of empty pots to fetch more water.

After the men came back with the water, the women served the food they had cooked in the early hours of the morning. Once everyone had eaten, Pandu and Soma went towards the tents, leaving the women and children relaxing under the tree. They returned after some time, carrying some prayer material and a brown goat.

'It's so cute!' Avinash exclaimed, running his hand over the goat's back.

Pandu laughed. 'Yes, and it'll taste very good too,' he said. Avinash got a strong whiff of liquor.

Soma laughed as well. 'Yes! After a long time, we'll have the privilege of eating all the organs of a goat.' He too, was clearly drunk.

'What? Are you going to eat it?'

The men laughed in unison, with the women joining in.

'What are we here for then?' Savitri asked.

Avinash was taken aback. 'I thought it was just a fun fair.'

'Yes, it is fun,' Pandu said with a broad smile. 'Fun and a feast.'

'Why didn't you tell me about this?' Avinash asked his mother.

She got up and approached him with a sheepish smile. 'Because you might not have come if I did.'

'It's good that you did not tell him,' Savitri said. 'He's becoming like his father, who has no respect for our traditions.'

'You are sacrificing an animal!'

'Nothing wrong with that,' Savitri countered. 'When you were born, I sacrificed five goats.'

'You killed five goats?' Avinash was stunned. 'Really? How could you do it?' he asked.

'I had prayed to the deity and promised that if your mother bore a child, I would sacrifice five goats,' she said with pride. 'And my wish was granted.'

'What has a goat's life got to do with these things?' Avinash asked. 'Do you really think the deity fulfils the wishes of any person who praises him and appeases him by killing animals?'

Suddenly, almost everyone started speaking all at once to defend their beliefs and customs. Avinash couldn't understand anything in the din. So, he walked away and sat on the lowered yoke of a bullock cart.

After a while, the women placed three stones in a rough circle on the ground and made a fire in the centre using cow dung cakes and wood. A utensil filled with water was then put over the fire. Then they started slicing onions, garlic and chillies.

Gradually, the noise of slogans, bells, music and the bleating of goats around them grew louder. Devotees, their faces smeared with gulal, were dancing as if in a trance as they thronged towards the temple.

Avinash saw Pandu discussing something with a huge, bearded man wearing a skull cap and dressed in a red shirt and a green-and-black chequered lungi. He was also carrying a leather bag. After a few minutes, Pandu and the others applied some vermillion on the goat's forehead and garlanded it while the bearded man took out a long, glistening knife and a chopper from his bag. The goat was then pinned to the ground by Pandu, Soma, Khandoo and another man. The bearded man bent down, pressed the goat's head against the ground and then looked at Pandu.

'Shall I?' he asked.

Pandu nodded and hailed the deity, with all the others joining him in the chant. The butcher stretched the neck of the goat with his left hand and swiftly slit its throat with the knife in his right hand. A jet of blood gushed out, and Savitri rushed forward with an aluminium plate to collect it—they would offer it to the deity later. The goat kicked and strained for its life as the men applied their full force to prevent it from moving. Soon, it became limp and lay motionless, and the men loudly hailed the deity again. Pandu took the blood Savitri had collected in the aluminium plate and left for the shrine.

The butcher and his assistant now demonstrated their skills with the chopper and the knife, working mechanically with the dead goat. First, its head was chopped off, then the skin was peeled, rolled into a ball of brown fur and kept aside, and lastly, the stomach was ripped open to pull out all the organs.

The bearded man then chopped up the goat's bones into smaller pieces. The decapitated head lay nearby, staring at them with its glassy eyes wide open. Once done with the bones, the butcher turned to the goat's skull. With a strong blow of his chopper, he first broke it and then removed the goat's brain and tongue, gouging out the eyes before breaking the face into pieces. Flies buzzed around the carcass while a few stray dogs waited patiently for the bits of flesh that were being thrown at them intermittently.

Gripped with nausea, Avinash quickly walked away from the spot. As he roamed around the fair, however, he saw many similar sights. In some places, he saw groups of devotees sitting in circles and enjoying a feast, gnawing the flesh off the bones served to them. Once done, they would throw the bones to the dogs milling around them. Avinash felt as if he was walking through a primitive world of hunters who had nothing else to eat and were, therefore, compelled to kill animals for food.

When he returned after about an hour, he found Godavari's temper running high. 'Where have you been?' she shouted. 'Don't go anywhere now. Stay here.'

Avinash did not argue. He stood a little distance away from the group, watching them helplessly. The mutton curry was cooking in a vessel over the fire, while the women were busy making bajra rotis. A little later, once the deity of the temple had been offered the meat, the feast began. Everyone sat in a circle to eat. Avinash was dragged in by his mother and made to join them. 'Give him the bigger pieces,' Savitri told Godavari. 'He's the light of your family.'

When a dish full of large pieces of mutton was placed in front of Avinash, he tried to guess which parts of the goat's body they had belonged to only hours ago.

'I don't want it,' he said. 'I can't eat this.'

Inevitably, his response invited the ire of all those around him. Even in their inebriated state, Pandu and Soma tried to convince him to eat, but he remained steadfast in his refusal.

'What's wrong with him?' Savitri asked Godavari. 'He eats meat at home, doesn't he?'

'He does—I don't know why he's behaving like this.'

'You shouldn't have allowed him to see the goat being butchered,' Savitri said. 'Avinash, remember that our ancestors used to dispose of dead cattle. They used to rip open dead bulls and cows, skin them and then eat their meat. Why are you shocked by this?'

Avinash was in no mood to argue. Ultimately, he ate a little rice with some sugar sprinkled on it, while the others ate to their heart's content.

On the journey back, he remained silent as images of the slaughter haunted him. He recalled the days he had relished eating meat without a thought about the cruelty behind it. He felt a deep sense of remorse. He knew that a food chain existed in nature and that animals killed animals for food. But human beings had other choices available to them most of the times.

By the time they reached Pandu's house, everyone was tired. There was another round of discussion, during which everyone criticized Avinash for being so weak-hearted. After staying overnight at Pandu's house, Avinash and Godavari returned to the city the following day.

When they reached home, Dagadoo was away on duty. It was only in the evening, when Avinash was busy with his homework and Godavari was cooking, that they heard footsteps at the door—Dagadoo had returned home from work.

'How was the fair?' he inquired.

'Horrible,' Avinash replied.

'Why?' Dagadoo asked, and all at once, Avinash blurted out the entire episode. Dagadoo shook his head in despair. 'We gave up these rituals after converting to Buddhism,' he said. He paused for a moment and then asked, 'But why didn't you join the feast?'

'I couldn't, not after watching the goat being murdered.'

'There's nothing wrong with eating animal flesh, son.'

'I don't understand this. On one hand, we talk about compassion towards all living beings, and on the other, we kill animals and eat them.'

'We don't kill animals,' Godavari interjected. 'The butchers do.'

Avinash shook his head. 'But the butchers kill the animals because people pay them to do so.'

'See, the majority of humans eat non-vegetarian food and still have compassion for animals,' Dagadoo said. 'Our ancestors were meat eaters.'

'Yes, the ancestors of all humans were flesh eaters—they had no other choice,' Avinash said.

'What would you do if you were marooned on an island or a desert, or let's just say a place where there is nothing to eat except the flesh of animals and birds?' Godavari asked.

Avinash thought for a while. 'In such a situation, I guess there would be no choice but to eat flesh,' he said. 'But there is a difference between eating flesh for survival and relishing it out of choice.'

His parents looked at each other. 'But the goat that was sacrificed for the deity, it was a religious ritual,' Godavari said. 'It has been our tradition.'

'If this is a tradition, then it's a horrible and outdated one,' Avinash said. 'I only saw a goat being killed and human beings feasting on it, all in the name of a deity. And some of the people were also drunk.'

'Our forefathers used to eat beef after skinning dead cattle,' Dagadoo said. 'Now, we've given up eating beef because we've stopped working as unpaid village servants. It was one of the things that had kept us oppressed in the village with its system of caste discrimination. Now, we are free citizens.'

Avinash nodded. 'In that case, let's make some humane choices that are aligned with the principles of non-violence, compassion and morality that we Buddhists always talk about,' he said, sitting on the threshold of the house and watching a plane fly overhead. 'How can the same people who claim that they are civilized and compassionate towards animals, relish mutton out of choice?'

'Err … theoretically, you're right. But practically, it's impossible to expect people to entirely give up animal meat because it's very nutritious and they are used to it.'

'But there are a lot of people who are vegetarians, and they are all healthy.'

'Yes, but they derive nutrition from dairy products, which also come from animals.'

Avinash fell silent for a moment. Then, he asked, 'Technically, dairy products come from animals, but aren't they a better option than meat, which requires killing animals? There are several categories of vegetarians. Some eat dairy products and some also eat eggs but not flesh. Similarly, some non-vegetarians don't eat beef, and some don't eat pigs.'

'Yes, food habits are mostly inherited,' Dagadoo said. 'But you have to draw a line somewhere. If you go to the extremes, then you can't even eat vegetables as they are also considered living things.'

'Perhaps so, but I find it strange that despite having several options, people eat flesh out of choice and then talk about compassion and non-violence.'

There was a long silence and the three of them looked at each other.

'But I think you should continue eating non-vegetarian food,' Dagadoo said finally.

Avinash looked at his father with a frown on his face.

'And you've always enjoyed mutton,' Godavari pointed out.

'Yes, I did, but that was before I realized there was so much cruelty behind it,' Avinash said. 'There is a food chain in nature, and we're at the top of it because of our intelligence. And *this* is what we do?'

'Oh God, please forgive him!' Godavari exclaimed.

'Why do you forget that nutrition is also a vital factor in this decision?' Dagadoo asked.

'You are right, but I think at least those who go on about compassion should not kill animals for food if there are other options that are easily available. I can't eat meat anymore,' Avinash said. 'I have a choice, so let me exercise it.'

His resolve was tested a few days later when Dagadoo bought home mutton. Avinash refused to eat it, compelling Godavari to cook some vegetables for him.

CHAPTER 5

Months later, the decision of the state government to provide some basic amenities in slums set in motion an unprecedented change in the residents' quality of life.

'The government is going to regularize slums and give us toilets, electricity and more water taps in the locality,' Dagadoo broke the news to his family.

'Really?' Godavari asked in disbelief.

'Yes. Now all those dark nights will be a thing of the past,' Dagadoo said, smiling. Then, turning to Avinash, he said, 'You can also study during the night now.'

'It'll be great for all of us,' Avinash said.

'A census will be conducted and each hut will be issued an identity card containing details about the area and the name of the resident,' Dagadoo added. 'We won't be treated as encroachers on government land anymore.'

The slum rehabilitation activity came as a blessing. Women were delighted as more taps were installed in the slum to ease their water woes. There was no longer any need for them to stay awake past midnight, waiting for the pressure to build up in the few taps in the slum after the city below had had its fill. There was a new water tank and pumps to bring water to the slum. The most glaring difference, however, came with the provision of electricity. At night, the slum now stopped resembling an ancient habitat, with tiny lamps flickering all over the slope of the hill, overlooking the splendour of the modern city spread out below. With electricity, the hill sparkled as lights came on in the irregular rows of huts that dotted its slope. Some residents even decorated their houses with tiny bulbs that glittered and changed colours at regular intervals.

Avinash and his parents' faces lit up when they switched on an electric bulb in their house for the first time. After the initial euphoria subsided, Avinash looked around the house and saw that it certainly looked different. The light had enhanced visibility in the house, but in the process, it had also exposed all the crevices and things previously hidden by the darkness. The tin-sheet walls were uneven, shabby and had many more holes than he'd expected. The rafters of the roof were worn out and broken in several places. There was dust on the pictures of Babasaheb and Buddha as well as on Avinash's certificates that were all framed and displayed in a row.

That year, Ambedkar Jayanti, the birth anniversary of Babasaheb, was brighter and more colourful than ever before. A loudspeaker in Buddha Vihar, the local shrine that housed idols of Buddha and Babasaheb, had been blaring songs about them the whole day, and it could be heard throughout Bhimnagar. But the highlight of the celebration, apart from the Panchsheel flags that were made of five strips of different colours, was the display of hundreds of tiny bulbs glittering in different colours on both sides of the road at the bottom of the hill.

Godavari had cooked puranpoli, a Marathi delicacy, for the occasion. Dagadoo had garlanded the picture of Babasaheb in the house and recited the Panchsheel. When the puranpoli was served to him, Avinash took a bite and enjoyed it thoroughly.

Dagadoo looked at him and smiled. 'Do you like it?' he asked.

Avinash nodded.

'Me too. I like it so much that once I was beaten up—'

'Not now!' Godavari interrupted her husband. 'Finish your meal first.'

Avinash's curiosity was piqued, and after the meal, he asked his father to narrate the incident.

Dagadoo opened a tin in which he kept betel nuts and leaves and prepared a paan. 'When I was a young boy, I was badly beaten up because I wanted to eat a puranpoli,' he said.

'*Beaten up?*' Avinash asked. 'By whom?'

Dagadoo stared blankly into space for a few seconds, and then he went down memory lane to narrate the incident. 'It was a cold winter night in the village. My uncle Kondiba and I were patrolling the village boundary as part of our traditional duty. Both of us had covered ourselves in coarse Ghongdi blankets and were carrying lanterns and sticks.

'The night passed without incident, and the cloak of darkness vaporized gradually at dawn, with the roosters in the village and the birds heralding a new day. There was mist all around us, and dew on the vegetation. The bells rang in the temple, indicating that the village had woken up.

'We folded our blankets and walked towards the village. It was time for our daily round of collecting leftover food before returning home. We went from door to door, maintaining a safe distance from the houses and the people.

'As usual, my uncle stopped outside every house and shouted, "Johar, mai baap, johar." He would wait for a minute for the people inside to come out and give him leftover food, if they had any, and then move ahead. We got no response from the first couple of houses, but then we saw a lady coming out of a house, carrying some leftover food. She put the food on the ground just beyond the door and quickly went inside, throwing a cursory glance at us. My uncle collected the food in a cloth bag and moved to the next house.

'Soon, we came to a multi-storeyed house built with black stones. Several oxen and cows were visible in a shed in the courtyard, and a couple of horses were tied in a stable adjacent to the shed. There were two bullock carts and several agricultural implements lying in one corner of the courtyard.

'"Johar!" my uncle called out loudly to make his presence known. A huge man dressed in a white dhoti and kurta, with a thick twirled-up moustache and a fat gold chain around his neck, was sitting on a swing in the veranda of the house. He turned and looked through us, and then went inside the house with a contemptuous expression on his face. A plump lady in a bright-red sari, bedecked in jewellery and sporting a big red bindi on her forehead, appeared a few seconds later with some leftovers and put them outside the gate. My uncle collected the food and moved ahead. But I lingered—the villagers had celebrated a festival the previous day and I was hoping to eat some of that food.

'The lady looked at me and narrowed her eyes. I said johar, again.

'"What?" she snapped.

'"Is there any leftover puranpoli from yesterday's festival?" I asked.

'She was shocked. "Oh my God! You want puranpoli?" she asked.

'I nodded.

'"Wait," she said and went inside the house. Within a few seconds, she came out with the huge man and pointed at me. The man clenched his teeth and picked up a stick lying nearby.

'"You want puranpoli, eh?" he shouted, and the next instant, he started hitting me with the stick, hurling expletives. My uncle, who was in front of the neighbouring house, rushed back on hearing the commotion. He apologized to the man and slapped me hard before pulling me away. The man continued to curse us till we were out of his sight …' Dagadoo paused after narrating the incident.

Avinash was shaken by the story. 'But why were you so desperate? Did you not get to eat puranpoli at home?' he asked.

Dagadoo sighed. 'It was a luxury we couldn't afford,' he said. Then, after a pause, he smiled. 'But not anymore. Now we can eat it to our heart's content,' he said.

Avinash was stunned. He looked at the puranpolis Godavari had kept aside for dinner and recollected the lingering sweetness of the festive delicacy. 'I don't think I can enjoy puranpolis again,' he said. 'They will always remind me of this incident.'

'What?' his parents exclaimed in unison.

'Are you crazy?' Dagadoo asked. 'That was in our past. Forget it and move on.'

Avinash shook his head silently.

'Why do you share such things with him?' Godavari shouted at her husband. 'He always takes them to heart!'

'I just wanted him to know the truth about how our community was treated then—nothing else.'

'It was inhuman,' Avinash said. Then he paused for a minute before asking, 'And what is "johar, mai baap"?'

'Johar, mai baap,' Dagadoo muttered, staring at his hands for a few moments. 'It was a salutation a servant used when greeting his master. "Mai baap" literally means mother and father. We used it because we were treated like servants; we were at the mercy of our village masters,' Dagadoo said. 'We had to bend and touch our foreheads with our right hand, like saluting a king.'

'But now we don't say johar.'

'Yes, now we say "Jai Bhim" to salute our liberator, Bhimrao Ambedkar, and to greet people of our community and others who are Ambedkarites.'

Avinash nodded. 'But I can't forget the puranpoli incident,' he added.

'Get it out of your mind, son,' Godavari said.

But Avinash could not put the story aside. 'Did you suffer more because you were poor or because you were an untouchable?' he asked his father.

'Both. We were at the mercy of the villagers because of the "divinely-sanctioned" caste system,' Dagadoo said. 'But things have now changed.'

'Changed?' Avinash asked, suddenly remembering his visit to the village. 'What do you mean? The traditional landlord continues as the village headman even today by getting elected as the sarpanch,' he said.

Dagadoo nodded. 'Yes, some traditionally privileged communities have appropriated the democratic system,' he said. 'But there is political reservation for us in the legislative assemblies and the Parliament. It may get extended to the village panchayats in the future.'

Avinash nodded. 'But has it really changed things?' he asked after a while.

Dagadoo took a deep breath and then said, 'To some extent, yes. But sometimes, the traditionally privileged families ensure that their candidates get elected on the reserved seats in order to rule by proxy.'

'Oh! But why do the marginalized people agree to become proxies?'

Dagadoo laughed. 'You cannot liberate a slave without his consent,' he said. 'Some are motivated by loyalty to dynasties, and some by fear or greed.'

Avinash shook his head. 'Then why do we celebrate our rights?' he asked. 'This is just a make-believe world.'

Dagadoo didn't reply immediately. He was folding some newspapers and arranging them neatly in a pile. A couple of seconds passed before he finally replied, 'We are jubilant because we can now access education, choose what sort of work we want to do and live with dignity. You are living a much better life than all the previous generations of our family did.'

Avinash was not totally convinced by his father's words, but he did not argue further.

When dinner was served that day, he looked at the puranpoli on his plate. It had the usual irregularly shaped golden-brown spots on it. As he stared at them and tried to connect them, they seemed to form the rough outline of a young boy being beaten up. Avinash immediately lost his appetite. 'I can't eat this,' he said. His parents tried to persuade him, but in vain. The sweet delicacy had turned bitter.

With sustained effort, Avinash's academic scores kept improving every year and when he became one among the top three students in the class, the teacher shifted him to a front-row bench. Sitting on a front-row bench had its own advantages. The teachers were more audible, and the blackboard was closer. It was also airier as the ceiling fan was right overhead. But he was away from the window now and missed the fresh air and the privilege of looking out when bored. Also, he had to be attentive all the time and could not doodle in his rough notebook without getting caught by the teacher. Another hitch was the temperament of the scholars, who got annoyed whenever he shared his notes with the backbenchers.

Once, during a free period, when Prasad borrowed Avinash's notebook and went back to his seat, Atharva turned to him, clearly furious. 'Why do you give your notebooks to the backbenchers?' he snarled through clenched teeth.

'I'm helping a classmate and a friend,' Avinash said. 'What's wrong with that?'

'You don't understand, you fool. Don't help the backbenchers—they are brainless and rude. Just let them rot.'

Avinash was taken aback. 'I think it's our duty to help them; I've helped you too.'

Atharva stared at him for a moment. 'It's all right if you help people like me. Just don't go around helping anyone and everyone,' he said finally. 'Don't increase the competition.'

'Don't be selfish, Atharva. Knowledge should be distributed widely, not hoarded.'

'No! Knowledge is power. It must be protected and utilized carefully.'

Avinash shook his head. He saw Prasad, who was watching them, gesture to ask if anything was wrong.

'Don't tell him about our conversation,' Atharva whispered. 'He's short-tempered and gets into physical fights quickly.'

Avinash broke into laughter and waved at Prasad, indicating that everything was all right. He realized then that there was something fundamentally different between him and Atharva. It was so deep-rooted a difference that it was going to be difficult to build an unconditional solidarity.

The next day, during a free period, Atharva opened his rough notebook and pointed to a column of words, one piled over the other, that he'd scribbled in it. The word at the top was 'universe' and below it was, 'Milky Way Galaxy', followed by 'solar system', 'sun', 'earth', 'Asia', 'India', 'Maharashtra', 'Bombay' and, finally, 'Atharva'.

'Have you ever thought about your place in the universe?' Atharva asked Avinash. 'You can replace "Atharva" with "Avinash" on this page and see for yourself.'

Avinash looked at the page and smiled. 'I think this is incomplete,' he said.

'Incomplete?'

'Yes, because below your name, you should also note down your personal and family details, because they determine your privileges on earth,' Avinash said. 'If I replace your name with mine, I'll have to add a few more details about my economic status, caste and religion. It makes a lot of difference.'

Atharva narrowed his eyebrows and looked at Avinash for a while before closing his notebook. 'Why do you keep harping on these things?' he asked.

Avinash shook his head. 'Because we come from different backgrounds,' he said. 'We live in different worlds by virtue of our births.'

'So, you mean we can't be good friends?'

'No, we can be friends, provided you try to understand my situation and stop insisting that I accept everything you say as the ultimate truth.'

Atharva stared at him for a moment and shrugged.

On reaching home that evening, Avinash recounted both the conversations to his parents. Dagadoo lauded him for helping out the weaker students. Godavari, however, had some reservations. 'It's all right, but I think you should not antagonize the scholars in your class,' she said. 'They can help you improve your marks further.'

Avinash looked at her and then at his father. 'Most of the scholars are friendly with me only when they need my help.'

'You will meet a lot of people who will either be blind to your condition or they will ignore it,' Dagadoo said. 'It's their failing, not yours, so don't let it bother you. They have a different narrative.'

Avinash nodded and sat on the threshold of the house, looking at the fascinating world spinning around in the distance, with its own terms and conditions.

He recalled his visit to the village, where he had watched its vibrant life from his uncle Soma's house on the outskirts. The schism between the castes existed everywhere, but the city offered a better chance of being upwardly mobile through economic success. Though he could change his class, he could not change his caste, a fact that was rigidly enshrined in the minds of a large section of Indians.

PART TWO

The Factory

CHAPTER 6

Emergency was imposed in the country in 1975, creating a commotion in the polity, economy, media and society. A welfare programme was announced the same year, promising succour for the poor and the marginalized. However, Godavari and Dagadoo continued to toil hard to manage the growing expenditure of the family. Avinash did some temporary petty jobs, whenever available, like delivering groceries and assisting Gopal in painting walls.

He completed his schooling in the middle of the Emergency, and his parents were ecstatic. They celebrated his matriculation by distributing sweets among their neighbours. 'You are the first matriculate in our family,' Dagadoo said, patting Avinash on the back. Godavari ruffled his hair and looked at him with eyes brimming with tears.

Things seemed rosy but the family was actually faced with a dilemma about whether Avinash should find a job or join a college. He wanted to study further, but the financial situation at home was dire.

Dagadoo had gotten Avinash's matriculation certificate framed and he decided to display it alongside his other certificates. He was putting up the frame when his cousin Hari arrived at the door.

Dagadoo smiled at him. 'Come in,' he said, hammering the nail.

'What are you doing, brother?' Hari asked.

'Displaying Avinash's certificate on the wall,' Dagadoo replied. 'He has completed his schooling.'

Hari was a crane driver at the century-old Bombay harbour. He had a bulky body and was clean-shaven. Dressed in a spotless white shirt and trousers, he entered the house and slowly lowered himself to the floor. A thick gold chain dangled from his neck as he sat down.

'Well done, Avinash!' Hari said with a broad smile, looking at the row of certificates on display.

Godavari offered him a glass of water and then started pumping air into the kerosene stove to make some tea.

'So, what do you want to do now?' Hari asked Avinash.

Avinash looked at his father and then at his uncle. 'I want to study further, Hari kaka,' he said.

Hari grimaced. 'I have a better idea. Find a job and start earning. I can fix one up for you in the port. I know people who can pull some strings,' he said. Then, looking at Dagadoo, he asked, 'Have you had his caste certificate made? It will help him get a job quickly.'

'Hari, my son was in a private school and we paid his fees all these years,' he said. 'We have not applied for a caste certificate.'

Hari was amused. 'No? Not a problem. I can fix even that. I know people who can do it quickly if you are willing to pay,' he said.

There was a long, uncomfortable silence as the two cousins stared at each other.

'There's no need. Avinash was born after I converted to Buddhism, and I've listed him as a Buddhist in all his documents,' Dagadoo said. 'We've not taken advantage of caste reservation.'

'But he'll need it now,' Hari said.

Dagadoo shook his head. 'I don't want to label him as a member of the untouchable Mahar caste, especially now that we've converted to Buddhism. I don't want him to be identified with the caste and religion we left behind.'

'Are you out of your mind?' Hari shouted. 'Reservation is our birthright.'

'Yes, I know. I'm not against reservation—a lot of people need it.'

'Then why are you depriving your son?'

'Many of our people retain their identity as Hindu Mahar in their official records to claim the benefits of reservation, but they strut around as Buddhists. I'm not comfortable with it.'

'So what if you are uncomfortable? You are only ruining Avinash's future.'

'I don't want him to use victimhood as his identity; he can create his own.'

Hari shook his head in despair. 'You are insane,' he said. 'You'll regret this.'

Godavari served tea as Dagadoo glanced at Avinash and then at Hari. 'Avinash is getting used to fighting it out on his own,' he said. 'Let him do it. As such, reservation is not going to last forever. We should start training the next generation to live without it.'

Hari chuckled. 'It's useless talking to you,' he said, gulping his tea down quickly and heaving himself to his feet.

'I think we should seek his help,' Godavari said after Hari had left. 'He can find Avinash a job.'

'Hari is a shady character, and he's certainly mixed up with crooks,' Dagadoo said. 'Avinash will get a job on his own merit.'

'But I also want to go to college,' Avinash said.

There was an uneasy silence for several minutes. Then Godavari asked, 'How is that going to be possible?'

Avinash thought for a moment. 'I'll enrol in a college and take up a job as well,' he said.

And so, two weeks later, Avinash got enrolled in a college and also started looking for a job. The college was far away, requiring a long commute in a local train from Ghatkopar to Victoria Terminus (now Chhatrapati Shivaji Maharaj Terminus). But Avinash didn't mind it. Being in college opened completely new doors for him. He had access to a library with thousands of books, all of them waiting on the shelves for him to explore the knowledge hidden within their covers. The fact that he could now read and even borrow these books was exhilarating—it was a dream come true!

Attending classes in the college was a new experience for Avinash since the professors simply delivered their lectures and then went away. Most of these lectures were, however, monologues, during which students could walk out at will, and many of them derived pleasure in doing just that to celebrate their newfound 'collegian' status, which mostly meant liberation from school discipline and uniforms.

On the threshold of adulthood, most of Avinash's classmates were starry-eyed lovers on the lookout for potential romantic interests. They were obsessed with films, music and the latest trends in clothes, hairstyle, language and gestures. Many carried only a notebook, which they liked to spin on their fingertips.

Gradually, Avinash became acquainted with some of his classmates. Among them were Gauri, Ravi and Nisha. Gauri was short, plump and talkative, while Nisha was tall, slim and fair, with a taste for the latest fashion trends. Ravi was tall, fair and thin, and wore gold-rimmed spectacles. They would all hang out together either in the college canteen or in the lobby. But Avinash felt a bit trapped whenever they planned to go to a movie or a restaurant. He preferred to accompany them to the college canteen, which was sort of affordable. He still hadn't found a job, and the thought of it nagged at him. He kept sending out applications and even visited some factories seeking employment.

A few months later, he received a letter from a reputed private company that required temporary unskilled workers at its factory. When he reached the factory, he saw that he was one amongst hundreds of unemployed young people there. During the screening formalities, most candidates were rejected on the grounds of physical fitness, and many others were turned away after the subsequent written test. Of the remaining, only about a dozen were selected after a skill test to measure their speed and accuracy in handling mechanical activities. Avinash cleared all the tests and was asked to report for duty the next day in the company's bottle caps manufacturing plant

The world of the factory was different from anything Avinash had ever experienced. Located in the industrial zone in the western suburbs of Bombay, the multinational factory was an industrial complex sprawling over a vast area. Signboards pointed towards various plants, warehouses, parking areas, office blocks and canteens. Monstrous metal structures, with a network of pipes around them, towered over the warehouses and the workshops. The whole thing looked like the intestines of a disembowelled mechanical giant.

The noise of machines running became louder as Avinash approached the unit making the bottle caps, and the smell of hot metal and chemicals hung in the air. A timekeeping machine had been installed near the door, and a wooden board mounted on the wall contained the workers' attendance cards. Huge fans, whirring on iron pillars across the floor, were adding to the noise level.

Avinash approached the nearest machine, which was busy punching holes in printed metal sheets. A bulky, middle-aged man wearing a blue boiler suit was standing on a raised platform and monitoring the process. His assistant was a boy of about Avinash's age, and he was standing below, using a sponge to apply some lubricant on the metal sheets before inserting them into the machine. They barely spared him a glance and continued with their work.

'Where is the manager?' Avinash asked, but his words were gobbled up by all the noise on the floor. He repeated the question in a louder voice and this time, the assistant looked at him and raised his eyebrows.

'Manager?' Avinash asked again.

The assistant read his lips and pointed to a glass cabin in the centre of the shop floor. The smell of chemicals, machine oil, hot metal and paint was beginning to go to Avinash's head, and walking through the rows of machines was like moving through the irritated entrails of a mechanical monster.

When he reached the glass cabin, Avinash saw that there was nobody inside. Some instruments and machine components were lying on a table along with some files, rolled-up charts, screwdrivers, Allen keys, micrometers and spanners. He waited at the door, wondering whether he would be able to work in such a noisy atmosphere. Closing his eyes, he tried to shut out the noise pounding at his ears.

When he opened his eyes a few seconds later, he found himself looking at a short, bald man wearing a white apron with the company's logo stitched on it. The man raised his eyebrows.

'Hello, sir. I'm a new recruit,' Avinash said, handing over his appointment letter, but his words were inaudible in the din. The man read the letter, pushed open the door of the cabin, and a gush of cold air swept over them. Avinash followed him inside and the door closed behind him automatically, guillotining the noise and the heat.

'We work in three shifts and need hardworking people,' the man said, looking at Avinash from head to toe.

'Sir, I'm ready to work hard.'

'Okay, you can work in the first shift today, but from tomorrow, join the second shift. The shifts change every fortnight.' He pulled a blank attendance card out of a drawer and scribbled Avinash's name and employee number on it.

'Yes, sir,' Avinash said, looking at the shop floor through the cabin's glass wall. He could see the machines running but couldn't hear anything. It was like watching an action-packed film with the audio track switched off.

'Take this—remember to punch it at the beginning and end of your shift,' the man said, handing over the attendance card.

When Avinash opened the door of the cabin to leave, the noise of the machines poured back into his ears like an ocean breaching the hull of a ship. The manager followed him out. Avinash could see his lips move but he couldn't hear a thing. 'Sorry, sir. I can't hear you!' he said, but he was not sure whether he was audible.

The manager smiled, came close to him and shouted, 'You'll get used to this noise, don't worry.'

The two of them walked to the timekeeping machine at the door. The manager demonstrated how to punch the card and then put it in a slot on the wall-mounted board. He then took Avinash to the shift supervisor, who gave him instructions about what he was to do that day.

Avinash spent the first day cleaning the shop floor, carrying boxes and stacking them in a corner and collecting and carrying metal scrap from behind the machines in a handcart to a dumping yard within the factory compound. It was hard labour, and the noise soon gave him a headache.

At noon, a siren pierced through the deafening mechanical noise, signalling the start of the lunch break. The thundering of the machines, the shrill noise of the friction between metal sheets, the hammering of punching pistons and the roaring of motors all stopped. The only sound remaining was of the flywheels humming, and it came as a relief to Avinash, who had feared that he would go deaf before the day ended. Human voices started mushrooming in different parts of the shop floor. The overall sound changed from being metallic to human. Workers walked towards the washroom, the break room and the canteen. Avinash ate the meal he had brought with him in the break room, which was adjacent to the washrooms near the shop floor entrance.

As he ate, he made a few acquaintances, mainly young casual workers like him. Most of the older workers were not keen to befriend daily wagers and preferred to ignore them.

'Avinash Gaikwad? What is Gaikwad?' a senior machine operator asked when Avinash introduced himself.

'It's my surname,' Avinash said.

'I know, stupid. But who are you?'

'Hungami rojandari kaamgaar,' Avinash said, 'temporary daily wage worker.'

A few workers standing around started laughing. 'Silly boy, he wants to know which community you belong to,' one of them said.

'Oh! You want to know my caste. Does it matter?'

'No. I'm only asking since your surname exists in many communities.'

'Well, my ancestors were untouchables, and my father converted to Buddhism before I was born.'

Many heads turned their way, and Avinash could see the expression on people's faces changing.

'Oh! So, you are a Jai Bhim guy,' the operator said.

'Yes.'

'My name is Shirke, and I'm a Maratha,' he said, his chest expanding with pride.

Avinash smiled and moved away. Some workers were sitting in groups and playing cards while others were just fooling around with each other or napping. The lull continued till the siren ripped through the silence.

CHAPTER 7

The hard manual labour on the shop floor continued through the day, and by the time Avinash reached home, he was exhausted. His parents, however, had excitement writ large on their faces. 'How was your first day?' Godavari asked.

'Good.'

'If it's too tiring, you can find another job,' she said. 'You can get a clerical job somewhere.'

'It's not very tiring, but I'll have to get used to all the noisy machines on the shop floor and the constant change in shifts.'

'If you are comfortable there, then you can continue,' Dagadoo said. 'But how will you attend college?'

'I'll miss lectures during the day shift. From tomorrow, though, I'll be working in the second shift which begins at 4 p.m. and ends at midnight. So, for a fortnight, there won't be a problem.'

'If it clashes too much with your college timings, you can leave this job and focus only on your studies,' Godavari said.

'Don't worry, I'll manage,' Avinash said. 'In fact, I want *you* to stop working now. I've started earning, after all.'

Her face lit up for a moment, but then she shook her head sadly. 'I would like to,' she said in a low voice. 'But your job is temporary. What if they don't renew your contract after three months?'

Avinash pursed his lips. She was right. He was just a temporary, unskilled worker hired for a period of three months with no guarantee of regular employment.

'When you get a permanent job, I'll stop working,' Godavari said with a smile. 'And it will be marvellous if you get a government job.'

Avinash nodded.

After dinner, he went straight to bed and closed his eyes. When he woke up next, it was already morning. The neighbourhood had woken up with its usual noises. Avinash had some mild pain in his limbs, reminding him of the previous day's labour. He was tempted to sleep a little longer, but he resisted the urge since he had to rush to college.

After completing his morning chores, he reached college well in time for the lectures. The smell of overboiled tea, noisy conversations, cigarette smoke and laughter greeted him as he passed the canteen. He stopped to look over his shoulder and saw some of his classmates coming out of the canteen, cheerful as ever. All of them were dressed in casual shirts and jeans.

'Where were you yesterday?' they asked him almost in unison. He stopped and smiled.

'Is everything all right?' Ravi asked.

'Yes.'

'We are bunking lectures today to go for a movie now, join us!' Nisha said as the others nodded.

'No, I can't,' Avinash said.

'Why?' Ravi asked.

'I'll tell you. Come, let's sit on the stairs,' Avinash said, leading them to the wide stairs at the entrance of the college building.

'Why aren't you coming with us?' Nisha asked as they all sat down.

'That's because I'm not free,' Avinash said.

'What?'

'I'm also working in a factory apart from attending classes,' he said. 'I have to earn and learn simultaneously.'

'Oh no! That's bad luck,' Nisha said. 'This is when we should be having fun! Too bad you'll miss it!'

'It's all right,' he replied. 'We live in different worlds.'

'But I'm sceptical about whether or not you'll be able to do both things at the same time,' Ravi said, shaking his head. 'At least try and find a clerical job somewhere, otherwise you'll tire yourself out.'

'There's no choice at the moment.'

'I guess this is just your destiny,' Gauri said curtly. 'Just face it.' Turning to the others, she said, 'Let's go. Best of luck, Avinash.'

After his friends left for the movie, Avinash went to the classroom. As the professor began his lecture, Avinash thought of his friends enjoying themselves at the movie hall. But then, attending lectures and getting a higher education was more important than bunking lectures for the sake of watching a movie. His background was different from theirs and hence, his life would be different too.

After classes were finished for the day, he rushed to the railway station to get to the factory in time for his shift. A group of five college students—three boys and two girls—were travelling in the same train compartment as him. All of them were clad in jeans and shirts, talking and giggling like overgrown school kids. Looking at them, the thought of having to miss the joys of college life came back to his mind. He tried to imagine what it would feel like to live a carefree life, with everything taken care of by his parents. It must be an enjoyable and, probably, a necessary experience before leaping into the responsibilities of adulthood. But he brushed the thought aside. Going by what his father had told him, he was still in a better situation than so many others like him. He was privileged to receive a higher education and have access to libraries. Ultimately, it was going to help him catch up with the world, which had left his family and communities like his behind.

When he reached the factory and punched his card, he found the workers he had met the previous day preparing to leave as their shift was over. Those in the second shift kept pouring in, and Avinash found himself moving among total strangers again. The siren sounded, and the new batch of workers took over the machines. The shift supervisor called the temporary workers and assigned them manual work. Avinash made some new acquaintances in that brief window of time. Like the previous day, the permanent workers and the technicians avoided talking to them and spoke only in curt monosyllables when approached.

The work was the same as before, with a break in between for dinner. The shift ended at midnight, and about an hour later, Avinash was walking home after having taken a local train and then a bus to reach the slum. All the roads and bylanes in the slum were deserted. The stray dogs were either sleeping on the pavement or roaming around. Intermittently, a car or a bike would whizz past.

His footsteps echoed in the silence, attracting the attention of some dogs, who looked at him, their ears raised in attention. Two men emerged from the shadows behind a couple of shops lining the street. Avinash saw the flash of a knife blade in one of the men's hands as the streetlight fell over it for a second.

'Hey, wait!' one of the men called out. As Avinash approached closer, the man exclaimed, 'Oh, he's one of us!'

There was a whiff of liquor in the man's breath. Avinash recognized him—he had seen him several times at Zende's liquor den. 'What are you doing here at this hour?' Avinash asked. The other man, a stranger, hid the knife behind his back.

'Nothing,' he said. 'But where are you coming back from so late?'

'I've got a job in a factory,' Avinash said. 'I'm returning from my shift.'

'Oh, that's good! Go home and sleep now.' Then, turning to his companion, the man said, 'Let's go.' The duo crossed the road and vanished into a dark alley.

Avinash continued walking towards the hill slope. As he climbed the stairs to his home, he saw that the light inside was still on, and his parents were waiting up for him. 'Why are you still awake?' he asked.

'We were worried because it's so late in the night,' Godavari said.

'Don't worry,' he said, unbuttoning his shirt. 'I'm not a kid anymore. Don't wait for me from tomorrow.'

She nodded.

'Is everything all right?' Dagadoo asked.

'Yes.'

'Do you want to eat something?' Godavari asked.

'No,' he said. 'I just want to sleep.'

He quickly changed his clothes, splashed some water on his face and dried it with a towel. Then, after drinking some water, he switched off the light and went to sleep.

Some weeks later, Avinash was given the night shift from midnight to 8 a.m. He was overjoyed at the prospect of having the entire day to himself. Back from duty in the morning, he would have breakfast and rush to college. After attending lectures and visiting the library, he would spend some time with his classmates, then return home in the afternoon, eat a late lunch and sleep for a few hours. In the evening, he would spend some time at Buddha Vihar, where Raja, Sudhir and some of his other friends would be whiling away their time. After dinner, he would leave for the factory.

But the jubilation of having the entire day to himself did not last long. He realized soon enough that sleeping during the day was poor compensation for staying awake all night. His sleep backlog kept piling up, and he began to feel dizzy round the clock. It was especially worse in the wee hours between 2 a.m. and 4. a.m., when he felt an irresistible urge to sleep, regardless of how much he had slept during the day. His body clock was in a tizzy, which affected his digestion.

Avinash felt it was unnatural and inhuman to make people toil overnight because it meant moving them away from the cycle of nature. In the morning, while returning home, he met many people on their way to work. They were all starting their day with a fresh mind, while he was sleep-starved and walking slowly like a sick man. The worst thing about shift duty was that by the time he got a little accustomed to the working hours, the shift changed.

During the day shift, Joseph, the floor supervisor, moved him to the knurling section, where machines processed punched bottle caps to create the crown at the top and the sharp line cuts at the bottom to seal bottles at the consignee's end. Avinash carried boxes of punched caps on his shoulder and climbed up the narrow ten-feet high iron ladder attached to each knurling machine to pour the punched caps into the hopper above. There were twelve machines in a row, and by the time he finished filling the hopper of the last machine, the hopper of the first machine would be almost empty. The work was physically taxing, but the saving grace was that sometimes, some machine operators allowed him to operate their machines when he was free for a few minutes. He was curious about the mechanical process and did not mind handling the machines.

One day, as he was preparing to leave at the end of the shift and had punched his attendance card, Joseph called him. 'Can you work overtime for four hours today?' he asked, pulling out a red attendance card from a drawer. 'You'll earn double the wages.'

'Thank you for asking, sir, but I'm sorry,' Avinash said. 'I can't.'

'No? But why not?' Joseph asked. 'I'm asking you to work overtime because you work sincerely.'

'Sir, I also study in college, and I need to spend some time with my family and friends.'

'Well, I just wanted you to earn some more money.'

'Thank you, sir, but there are other things that are equally important.'

Joseph narrowed his eyes and shook his head. 'You are different,' he said. 'Some of your colleagues fight for overtime work.'

Avinash smiled and took his leave. Between his shifts in the factory and the lectures in college, things were already too hectic, and he wasn't left with enough time for his family.

Even as he was trying to adjust to his ever-changing schedule, three months passed and his contract with the factory expired. His parents told him not to worry, but Avinash felt guilty about being jobless and having to depend on them.

A couple of days after his stint at the factory ended, Avinash was walking with Raja near the railway station. It was rush hour and the station was swarming with people going to work. Autorickshaws, taxis and buses were crawling along the congested road leading to the station, and there were long queues at the bus stop.

Suddenly, they saw that a crowd had formed around a hawker and a middle-aged commuter just outside the station. The two were screaming at each other. The commuter was wearing a silky white kurta-pyjama and had a gold chain around his neck. He was also carrying a briefcase. 'How dare you argue with me?' he shouted. 'I can buy you, along with all your fruits, right now!'

The hawker, dressed in a pair of brown trousers and a shirt with yellow-and-blue stripes, retorted, 'Are you blind? Can't you see that your briefcase knocked some apples off my basket?'

Some of the onlookers tried to pacify both of them, and soon, the commuter hurried into the station, muttering expletives.

'Go, get lost! I've seen many like you!' the hawker shouted after him.

As the commuter disappeared into the crowd, some of the people sympathized with the hawker. 'It's always like this,' one of them said. 'People with money are so arrogant.'

'It's always the poor man who suffers,' said another, expressing solidarity.

Nodding, the hawker began collecting the apples that had fallen on the ground. Suddenly, there was a commotion as many of the other hawkers picked up their wares and ran helter-skelter. But it was too late for the apple vendor—he had not seen the truck belonging to the municipal corporation's anti-encroachment department approaching. As it pulled up behind him, two employees jumped down from the truck. They grabbed the apple basket, spilling some more apples onto the pavement, and threw it into the truck along with the wooden box on which the hawker had kept it. The hawker pleaded with the men to give his goods back, but in vain.

Meanwhile, the same onlookers who had sympathized with the hawker a moment ago, now pounced on the fallen apples, picking up as many as they could, and ran away gleefully.

Avinash picked the apples lying near his feet and held them up to the hawker. 'Why are you returning them to me?' the hawker asked. 'Take them away like the others did.'

'No, I won't do that,' Avinash said. 'It's wrong; it amounts to theft.'

The hawker took the apples from Avinash and sat down on the pavement. 'I've lost an entire day's earnings today,' he rued. 'Now I'll have to either pay a hefty fine or bribe them to get my things back.'

Avinash looked around for Raja, but he was nowhere to be seen. The crowd had dispersed and all the other hawkers who had scurried away with their wares, now returned to set up their makeshift stalls again.

Not knowing how to comfort the apple vendor, Avinash started walking home. He'd barely taken a couple of steps when Raja emerged from behind a shop.

'How many apples did you pick up?' he asked Avinash.

'Two.'

'I got four,' Raja said, beaming, and pointed at his bulging pockets. Pulling out two apples, he said, 'Show me yours.'

'I don't have them—I returned them to the hawker.'

Raja stopped and frowned. '*What?*' he exclaimed. 'Are you *crazy?*'

'I felt it was wrong to take those apples,' Avinash said. 'It's like stealing.'

Raja smirked. 'You are a fool,' he said. 'Take one from me—I know you like apples.'

'I don't want it, Raja,' Avinash said. 'I like apples, but not stolen ones.'

Raja stared at him contemptuously. 'You'll die hungry one day,' he snapped.

They walked in silence, the only sound coming from Raja crunching his apple.

Later, Avinash pondered over the incident. He was shocked by the behaviour of the people. What turned them from being sympathizers to looters? Were they just pretending to be on the vendor's side while sympathizing with him? How could they switch from being angels to demons in a second?

He liked apples, and he could've gotten a couple of them for free. But then, it would've weighed on his mind, and that was too heavy a load to carry around forever. It would've been illegal and immoral to take the apples without paying for them. Neither the Constitution nor Buddhist principles permitted it. On reaching home, he looked at the city below and found it pretentious, swarming with human beings who could put a chameleon to shame.

CHAPTER 8

A couple of weeks later, Avinash received a letter from the company, hiring him for another three months. It came as a wonderful surprise, more so as he'd been jittery about the company not calling him back for work. He did not want to remain unemployed, thereby burdening his parents financially.

They were also happy that he was earning and studying. The company continued to reappoint him, albeit with a break of a week or two between each contract, for the next two years. His monthly income was, therefore, almost regular, although he was only paid for twenty-six days a month and not for the weekly day-offs. But given the situation, it was the best option available. If things continued the way they were, he could continue working in the factory for two more years, till his graduation. He had already cleared the first year and the intermediate year examinations of his four-year degree course.

When Avinash reported for duty after a two-week break, he found the shop floor extended and some new machines installed in the newly created space in the compound.

Joseph greeted him with a broad smile. 'I'm glad you are back! I want you to work in my shift,' he said, taking him to the manager's cabin for the formalities. 'Have you seen the new machines?' he asked Avinash, pointing to the extended part of the factory. 'We have received a huge export order—we're going to move some regular machine operators there, and workers like you will be posted on the old machines.'

'But I'm just an ordinary worker,' Avinash pointed out.

'You won't be one for long. I'm told that some temporary workers will soon be trained and regularized as semi-skilled workers on higher salaries to operate the machines.'

Avinash smiled at the prospect of learning something new and getting regular employment with a higher wage.

Joseph took him to an old machine and told him to handle it under the supervision of the senior operators. It was a thrilling experience for Avinash, who had already learnt the finer details of running the machines from some operators. It gave him a sense of power, of having a mechanical monster at his command.

The new section in the factory started functioning properly much sooner than he had expected, and some of the seasoned operators were moved there to handle the work. Joseph took Avinash to an old machine and explained the various procedures involved, like filling up the worksheet, scheduling the work order and adhering to the timeline set for each consignment. Also, he was shown how to insert a production slip in every box, with details about the date, shift and muster number of employees at every stage of production, to ensure accountability in case of a complaint.

'Today, you can continue with Alpha Company's order on this machine. If you face any trouble, just stop the machine and call me,' Joseph said. He then called a new recruit and asked him to fill the hopper above with unprocessed caps.

The machine was in the idle mode with only the flywheel rotating with a hum. Avinash pulled a lever, and the machine responded promptly. Soon, he was busy monitoring the flow of caps in a row to the knurling piston inside. He was so engrossed in the work that it was only when the shrill siren cut through the noise that he realized it was time for lunch.

Joseph came over to check the output and smiled. 'Good! Keep it up,' he said.

Avinash pushed the lever to put the machine back in idle mode and then stepped down. The tremor in his legs made him realize that he had been standing for almost four hours, and as he sat down for lunch, he began to truly appreciate the comfort of sitting down, a luxury he had taken for granted all his life.

After the lunch break, Joseph advised him to take a small break in between his work to go to the washroom and drink water, provided someone else monitored the machine in his absence. Avinash nodded and switched on the machine after checking the hopper and the counter. A couple of hours later, when Joseph was around, Avinash signalled that he had to go to the washroom, and Joseph sent a fitter to fill in.

At the end of the shift, Avinash stopped his machine. Joseph came and checked the counter. He plunged his hands into the box in which the processed caps had been collected.

'Your machine's output is over 28,000 caps in this shift, which is higher than normal,' he said.

'Is it? But what happens if the output is lower because of a mechanical failure?'

'If you face any mechanical issues, stop the machine and inform me immediately. Then, mention the reason and the time in the production sheet,' Joseph said. Then, after a pause, he chuckled and said, 'Always remember: Machines don't fail—men do. If the creation, maintenance and use of a machine are done properly, it will not break down and will last as long as it's meant to.'

Avinash nodded, wiping his hands with some cotton wool. In the break room, while changing their clothes, the regularized workers discussed the new export order and spoke of their hopes for an increment as well as an annual bonus. The temporary workers, on the other hand, talked about how they would like to be absorbed as permanent workers.

When he reached home in the evening, Avinash told his parents about the new development at work. Godavari was delighted and considered it a promotion.

'I knew they'd promote you!' she said with a smile. 'Now they will regularize your employment and raise your salary.'

'I don't know,' he said. 'I'm just a temporary worker on a daily wage. And there are hundreds of workers like me who've been working for several years on the same wages across various units.'

She sighed and stared at him blankly.

The next day, when Avinash reached the factory, he saw a group of permanent workers having a conversation at the entrance of the shop floor. However, they stopped talking when he reached them.

'Avinash, come here,' Shirke, one of the men, said. 'Why are you tinkering with things?'

'What do you mean?'

'Yesterday, you operated a machine and gave more output than the regular operator,' Shirke said, staring at him angrily. 'Do you know the average daily output of that machine?'

'No.'

'It's below 25,000 caps. You produced over 28,000.'

'What's wrong with that?' he asked. 'I worked at a normal pace.'

Everyone laughed. 'Very innocent, aren't you?' Shirke asked sarcastically. 'Listen, son, we have fixed the average output of every machine, and all the operators follow it. The company is not going to give you a medal for giving more output.' All the regular workers standing around nodded their heads in agreement.

'I'm just doing my duty sincerely,' Avinash said. 'It's surprising that senior employees have a lower output.'

'I know you people,' Shirke said curtly. 'You like to upset things, but don't do it again.'

'Are you asking me to underperform?'

Shirke gnashed his teeth, trying to control his rage.

Thakur, another senior operator, pulled Avinash aside. 'Listen, boy, you may be working sincerely, but don't create trouble for others—it will only end up creating trouble for you. Follow the crowd and work like everyone else.'

Just then, the siren sounded, indicating the commencement of the shift and the men all dispersed. Avinash worked the way he had the previous day, and his output at the end of the shift was 29,500 caps.

Joseph smiled while filling in the production sheet for the shift. 'I think you are being too sincere,' he said.

'I'm just doing my job,' Avinash said.

From that day on, Avinash sensed that he was being followed by angry eyes everywhere he went in the factory. A few days later, when he alighted from a bus near the main gate of the factory, he saw a group of strangers standing outside the compound's wall. One of them was pointing at him.

He ignored them and was about to enter the factory compound when he heard his name being called out. He looked over his shoulder and saw one of the men beckoning him. When he approached them, a bulky middle-aged man chewing paan, spewed a jet of blood-red betel juice from his mouth, adding to the numerous stains on the road. 'Are you Avinash, from the bottle caps unit?' he asked, ruminating like a bull.

'Yes.'

'You think you are very smart, eh?' he asked, continuing to chew the remains of the paan in his mouth.

Avinash looked at him and then at the others. They were all staring at him angrily. 'What is the problem? Who are you?' he asked.

The man spit on the road again and stared at him for a few moments. 'My name is Patil, and I'm from the workers' union. We've received a complaint against you,' he said.

'Complaint?'

'Yes,' he said, spitting again. 'You are operating a machine and giving more output than the regular operators do.'

'I'm just doing my job.'

'Do you see these flags?' Patil asked, pointing at the red trade union flags tied to the lamp posts outside the factory gate. There were two larger flags on either side of the main gate, hanging limp.

'Yes.'

'And do you see that board?' he asked, pointing at the union noticeboard near the gate.

'Yes.'

'Don't mess with our men,' Patil said, raising his finger. The ruby set in the gold ring on his finger glittered for a split-second in the sun. 'Follow your seniors' rules and don't act smart—I am warning you.'

Avinash smiled. 'I'm surprised that the union feels this way,' he said. 'It appears that demanding higher wages is the only agenda the union has.'

Patil was flabbergasted. He looked at the others in the group, who appeared equally shocked.

'Are you a stooge of the management?' Patil asked sarcastically. 'Do you think the company will regularize you for working like this?'

'Not at all. I'm not doing it to impress anyone—I'm only trying to deliver my best in whatever I do.'

'Forget it. He will not listen,' one of the men in the group said. 'He's a Jai Bhim guy. People like him are rabble-rousers.'

Patil looked at Avinash, narrowing his eyes. 'Is that so? Why are you here then? Go find a government job where you'll be pampered—don't venture into the private sector!'

Avinash smiled. 'Sir, please don't forget that the laws protecting workers and trade unions were drafted by Bhimrao Ambedkar. Don't demonize him by calling me a "Jai Bhim" guy,' he said and walked into the factory.

❀

Avinash was punching his card when Babu, a co-worker, approached him. Babu had a wheatish complexion and was tall, hefty and curly-haired. He was wearing a dirty and worn-out boiler suit. 'Do you know what happened last night?' he asked.

'What?'

'There was an accident in the factory,' Babu said. 'One of our boys lost two fingers when his hand was crushed in a machine.'

'Oh! Who is the boy?'

'Chetan—he's in the hospital.'

Both of them walked over to Joseph, who was at his desk, filling some charts. He looked up when they approached him.

'How did the accident happen last night, sir?' Avinash asked.

'The boy was trying to remove the fragment of a damaged cap while the machine was still on. His hand got stuck and he lost two of his fingers,' Joseph said. 'He should've stopped the machine first.'

'But what about his future?'

'Well, an inquiry is in progress, and he'll receive medical treatment and a compensation package as per the rules. What else can we do?'

'He has been handicapped for life, sir. I think the company should absorb him as a regular employee on light duty. He was just an unskilled casual worker on meagre wages being asked to run a machine without proper training. The company is also accountable for the accident.'

Joseph pursed his lips and shook his head. Then, he looked up at the roof for a moment before turning to Avinash. 'I agree with you, but I can't do anything.'

Avinash looked at Babu. 'Come with me, let's go meet the manager.'

Joseph shook his head. 'Don't get into these things,' he said. 'I understand your feelings, but you are sticking your neck out for no reason. Just do your job and push off.'

Instead of responding to Joesph, Avinash looked at Babu and repeated, 'Let's go.'

'Wait,' Joseph said. 'Avinash, from today onwards, you'll not be operating the machines—someone else will do it.'

'Oh! Is anything wrong?'

'No, nothing. We just want to try out the other boys too. You'll be doing what you were doing before this—assisting the machine operators.'

Avinash nodded. 'Is this because some people are angry with me for giving a higher output?' he asked.

'Don't ask questions. You're only meant to follow orders,' Joseph said curtly. Then, after a pause, he added, 'We don't want any labour trouble, especially when we're rushing through this new export order.'

'As you wish, sir,' Avinash said and walked away with Babu.

The two young men then went to the manager's cabin and knocked on the door. They found him at his desk, leafing through a file. He looked at them and nodded.

Avinash opened the glass door and walked in with Babu behind him. The manager raised his eyebrows questioningly.

'Sir, I want to talk to you about yesterday's accident,' Avinash said.

The manager narrowed his eyes. 'What about it?'

'Sir, the boy is handicapped for life and—'

The manager raised his hand to interrupt him. 'He will get medical attention and compensation as per the company's rules.'

'I know, sir, but he may not be able to find another job,' Babu said.

'So?'

'The company should explore the possibility of absorbing him as a regular employee, possibly on light duty.'

The expression on the manager's face changed from nonchalance to anger. 'Who are you to tell me what to do?' he yelled. 'You are just ordinary helpers. Get out!'

'Please, sir, just listen to us.'

'Out!' the manager snapped, closing the file in his hand and banging it on his desk.

Avinash and Babu left the office, their faces sullen in the noise and heat. They walked back to the shop floor in silence. 'I have a suggestion,' Babu said finally. 'Shall we approach the union?'

'The union?'

'Yes, we can at least try it.'

'I don't mind. We'll go to the union office after the shift is over,' Avinash said. 'And then, we'll go to the hospital to see Chetan.'

Babu nodded and left to do his job. Some operators had already started working, and the noise from all the mechanical activity had picked up. Avinash went to the machine operated by Thakur and started oiling the metal sheets.

During lunchtime, Joseph called him. 'What did the manager say?' he asked.

'He sent us out of his cabin.'

'I told you not to get into these things.'

'Don't worry about me, sir. My conscience is clear.'

'I just don't want anything unpleasant to happen to you ...'

'Unpleasant?' Avinash asked. 'At the most I'll lose this job, which is anyway ill paid and temporary. Also, I don't intend to work here for a lifetime.'

Joseph shook his head and crossed himself.

After the shift got over, Avinash and Babu went to the union office. About half a dozen people were sitting on chairs scattered across the room while a couple of men were sitting behind a table littered with files and papers. The wall behind them displayed portraits of deceased union leaders with their names written at the bottom of the frames. Below these photographs, the names of the union's existing office bearers were painted on the wall. Once they got the union members' attention, Avinash and Babu narrated the entire incident.

'Are you members of the union?' one of the men asked.

'No, we are temporary workers on daily wages,' Avinash said.

'Wait here,' the man said, pointing to some vacant chairs.

Avinash and Babu sat down and waited. Soon, Patil and two others walked in. Everyone in the room stood up respectfully. Patil went behind the table and took his seat. Everyone else sat down after that. Patil looked around, nodding and smiling broadly. When he caught sight of Avinash, his smile disappeared. He gulped down the betel leaf juice in his mouth, wiped his lips with the back of his hand and asked, 'What brings *you* here?'

Avinash and Babu told him what the purpose of their visit was, and after listening to them attentively, Patil cleared his throat. 'I must admire your confidence. First, you irritate our workers by giving more output, and now you expect us to help you,' he said sarcastically.

'That issue has nothing to do with this case,' Avinash said.

Patil shook his head. 'You are just contract workers. We can't do anything.'

'But can the union at least write a letter to the management to consider the issue on compassionate grounds?' Avinash asked.

'Don't teach me what to do!' Patil shouted. 'And stop meddling in such things.'

'But, sir, we're just requesting you for help, as fellow workers,' Babu said.

Patil cleared his throat again. Then he looked at the others in the room. 'Kids born yesterday are teaching me what to do,' he sneered. 'Get out.'

Sensing that they would get no help from Patil, Avinash and Babu came out of the office.

'You seem to know Patil. Where did you meet him?' Babu asked. Avinash told him about his earlier encounter with Patil, and Babu shook his head sadly. 'Now what?' he asked.

'Let's first go to the hospital and meet Chetan,' Avinash replied. They bought some fruits and hired an autorickshaw.

At the hospital, they found Chetan lying on a bed with his hand heavily bandaged. His father was standing nearby. Chetan told him that Avinash and Babu were his colleagues from the factory, and Babu gave him the fruits they'd brought. They spent some time talking, and Chetan told them about the accident and his treatment.

'If you need anything, please don't hesitate to ask us,' Avinash said before leaving. 'And don't lose hope.'

In a dejected mood, Avinash and Babu left the hospital. They walked to a bus stop nearby and parted ways, boarding different buses to go back home.

When Avinash reached home, Godavari was cooking. 'Why are you so late today?' she asked. When he told her the reason, she was shocked. 'I think you should leave this job,' she said. 'Find another one. A safe job—where there is no risk of such an accident. Probably an office job, as a peon or a clerk.'

'Don't worry,' he said. 'I'll be careful. And don't think that accidents happen only in factories. They can happen anywhere.'

'Don't speak like that! It's inauspicious!' she shouted angrily.

Avinash did not respond to her, and instead went to sit at the threshold of the house. As always, he looked out at the urban habitation rising up from the dust and the noise and wondered why labour unions only focussed on monetary benefits and privileges for workers without making any efforts to instil in them a sense of responsibility towards their work. Why did the unions not ask the workers to give their best in return for their wages? But then there was the company which considered the workers merely as tools for making a profit, without empathizing with their plight and accepting the fact that its edifice was standing on the shoulders of these very workers.

CHAPTER 9

The Emergency was lifted in 1977, causing jubilation all over the country. The subsequent elections led to a change of guard in the country. There was an overall sense of elation among the people, caused by the promises made by the new leaders. At the ground level, however, people waited for change, as usual.

Babu went to several units of the company over the next few days, talking to other temporary workers who had been working there for several years. A few days later, about a dozen such workers assembled in a garden near the factory. Sitting cross-legged in a semicircle, they waited for more of their colleagues to join them. Some were smoking or chewing tobacco, while others were talking about mundane matters. About an hour later, they began the meeting.

Babu and Avinash opened the discussion, citing Chetan's accident and stressing the need for a platform to organize the temporary workers. 'I know it's a very difficult task to organize ourselves as we have no job security and privileges like the regular workers do,' Babu said. 'But it's even harder because nobody wants to invite the wrath of the management.'

'We are helpless! What can we do?' one of the workers asked.

'Yes, we are helpless, but we are not hopeless. Yes, we have many limitations, but we need to do something,' Avinash said. 'We'll start by organizing our boys and forming an association to interact with the management. It will take time and effort but let us at least make a start.'

Many of those present complained about the lack of safety gear, like gloves, while handling tin sheets on the printing machine, which led to cuts on their palms and fingers. One worker pointed out the bullying that the regular workers and the supervisory staff engaged in, while another said that there weren't enough lockers to put their clothes, lunch boxes and other belongings in, in the break room.

'We'll start by demanding safety gear and more lockers,' Babu said. 'Let's at least try that and see what happens.'

Everyone agreed, and during the hour-long deliberations, they resolved to canvass for support for their cause, along with preparing a list of potential members and specific problems. After the discussion, they had tea at a stall outside the garden before dispersing.

Over the next one week, Avinash and Babu met some union leaders who were active in the engineering and textile industries in the city. But the response was not encouraging. The terms and conditions of temporary employment left no scope for collective bargaining. Besides, most of the unions were affiliated with some political party or the other and functioned as political subsidiaries for their masters. Those associated with the ruling parties were not interested, while those linked with the opposition parties sympathized, but expressed their helplessness. To make matters worse, the temporary workers themselves were reluctant to join a movement, fearing that they would lose their jobs.

At home, Dagadoo was curious about what Avinash was doing. 'How is the response from the workers and the management?' he asked.

'Not encouraging,' Avinash said. 'I'm feeling quite helpless.'

'Don't give up,' Dagadoo said. 'When Babasaheb was the labour minister in the viceroy's executive council before independence, he enacted laws that dealt with duty hours, weekly offs, overtime wages, paid leave, maternity leave, the right to form a union, tripartite negotiations, pension, gratuity and so on, to prevent the exploitation of workers.'

'How long are we going to rest on his laurels?' Avinash snapped. 'You always say good things about Babasaheb's contribution to bettering the lives of people across caste, gender and religion. But then why do we still face such situations?' Avinash asked.

Dagadoo sighed and shook his head sadly. 'I've told you many times that the rich and the powerful appropriate constitutional provisions to suit their interests,' he said. 'Babasaheb cautioned us about two primary adversaries—the shetji and the bhatji, that is the greedy businessmen and the religious fanatics—dominating our lives. Today, the traditionally privileged have increased their dominance in business with help from various political parties that are eager to tweak the laws in their favour at the cost of the masses. To make matters worse, some political parties work to weaken communal harmony in our society, operating in tandem with fanatics from various religions, to either capture or retain power. Consequently, the masses get carried away by emotional issues and forget the value of their own votes in disposing off rulers who are destroying the constitutional principles of a welfare state.'

Avinash recollected his visit to the village as a child, where he'd learnt that the village headman, who was from a family of traditional landlords, continued to get elected democratically as the sarpanch. 'Is that why the sarpanch of our village is from a family of traditional landlords?'

'Yes. In rural areas, the dynasties of landlords become lawmakers even in the democratic set-up.'

'Then what has really changed?'

'Well, things have changed to some extent. Now, people's access to education and employment is better across caste and gender. We gained political independence from the British amidst communal bloodshed during the partition of the country, but social freedom came to us through the Constitution. It was a silent and peaceful revolution that empowered everyone, especially women and the marginalized and minority communities.'

'But there are still so many problems!' Avinash exclaimed, sounding frustrated.

'Of course! Issues like the henchmen of the traditionally privileged being elected on reserved seats, and industries preferring the contract system to circumvent labour welfare laws in connivance with the government still persist. The dominance of certain upper-caste communities and dynasties in businesses, politics and religious institutions continues as well.'

Avinash sighed deeply.

'Don't be disheartened, son,' Dagadoo said. 'There's still a long way to go, but we've made a beginning. We can agitate and use all the democratic tools at our disposal to seek justice without resorting to violence or breaking any laws.'

Avinash was not convinced. 'It sounds too simplistic, especially when you look at the delays in the delivery of justice. Many a times, the process itself becomes the punishment,' he said. 'And laws are made or changed to suit the ambitions of those in power, rather than to work for the welfare of the people.'

Dagadoo shook his head. 'But every citizen has the right to vote corrupt lawmakers out of power. Our need is for enlightenment and consensus among majority of the voters to rise above narrow emotional barriers,' he said. 'Then, a day will come when there will be proportional representation of all stakeholders in lawmaking.'

'But the privileged ones, who are, in fact, a minority segment in the population, are always being voted into power by the socially underprivileged majority.'

'Yes, but that's because the underprivileged are yet to realize the value of their votes.'

Avinash knew that Dagadoo was making a lot of sense, but considering the mindset of the gullible masses, such a transformation seemed very difficult, albeit not impossible.

The next day, it was noisier than usual in the slum, with songs praising Dr Ambedkar and the Buddha playing loudly in many houses. Avinash had his lunch and left for Buddha Vihar. The fragrance of meat being cooked was in the air as it was Sunday, the day when most of the slum's residents ate non-vegetarian food. Zende's liquor den was overcrowded, and the stench of liquor was more pronounced than usual.

At Buddha Vihar, about a dozen school students were waiting for Avinash for their weekly coaching class; he'd started it a while ago. 'Jai Bhim, bhau!' they greeted him. Then they removed their footwear and entered the vihar. As they sat on the floor in a circle around him, Avinash discussed and reviewed their weekly progress one by one, giving instructions and clarifying doubts by drawing figures and diagrams in their rough books. Intermittently, someone would peep in through the door and say 'Jai Bhim'. On seeing what was going on inside, the person would go away after telling them to carry on.

After about half an hour, a shabbily dressed man staggered to the door. He balanced himself by holding on to the door frame with both his hands and then proceeded to remove his footwear. He was a lanky, middle-aged part-time worker with untidy hair. On seeing Avinash and the students, he stopped. 'Jai Bhim,' he said, and Avinash and the students got a strong whiff of alcohol. Avinash stood up.

'I said Jai Bhim. Why aren't you responding?' the man demanded.

'No,' Avinash said. 'I will not respond. Please go home.'

'What? You will not say Jai Bhim?' the man asked, raising his voice.

'No.'

'You are insulting Babasaheb! Aren't you ashamed of yourself?' the man fumed.

Avinash could sense anger building up inside him. 'It is you who is insulting Babasaheb. He was a teetotaller. How can you say Jai Bhim in an inebriated state?'

The man narrowed his eyes and paused. 'But I want to pray to Buddha,' he said.

'Buddha is not God, and the Panchsheel mentions keeping away from alcohol.'

The man mumbled something and took a step back, struggling to maintain his balance and holding on to the door frame for support.

Some of the students stood up and approached the man. 'Uncle, please go home. You are interrupting our class,' one of them said, and the others joined in.

The man looked at them and then at Avinash, who folded his hands. 'Please leave.' The man smacked his lips and staggered away, mumbling something. Avinash and the students resumed their class.

About an hour later, as they were preparing to leave, one of the students took Avinash aside. 'One of my classmates wants to join our class. Can I bring him with me?' he asked.

'Sure, ask him to join us.'

'But ...' the student paused for a while and then said, 'He's not one of us.'

'What does that mean?'

'He's not a Buddhist.'

'So what?' Avinash snapped. 'How can we discriminate on the basis of caste, gender or religion when we ourselves have been historically discriminated against?'

'Okay, then I'll ask him to join us,' the student said. As they walked out, he pointed to a teenager standing outside. 'There he is.'

The boy came forward. 'Bhau, I'm Anil Kale. I live two rows behind this house,' he said, pointing to a house down the road. 'I want to join your class.'

Avinash patted his shoulder. 'You can certainly join us. The only problem is that this is not a daily class with a fixed time; it's a weekly one. I'm here every Sunday, but if you need me on any other day, I'm available at home, depending on my shift.'

Anil nodded and joined the other students who were chatting nearby. Avinash then spotted Raja standing with a group of young men nearby. He spent some time with them and then Raja and he walked towards the market.

It being a Sunday, the streets were less crowded and the traffic scant. They were walking along the main road when a white sedan whizzed past them, but then it suddenly slowed down and stopped ahead of them, its tail lights blazing. As they reached the car, the backseat window slid down and a head popped out. It was Atharva! A fair-skinned man was at the steering wheel, and an obese lady was in the passenger seat next to him.

'Avinash! How are you? Where have you been? What are you doing nowadays?' Atharva asked, opening the door and getting out. Cold air gushed out of the car as if the door of a refrigerator had been opened. Avinash could immediately smell Atharva's perfume.

'I'm fine,' he said once they had shaken hands. 'I work in a factory.'

'Oh! Have you given up on your education?'

'No, I've also enrolled myself in college.'

'Really? How do you do both?'

'Well, I can attend college only while working the evening or night shifts.'

'Oh, poor chap. Then you must be in an arts college.'

'Yes.'

'I'm studying in the Lord's College of Science. You must have heard about it? It's one of the elite colleges in our city.'

'Yes, I have. That's good.'

'I have everything planned! I'll specialize in information technology and join my uncle who is settled in the United States. There is nothing in this country worth staying back for.'

'Do you really think so?' Avinash asked. 'Then we need to make it worth staying back for by doing something here ourselves.'

Atharva sneered. 'I want to live a better life ... one that matches global standards,' he said.

'Think over it.'

'No. I don't think it's a possibility worth pursuing.'

Avinash shook his head. 'Your choice, after all. Best wishes,' he said.

They shook hands again. Then Atharva opened the car door, sat inside and rolled up the window. The next instant, the car zoomed away and vanished round the corner ahead.

'Who was that?' Raja asked.

'Atharva, my classmate from school.'

'Hmm. Lucky chap,' Raja said, jerking his head to toss back the hair falling over his eyes. 'Living on the legacy of his privileged ancestors. Baap kamai.'

'Depends on how you look at it,' Avinash said. 'It's indeed baap kamai, inherited privilege, but instead of wasting time and energy on comparing ourselves with him and whining about the things we lack, we should focus on how to make the best use of what we have today. We are also lucky, Raja.'

'What? *We* are lucky? How?' Raja asked, halting to look at Avinash with wonder.

'We are normal, healthy human beings who have access to education and employment with the privileges granted to us by the Constitution,' Avinash said. 'We have it many times better than our ancestors did.'

Raja smirked and then said, 'Yes, but what about Atharva's ancestors? They have always had the upper hand. They have the gods on their side.'

Avinash smiled. 'So what? We have the Constitution on our side. The only thing is that it should be implemented properly in both letter and spirit.'

Raja narrowed his eyes. 'You mean, our god is the Constitution?' he asked.

'Yes, if it pleases you or boosts your morale to think that way.'

Raja fell silent, lost in thought.

CHAPTER 10

The second meeting of the temporary factory workers was called two weeks later. It received a better response than the first one, with about thirty workers attending. Yet, it was a fraction of the temporary workforce. During the deliberations, six workers from different units took on the responsibility of reaching out to more workers.

Eventually, a petition was drafted, enlisting the issues the temporary workers faced as well as Chetan's plight. However, getting the workers to sign the petition was a major challenge as most feared punitive action by the management. To make matters worse, most of the permanent workers and the supervisory staff had warned them against taking part in any such activity. Ultimately, the petition turned out to be an exercise in futility as only four workers signed it. Nevertheless, Avinash, Babu and two others decided to meet the general manager of the factory.

Seeking an appointment with the general manager proved to be a difficult task, and they were turned away several times as he was always busy in meetings. Finally, after half a dozen postponements spread over a week, the general manager's secretary said that he would finally meet them. When they entered his spacious cabin in the administrative block, it was so cold that they felt like they were entering a huge freezer. There were several charts, demonstration boards, files, machine components and electrical devices in his office. He was on a phone call, and they waited at the door till he nodded for them to approach. They stood behind a row of chairs in front of his desk.

The general manager looked at their petition, which lay on his desk, for a while and then said curtly, 'What is this? How dare you come to me? You have no right to ask for anything.'

'But, sir, these are genuine problems,' Avinash said.

'Please leave,' the general manager said.

'Sir, one of our temporary workers has lost his fingers in an accident and his case needs to be considered sympathetically,' Avinash said. 'And there are hundreds of temporary workers like us who have genuine problems.'

The phone rang just then and the general manager picked it up, looking at them contemptuously. 'Out!' he shouted before speaking into the phone.

Avinash tried to speak again, but the general manager gestured for him to stop and rang the bell on his desk to summon his secretary. The secretary walked in a second later. 'Bring me the quarterly statement and send this lot out,' he said, burying his head in a file.

The secretary waved them towards the door and opened it. A wave of heat embraced them as they came out of the cold cabin.

'I don't think anything will happen,' Babu said.

Avinash shook his head in despair. 'You're right, but we need to do something. We can't just give up.'

✿

A week later, during the Sunday class in Buddha Vihar, Avinash noticed that Anil was not there. 'Where is Anil?' he asked. But none of the students had any idea. After class, some of the students volunteered to find out where Anil was and went to his house while Avinash waited at the vihar. After a while, the students returned and told him that Anil's parents were not willing to send him to Buddha Vihar.

'Let's go meet them,' he said, and all of them walked towards Anil's house, entering the narrow passage leading up to the place.

When they got there, they found Anil sitting on the floor with his books spread all around him. His father, who was sitting near him, stood up. He had a vermillion tilak on his forehead, a black thread around his neck and a black tabeez, a charm, tied around his arm. There was smoke hanging in the air from a lamp and some incense sticks that had been lit in front of an idol of a deity. Several garlanded photographs of different gods and goddesses were displayed on the wall.

After exchanging pleasantries, Avinash asked Anil's father, 'Anil was to join our class today, but he didn't. Is there a problem?'

Anil closed his books and looked at his father, who hesitated and avoided making eye contact with Avinash. 'No, it's nothing,' he said, shaking his head. 'Anil will study at home.'

'All right,' Avinash said, looking at Anil. 'If you want him to study at home, I don't mind. But if he has any questions, he can always contact me.'

Anil's mother, who had been cooking, now stood up and looked at her husband. 'Let him go to the class,' she said.

Anil's father looked at her and then at Avinash. 'But I feel awkward,' he said.

'Why?' Avinash asked.

'Err, well, the class is held in Buddha Vihar.'

'So?'

'Perhaps there might be some objection to Anil being there.'

Avinash was taken aback. 'But why would anybody object? It's the only peaceful public space we have in our locality.'

Anil's father kept quiet for a second, and then he said, 'But we are not Buddhists, and I thought that may create problems.'

'Are you crazy? There is no such restriction about entering a vihar. We have no caste, gender or religious barriers.'

'Oh, is it? But there is another issue.'

'What?'

'If somebody from our community comes to know that Anil goes to Buddha Vihar, it may create problems for us.'

'Brother, Anil will neither lose his religion nor become a Buddhist just by entering Buddha Vihar. We won't ask him to pray or perform any rituals. Buddhism is simply a godless path towards a moral life.'

Anil's father stared at Avinash blankly. 'Err, all right,' he said finally. 'Let me think it over.'

'Sure, if you're still not sure, your son can come to my house.'

Anil's father appeared lost in thought. After a few moments, he said, 'No, that's all right, I'll send him to Buddha Vihar. But what fees will you charge?'

'I don't charge any fee.'

'Is it?' Anil's father asked, looking at his son and then his wife. He folded his hands and said, 'In that case, you will be doing us a great favour—'

'No, not at all.' Avinash interrupted him. 'I'm just giving back what I got.'

Beaming, Anil looked at his parents. The students accompanying Avinash were also delighted.

As they left the house and turned to descend the uneven steps that led down to the road, Avinash spotted his friend Sudhir coming towards them from the opposite direction.

'Avinash, Jai Bhim!' Sudhir said and Avinash returned the greeting. 'What are you doing here?' Sudhir asked.

Avinash told him about Anil and the concerns his parents had.

'Oh!' Sudhir exclaimed. He turned to Anil's father who was standing at the door and said, 'Kale, don't worry. Send your son to the class, and if anybody objects, tell us—we are here. Don't ruin your son's education.'

Kale smiled and nodded as Sudhir walked away towards his house.

Avinash continued to work at the factory, making efforts to organize his co-workers. On the last day of his three-month contract, when he reported for work, the factory was bustling with noisy mechanical activity as usual. Avinash walked in, picked up his attendance card from the slot, punched it and put it back. He walked towards the rows of machines on the shop floor and found Joseph sitting with a pile of letters in front of him.

'I have some bad news for you,' he said, flipping through the pile and pulling out a couple of letters. 'Your three-month contract is over—this is your termination letter,' he said, handing over a letter in duplicate. 'Sign a copy and give it to me.'

'I was expecting this,' Avinash said, signing a copy. 'Time really flies. I don't think the company will hire me again now.'

Joseph looked up and stared at him blankly. Then he shook his head. 'I don't know,' he said. 'It's beyond my control. But if that happens, I'll miss a sincere and hardworking employee.'

'Don't worry about me. I'll find some other job,' Avinash said and turned to leave.

'Wait. There is a piece of good news,' Joseph said, smiling. 'Chetan is likely to be absorbed as a permanent employee on light duty, most probably as a peon.'

'Wow! That's great news.'

'After you met the general manager, a delegation led by union leader Patil also met him about the same issue,' he said. 'Chetan's case was subsequently discussed by the senior management and a decision was taken.'

'Has Chetan been informed?'

'He has been verbally intimated, but the formalities will be completed only after he is declared medically fit to resume work.'

Avinash was jubilant and hurried to inform Babu, who was in the break room. The news spread quickly among the temporary workers, who were all thrilled. They organized a meeting a couple of days later, and it evoked a better response than ever before. Most of those who spoke that day boisterously vowed to build up a united front. Some of them even suggested the names of some professional trade union leaders to lead them. Babu concluded the meeting by summing up the issues and stressing the need to reach out to all temporary workers. In the evening, Avinash and Babu went to the hospital to see Chetan, who welcomed them with a big smile.

'An official from the personnel department came yesterday to tell me that I'll be absorbed as a regular employee. After he left, Patil and a couple of men from the labour union also visited me,' he said. 'They sympathized with me and said they would support me. And they also said that they had made tremendous efforts with the senior management to plead my case.'

'Is that so?' Babu interrupted. 'They are lying—they only want the credit for our work.'

'Babu, the question is not of credit. Chetan being absorbed as a regular employee is more important,' Avinash said. 'We're just ordinary, dispensable workers. And remember, even Joseph had told us about Patil's meeting with the manager.'

'But we had taken up the issue first,' Babu said firmly. 'You don't know these people. They only want Chetan to join their union.'

Avinash shook his head. 'Why are you talking as if we are rivals or are at war with them?' he asked.

'One more thing,' Chetan said before Babu could reply. 'They said that the moment I join work as a regular employee, I should become a member of their union.'

'See, I told you! They have a hidden agenda!' Babu exclaimed. 'They're just like politicians.'

'Relax, Babu,' Avinash said.

Before parting ways after the hospital visit, Avinash and Babu had some tea at a roadside stall nearby, where they decided to organize meetings of the temporary workers more regularly and build up an organization to represent them. Their first demand would be the allocation of safety gear for the temporary workers.

With this break in employment, Avinash felt like a free bird again—a bird which could spread its wings and soar in the sky at will, enjoying its view of the world. How he wished that he were indeed a bird. The only problem was that irrespective of the altitude and duration of its flight, a bird could not remain airborne forever—it would have to descend to the earth for food and shelter. His elation over his freedom was overshadowed by the worry of being jobless for who knew how long.

And so, even as he looked around for a job, Avinash started spending long hours at the college and in the library. Several weeks later, an opportunity sprung up—the port authorities were hiring tally clerks for supervising cargo loading and unloading operations. He applied immediately, cleared the written test and got called for an interview.

PART THREE

The Docks

CHAPTER 11

A week later, when Avinash visited the docks early in the morning for the final interview, he found the harbour bustling with activity. Quay cranes were peering into the cargo holds of docked ships. Gantries were handling containers on some ships, with trucks waiting on the wharves below. Huge transit sheds along the berths displayed 'No Smoking' and 'Keep the Docks Clean' messages in big letters on their walls. A peculiar stench, akin to a barrel of paint dripping over a pile of garbage on the seashore on a sunny day, hung in the air.

Avinash was waiting at the dock office on the first floor. There were other candidates along with him, but he was confident of being selected as his name was third in the merit list of candidates displayed on the noticeboard of the office. The foghorn of a ship ripped through the silence, and Avinash looked out the window. A tugboat was moving in the dock basin, toeing a crease in the still water as it pulled a huge cargo ship in to dock. Another tugboat was at the stern of the ship.

'Avinash Gaikwad!' a clerk standing at the door to the manager's cabin shouted. Avinash stood up and rushed forward, clutching his file. The clerk held the door open for him.

Inside, three people were sitting behind a huge wooden table. The person in the centre was in his fifties—fair, bespectacled, clean-shaven and thin. He was wearing a cream-coloured safari suit which looked a bit oversized. He'd left the shirt unbuttoned at the top, revealing a gleaming gold chain. Clearly, he was the manager.

On his right was a middle-aged, round-faced, chubby woman in a pink floral sari, and on his left was a fat, bald, bearded man in a brown shirt.

Avinash paused at the door. 'May I ...'

The manager looked at him and nodded. Avinash noticed his probing eyes as he approached the table. 'My name is Avinash Gaikwad,' he said, handing over his file.

'Sit down,' the manager said, opening the file and browsing through it.

Thanking him, Avinash pulled a chair and sat down. There were several maps mounted on the walls—among them was a map of the world, a map of India and one of the layout of the port. There were also several cupboards stuffed full with files. Some more files, a desk calendar, a pen stand and a plastic globe lay on the table in front of the manager.

'Hmm ... You're in the top three among those who've cleared the written test,' the manager said, glancing at a sheet of paper on the table. The other two looked at Avinash and smiled.

Avinash could see a twinkle in the manager's eyes as he leafed through his file. Suddenly, he stopped, and the gleam in his eyes vanished. He frowned as he read something in the file and looked up at Avinash. 'You're a Buddhist?' he asked.

'Yes, sir,' Avinash said. 'My ancestors were untouchables, and my father converted to Buddhism.'

'Hmm ...' The manager turned over some more pages hurriedly. 'Where is your caste certificate?' he asked. The expression on his face had changed from appreciation to disdain.

'Caste certificate?' Avinash asked. He had not been expecting that question.

'Yes, you will have to submit a caste certificate.'

'But, sir, I've applied in the open category. I'm not seeking employment in the reserved category,' he clarified. 'My performance in the written test was good. I'm among the top three candidates in the merit list. Please treat me as a general candidate.'

The manager frowned and looked at Avinash and then to his right and left. The other panellists, too, seemed shocked.

'Why?' the manager asked in a raised voice. 'Don't you want reservation?'

'No, sir.'

'This is bizarre. Who do you think you are?' the lady asked. The second man just nodded along and looked at Avinash with cold eyes.

The manager closed his file. 'See, you will have to produce your caste certificate.' The other two nodded along mechanically.

'But, sir, please treat me as a general candidate,' Avinash said. 'I haven't got my caste certificate from the government yet.'

'Then get it,' the lady said curtly.

Avinash felt irritated. 'But I don't want to,' he said.

'Why not?' the trio asked almost in unison, looking at each other in confusion.

'Because I don't have to, not when I've applied as an open-category candidate,' Avinash said.

The trio looked at one another again. 'Are you against the reservation policy?' the manager asked.

Avinash smiled. 'No, I'm not against it,' he said. 'There are many other people who genuinely need it—I can get a job without using it and can leave a reserved seat vacant for them.'

'Oh, very clever,' the manager grinned. 'You can go,' he said, pushing Avinash's file back towards him. The lady and the bald man stared at him.

'I thought you would appreciate someone declining reservation,' Avinash said. 'But you are not even acknowledging my merit.'

There was an uncomfortable silence in the room for a few seconds. Then the manager said coldly, 'We need to seek legal advice. We'll get back to you.'

Avinash rose, picking up his file. 'I'll wait to hear from you, sir. And in the meanwhile, I'll also check up on the legal aspects of this case,' he said. 'Thank you.'

He left the cabin, and the other candidates anxiously awaiting their turn looked at him. 'Chintaman Joshi!' the peon shouted, reading from the list of candidates in his hand.

A tall, thin, bespectacled youth, with a thick red tilak on his forehead, immediately came to his feet. With his closed eyes, he quickly murmured something under his breath and then hurried towards the manager's cabin.

Avinash looked out of the window before going down the staircase. The cargo liner had now been berthed. A gang of docking staff was mooring the ship with thick ropes thrown from the deck. He came out of the office building and walked towards the main gate. Security personnel from the port authority, city police and customs department were monitoring the movement of vehicles and pedestrians, and he was frisked before being allowed to exit.

Outside the docks, there was a flurry of activity. The road was thickly populated with trucks, trailers, cranes and forklifts. Labourers and handcart-pullers milled around. Some of them were pulling handcarts loaded with wooden cases and crates. They were all sweating profusely, but they didn't bother to wipe off the sweat dripping from the tips of their noses and chins. There were wet patches on their shirts. The smell of sweat hung everywhere; it was like being in a crowded gymnasium or the second-class compartment of a local train during rush hour.

'What happened?' Dagadoo asked as soon as Avinash came up the stairs of their house. Godavari and he had been waiting anxiously for a long while for their son to return home.

'What will happen?' Godavari asked with a smile. 'He must have got the job.'

Avinash looked at her. 'How do you know?' he asked.

'I know,' she said. 'I prayed to God. He knows our plight, and he will hear my prayer.'

Avinash laughed. 'In fact, I've not been selected,' he said. 'And the irony is that I'm among the top three candidates in the merit list.'

'Oh! Then why not?' she asked, her smile fading quickly.

'I thought you would be easily selected,' Dagadoo said. 'What went wrong?'

'They have asked me to submit a caste certificate,' Avinash said.

'Caste certificate? But you've not applied for a reserved seat.'

'I told them that—they are going to seek legal advice and then decide.'

'Oh,' Dagadoo sighed. 'But I think that if they seek a legal opinion, they'll be told to appoint you.'

'I hope so,' Avinash said.

'Dagadoo, are you home?' someone hollered from outside the house.

Avinash went to the door. It was Hari. 'Yes, Hari kaka, he's at home.'

Hari smiled and began ascending the steps slowly. On reaching the door, he removed his footwear and came inside, panting heavily. Dagadoo rose to greet him while Godavari brought him a glass of water, which he gulped down thirstily.

'It's good that you are all at home,' he said, wiping his face with a handkerchief. 'Have you applied for a job at the port?' Hari asked Avinash. 'There are some vacancies right now.'

'Yes,' Avinash said. 'They interviewed me today.'

'That's great! Don't worry, I'll ensure that you are selected,' Hari exclaimed. Then, turning to Dagadoo, he said, 'Your son has hit a jackpot. Your life is going to change for the better.' Dagadoo smiled.

'But they have put his appointment on hold,' Godavari said. 'They are asking for a caste certificate.'

'Then submit it,' Hari said.

'We don't have a caste certificate,' Dagadoo said.

'No problem! I'll help you; I have connections. I've told you this before as well!' Hari said. 'The only thing is you'll have to spend some money.'

'But I've applied in the general category, Hari kaka, where no caste certificate is required,' Avinash said.

Hari laughed. 'Why do you need to go in the general category?' he asked. 'Get a caste certificate—it's our right. Just come to my house tomorrow with all your documents.'

'Hari, stay out of it,' Dagadoo said. 'Avinash will get his appointment letter without a caste certificate and without spending money.'

Hari shook his head and stared at Dagadoo. 'Brother, don't ruin your son's future. Listen to me,' he said. 'I can get it done.' Then, turning to Avinash, he said, 'Don't pay me anything right now. Pay me later. After all, I can do at least this much for my nephew.'

'No, Hari,' Dagadoo said curtly. 'Please don't bother.'

'You are so strange, Dagadoo,' Hari said. 'You've made your own life miserable because of your impractical thoughts. Don't do the same to your son's life, too.'

Dagadoo stared at Hari. 'You will never understand,' he said.

'You were the first person from our village to migrate to this city and what have you earned?' Hari asked. 'Look at me—I own two apartments, two vehicles and I've recently bought some land near our village. I'm earning a lot of money, while you're still languishing in a slum.'

Dagadoo nodded. 'Yes, you are certainly wealthy, but what is the colour of your money?' he asked.

'The colour of my money?' Hari laughed mockingly. 'Nobody is bothered about the colour of money in this world. It may be white or black or any other colour—the only thing that matters is whether you have it or not.'

'It all depends on your values, Hari. I'm happy with mine, and you are free to choose yours.'

Hari shook his head in despair and sipped the tea Godavari had served him in silence. Then he slowly got up, balancing his obese body on his hands as he rose to his feet. The gold chain around his neck flashed. 'So, shall I expect you tomorrow, if you change your mind, that is?' he asked Avinash with a sheepish smile.

'No, Hari, we don't need your help,' Dagadoo said.

'All right,' Hari said. He went out of the door, slipped his feet into his footwear and slowly descended the steps.

After he left, Godavari said, 'You should've taken his help—he knows a lot of people.'

'You know he's mixed up with crooks,' Dagadoo said.

'But what will happen to Avinash's appointment?'

'Don't worry—just be patient.'

'But we're abandoning the easy way out and making his life difficult,' Godavari said. 'He's just a young boy.'

Dagadoo glanced at her and then at Avinash. 'Don't you realize that he's among the toppers in the merit list?' he asked. 'Have faith in the Constitution. Instead of overprotecting him and making his life easier, let him face difficulties and overcome them. Remember the difficulties faced by Babasaheb. He's our guiding light.'

Avinash felt dejected and unwanted. Brooding over his plight, he sat on the threshold of the house and thought about his father, his community and Babasaheb. Perhaps his father was right. If he had merit, there was no need to seek a reserved seat. Some other needy candidate could use it. There were enough people who were in worse conditions than him.

Avinash eagerly awaited the decision of the port authorities. A fortnight passed and just as he was beginning to lose hope, a letter arrived, informing him that his appointment had been confirmed, subject to a medical examination at the port hospital. His parents were both relieved and elated at the development.

'I knew he would be appointed,' Dagadoo told Godavari. 'Now he has a secure government job.'

'Yes, and once I join, I want you both to give up your jobs and relax. You don't need to work anymore,' Avinash said. 'Now it's my turn.'

'I would like to continue working,' his father said. 'But your mother can stop working now.'

'I don't know what to do,' Godavari said, looking bewildered. 'Let me think it over.'

Avinash visited the port hospital the next day for an examination and was declared fit for work. When he went to the dock office, the manager handed over his appointment letter. 'We consulted the legal department, and they cleared your case,' he said.

'I was hoping it would be cleared, sir,' Avinash said.

The manager smiled sheepishly. 'Err, well, we were hesitant because we were not comfortable with taking you in the open category,' he said.

'Why? Is there no merit in me?'

The manager shook his head. 'That's not the issue. Frankly speaking, you are blocking one seat in the open category, which would've otherwise gone to a general candidate from the upper castes. You have now reduced the seats in the open category by one.'

'Oh! So, clearly, even if a person from a lower caste refuses reservation, you don't consider him at par with his upper-caste counterpart, despite his merit,' Avinash said.

The manager rose from his seat. 'Let's not get into all this,' he said. 'The Constitution is on your side, and your appointment has been cleared. Report to the timekeeper's office for duty tomorrow.'

Avinash left the dock office with mixed feelings. While he was elated that he had got a permanent white-collar job in a central government concern, he was anguished by the attitude of people occupying key positions. Later that day, when he broke the news of his confirmation to his parents, they were ecstatic.

'They had no valid reason to reject you,' Dagadoo said.

'They had an unofficial reason,' Avinash replied, narrating his conversation with the manager.

Dagadoo shook his head in despair. 'These prejudices suit their convenience,' he said. 'But don't let that bother you. It's their problem—don't make it yours. Just remember that you are in a better position than your ancestors and that you should perform your duty sincerely and work hard.'

That day, Dagadoo and Godavari went around distributing sweets to their neighbours.

'Most of the neighbours are saying that our life is going to change for the better,' she told Avinash when they returned home. 'Some of them are even saying that now there is no need for you to study further.'

'But I would still like to continue with college,' Avinash said.

'He's right,' Dagadoo said. 'Let him graduate if he's willing to slog it out.'

'But how can he attend college now?' she asked.

'I'll be working in shifts and whenever possible, I'll go to college,' Avinash said. 'It'll be the same routine as in the past, except that instead of being a factory worker, I'll be a clerk in a central government entity.'

Godavari nodded, smiling.

'But when are you going to stop working?' he asked her. 'You said that you'll give up your job if I get a permanent one.' His mother looked lost in thought, and he kept gazing at her, waiting for an answer.

'Yes. Give up your tiring work and stay home now,' Dagadoo said.

'All right, if you both insist,' she said finally, beaming. 'I guess it's possible now that you have a secure government job.'

Their conversation was interrupted soon because word of Avinash's appointment had spread through the slum, and many people, including Raja and Sudhir, came visiting to congratulate them. Godavari made some tea for them as she had run out of sweets.

The next day, Avinash reported for his first day of duty at the dock office. Many others like him were waiting with their appointment letters. They were taken to the Yellow Gate Police Station to record their fingerprints before being issued dock-entry permits. Back at the dock, Avinash was amazed when he saw the huge cargo ships at close quarters. Most of them were foreign cargo ships, flying the flags of the countries of their origin on their stern and the Indian flag on the mast. For an entire week, the new recruits were divided into batches of four and assigned to an instructor for training. They learned how to examine and tally imported cargo discharged from a ship, as well as how to check the documents for export cargo consignments before they were loaded onboard. They were also made familiar with the procedures involved in the warehousing of cargo that was lying uncleared after a specific period and the rules of verifying cargo and its documents before issuing gate passes to importers' trucks taking delivery.

Before the week was over, the names of Avinash and the other new recruits were put into the roster of the tally pool on the noticeboard. Tally clerks had to report for duty at one of the three booking points set up at different locations along the length of the docks as per their shift timings. The timekeeper's office staff at each booking point posted them at a different berth everyday according to the number of hatches of a ship being worked in that shift. The different locations of the booking points ensured that the tally clerks were not required to walk long distances to the berth assigned to them. If a ship was loading or unloading cargo from three hatches, three tally clerks would be posted at that berth to tally the cargo being handled at each of the hatches. The shifts would change every week and the roster of their booking point for the following week used to be displayed three days in advance at all the three booking points.

CHAPTER 12

It was a hot, sunny morning, and cargo activity at the port was yet to begin. Shore labourers were walking towards their specified work points. Avinash and one of his colleagues, Mohan, were posted at berth number six for the day. Mohan was tall, thin and dark-skinned, and his hair was carefully groomed like that of a film actor's.

At the transit shed along the wharf, fire extinguishers and buckets of sand had been placed near the gate. A blackboard stood opposite the entrance, displaying the particulars of the docked ship including its name, tonnage, import general manifest (IGM) number, type of cargo, shipping line, agents, stevedores and sailing date. The stevedoring staff was busy handling all the documents related to the ship's cargo movement. The superintendent's enclosure was near the entrance. A room resembling a huge cage was located opposite the enclosure. It was locked and a signboard hanging from its door read, 'Lockfast Cargo'.

The superintendent, dressed in a spotless white uniform with silver stripes and two crossed anchors stitched on black epaulettes, was busy with his morning rituals inside his office. He stood facing the wall, with his hands folded and his back towards Avinash and Mohan. Near him stood the labour supervisor in a white uniform, also with his hands folded. Both were mumbling some prayers.

There were photographs of several gods, prophets, godmen and religious places arranged on a wooden plank affixed to the wall. The superintendent lit some incense sticks and, as the aromatic smoke spread, he waved them in circles in front of the photographs, invoking the deities and murmuring something.

Then he turned around, opened all the four drawers of his table and held the incense sticks inside each one, filling them with the smoke. He even tried to wave back the smoke coming out of the drawers to ensure that it remained inside for longer. Then he inserted the incense sticks into a holder and placed them below the row of photographs on the shelf. Before sitting down, he touched each drawer with folded hands and closed his eyes, seeking divine blessings.

Avinash produced the duty slip issued by the dock office. The superintendent, Keshav Phadke, was a short, plump man in his fifties. He looked at Avinash and then at Mohan. 'New recruits?' he asked, narrowing his eyes.

'Yes, sir,' Avinash and Mohan said in unison.

He wrote their names in the huge logbook spread out on his table. Avinash noticed threads of black, yellow and red tied on Phadke's right wrist as he was writing.

'Two hatches are working today, number two and three,' he said. 'Avinash will work at hatch number two and Mohan at number three. Be careful while tallying the cargo. The tally sheet is a legal document that is submitted in court in case of any litigation; so, there should be no overwriting or smudging.'

The duo nodded and left the superintendent's office. They came out on to the wharf and saw that the ship docked was painted black, with a huge red stripe running along its length. The American flag flew on the stern and the Indian flag on the mast. The ship's name was painted in white on both sides of the stem in large capital letters. On the stern, the name of the mother port was also painted below the ship's name. The ship was moored to the wharf with thick nylon ropes with circular rat guards clamped midway around them to prevent rats from entering the ship. The upper deck towered almost twenty feet above the wharf. A metal gangway with a safety net around it was lowered from the deck, almost touching the wharf.

Avinash went and sat on the wharf on a folding chair with his tally sheet on a clipboard. A quay crane picked up some wooden cases in a sling from the hatch and as it was being lowered on to the wharf, the shore workers surrounded it and shouted, 'Aaryaa, aaryaa!', signalling the crane driver to land the sling on the wharf. They took the sling off the hook of the crane and shouted, 'Haabays, haabays!', signalling the crane driver to pull up the hook. The crane rotated on its axis and seemed to peer into the ship's hold for another sling of cargo.

Avinash recorded the shipping marks, counted the wooden cases and noted their condition before they were carted inside the shed by the dock workers. He saw Mohan doing the same at hatch number three. Intermittently, they waved or walked over to each other when the cargo on the wharf was cleared by the workers and the next sling was yet to arrive.

During his lunch break, Avinash went inside the superintendent's enclosure to submit the tally sheet and collect his lunch box. It was crowded with clearing agents and importers, and the superintendent was busy thumping his rubber stamp on documents and signing them. Avinash was impressed by the speed with which he was working.

As Avinash turned to leave, he saw a drawer of the superintendent's table lying open, and every clearing agent and importer was dropping notes into it before getting his documents signed. Each time, the superintendent would look down at the drawer before signing a document to ensure that money had been dropped. Avinash found himself feeling embarrassed. Just then, the superintendent caught his gaze and smiled. 'Going for lunch?' he asked.

'Yes.'

'Wait, I've sent the peon to bring us biryani.'

'No, thank you, sir,' Avinash said.

'It's chicken biryani from Hotel Biryani Darbar.'

'Sir, I'm vegetarian.'

'Oh, really? But how is that so when you're a Gaikwad?'

Avinash smiled. 'My family eats non-vegetarian food, but I don't.'

'Strange. You are making me feel guilty.'

'Not at all, sir—this is just a personal choice.'

'Are you from the Warkari sect?'

'No, sir. My ancestors were untouchables. My parents converted to Buddhism.'

'Oh. So, you're a Jai Bhim guy.'

'Yes, sir.'

'Oh! Wait a minute then, I'll order some vegetarian food for you.'

'No, thank you, sir. I prefer to eat home-cooked food,' Avinash said, showing him his lunch box. Phadke shrugged and Avinash walked out.

'Why are you going to the canteen?' Mohan asked. 'Saheb has ordered biryani.'

Avinash smiled. 'I don't want it. You can wait and eat it.'

While on his way to the canteen, he saw a vessel docked at berth number seven, flying the flag of Panama on its stern. However, he was shocked when he looked up at the mast. The Indian flag was flying upside down, with the green strip on the top and the saffron strip at the bottom. He entered the shed and went to the superintendent's enclosure, where some businessmen were waiting with briefcases and documents in their hands. Inside, the superintendent, a tall, lanky man dressed in a white uniform, was signing some papers. On the wall behind him was a row of pictures of various deities, just like the ones he'd seen in the morning in his own shed. The man looked up at Avinash questioningly, and he then told him about the flag.

'What?' the superintendent asked. Avinash repeated that the Indian flag was hoisted upside down.

'Who are you?' the superintendent demanded.

'Sir, I'm a tally clerk.'

'Where are you posted today?'

'Sir, at berth number six.'

The superintendent put his pen down and looked at Avinash with contempt. 'Do you have no other work? What are you doing in my shed?' The clearing agents around him giggled.

Avinash was shocked. 'Sir, I was just going to the canteen for lunch when I saw the flag flying the wrong way and thought I should tell you.'

The superintendent got up from his seat. 'Do you think I have no other work?' he asked. 'Go away, or I'll make a complaint about you entering my shed without authorization.'

Avinash left the shed and stood staring at the upside-down flag. The office of the assistant docks manager for that section of the docks was nearby. Making a quick decision, he hurried over to the office, where a couple of clerks were having lunch. The door to the single cabin within was closed, and a black wooden nameplate on it read 'A.B. Kulkarni, Assistant Docks Manager'. Avinash knocked on the door and then pushed it open. A middle-aged man wearing glasses was sitting behind a desk on which piles of papers were lying with paperweights on them. There was also a pen stand on the table with a couple of pens in it. The man was reading some documents. A fragment of the harbour was visible from the window behind him. He looked up and nodded on seeing Avinash, and then asked him what the matter was.

When Avinash told him about the flag, Kulkarni stared at him for a moment. 'Why have you come to me for such a trivial matter?' he asked. 'The shed superintendent, the ship's agent or the stevedore would've taken care of it.'

'Sir, I met the superintendent and told him about it.'

'Oh! Then why did you come to me?'

'Because he refused to do anything and sent me away.'

Just then, the phone on the desk rang. Kulkarni picked it up and started talking to the caller. Avinash waited for him to say something until Kulkarni waved his hand, signalling him to leave.

Disappointed, Avinash went to the canteen, where he met a few acquaintances, and after exchanging pleasantries with them, he ate his lunch alone. While returning to his shed, he glanced at the ship at wharf number seven and felt relieved when he saw that the national flag was now flying in the proper position, with the saffron strip on the top.

Back at his shed, the shore workers were either playing cards or taking naps on the cargo stacked inside. The superintendent and some other staff members were eating lunch in the export cargo receiver's office on the mezzanine floor. Avinash put his lunch box in his bag, pulled out a book and went to sit on a chair on the wharf.

A little later, Mohan came out of the shed and, pulling a chair, sat beside him. 'The biryani was tasty,' he said. 'You should've joined us.'

Avinash smiled and closed the book.

Mohan looked at the book and asked, 'You're reading Ambedkar?'

'Yes.'

'Are you from the Jai Bhim community?'

'Yes.'

'Oh! But your name was in the general category on the recruitment list.'

'That's right. I had applied through the open category.'

'That's very strange and unusual. But I don't care—I'm from a higher caste, but I don't believe in the caste system. As a matter of fact, I have some friends from your community.'

Avinash smiled in response. He knew that what Mohan had said was meant to be a compliment, to claim that the speaker was above caste prejudice. But it was usually just a formality. Moments later, a siren signalled the end of the lunch break.

That afternoon, cargo unloading was in full swing. Avinash was checking the shipping marks and the condition of the cargo on the wharf when he found the superintendent standing next to him.

'Gaikwad, some special cargo is being offloaded from your hatch. Be careful while tallying it.'

'Special cargo?'

'Yes. It's lockfast cargo—it will be kept in a separate, locked enclosure to prevent theft.'

'All right, sir.'

'Good,' the superintendent said and went back into the shed.

After a while, the quay crane lowered a pallet of cartons onto the wharf amidst cries of 'Aaryaa'. Avinash got up from his chair as the shore labourers unhooked the sling. It was a consignment of cartons containing international brands of liquor and cigarettes. The labourers unloaded the cartons and carted them inside the shed after Avinash had counted them. He recorded the shipping marks, quantity and condition of the cartons. The crane swung towards the hatch for another sling of the consignment. With the cartons cleared from the wharf, Avinash looked over his shoulder. The superintendent and a handful of other staff members had opened the lockfast room, and the cartons were being stacked inside.

Mohan came to stand next to him. 'Wow, these are expensive brands of liquor and cigarettes!' he said with a broad smile, looking at the cartons. 'I wish this consignment had been offloaded from my hatch.'

'Why?'

'I would've tried to get a couple of bottles at a discount from the consignee.'

At the end of the shift, Avinash completed the tally sheet after calculating the total number of cartons per consignment and recording the condition in which they had landed on the wharf. When he went into the shed, he saw the superintendent, the labour supervisor and the export cargo receiver coming out of the lockfast room. The superintendent locked it and returned to his chair.

'Show me your tally sheet,' the superintendent said, and Avinash placed it on the table.

'Oh my God!' the superintendent exclaimed. 'What is this?'

'What is it?' Avinash asked and looked at the tally sheet.

'In the remarks column, you've mentioned that only two cartons were received in a torn condition and that only one was completely damaged.'

'Yes, that's right. I examined the cartons before recording their condition. I've recorded their serial numbers also.'

'Oh God! That's not enough! You should've marked at least twenty to thirty cartons as damaged or torn.'

'But, sir, that's not true.'

'You may have missed some of the damaged cartons; you must've gone for tea while the consignment was being offloaded.'

'No, sir. I was there all the time. My tally is perfect.'

'Oh, is that right? But we have to be very careful with lockfast cargo. What if someone opens the cartons and takes away some liquor bottles or cigarette packets?'

Avinash was shocked. 'How is that possible, sir? The consignment is in the lockfast room and only you have the key.'

Phadke grinned. 'You don't understand, Avinash! We have to play it safe,' he said.

The labour supervisor walked in just then. 'Is there a problem?' he asked.

'He has not written enough remarks in his tally sheet about the lockfast cargo,' Phadke said.

'Oh, really? I'll talk to him,' the supervisor said and turned to Avinash. 'See, Avinash, there is going to be no problem if you make some changes to your tally sheet. You won't lose anything. Come on, do it.'

'But why? No, sir, I'm sorry, I can't.'

The supervisor wrapped his arm around Avinash's shoulders. 'Come with me, let me tell you something,' he said.

The two of them stepped out onto the wharf where the cargo movement had been paused before the start of the next shift. The supervisor was dark-skinned, bulky and short. He was wearing a gold chain that had a tiny sapphire pendant. 'You're new here, right? What is your full name?' the supervisor asked.

'Avinash Gaikwad,' Avinash replied.

'Gaikwad?' the supervisor asked and scratched his head, narrowing his eyes. 'That's a surname that's used in several communities. Which one are you from?'

'I'm a Buddhist.'

The supervisor's face lit up. 'Oh, that's great!' he said. 'That means you are from the Jai Bhim community.'

'Yes,' Avinash said curtly. 'Is that a problem?'

'No, no! I'm also from your community,' the supervisor said, smiling broadly and reaching out to shake Avinash's hand. 'Jai Bhim! My name is Vikas Kamble.'

'Oh! Well, I saw you worshipping gods with the superintendent in the morning,' Avinash said, 'when there are none in Buddhism.'

The smile vanished from Kamble's face. He looked around to ensure that nobody was within earshot and then whispered, 'Oh, that? I know there is no god in Buddhism, and you must've noticed that the Buddha's picture was not displayed there. What I did was just an act. We have to do it so that the system works smoothly and everyone benefits.'

Avinash was appalled.

Kamble winked at him. 'Here, we believe in the live-and-let-live principle. We are all here to make money. So, you just follow the traditions quietly. For example, there is no problem if you mention a larger number of torn and damaged cartons.'

'But why should I do such a thing when it's not true?'

'I know it's not true, but what if a thief steals some bottles or a couple of cartons?'

'How is it possible when the consignments are locked?'

Kamble scratched his head. 'You don't understand, boy. Suppose we want to taste the liquor and take away some bottles, it will be safe to do so if the record says that more cartons had arrived damaged.'

'Isn't that theft?'

'No, no—think of it as our perquisite! And these privileges will not last forever because soon, entire cargos will be moved in containers.'

'But this is just ridiculous! How can you justify such blatant thievery? We are the custodians of the cargo, and we get salaries for working on behalf of the government.'

'Yes, but who is the government here? We are! You don't lose anything. Instead, you gain something extra!' Kamble winked and smiled. 'You can also take a bottle for yourself.'

'What are you saying? I would never do that,' Avinash snapped. 'And by the way, I don't drink.'

'Well, you can gift a bottle to someone or even sell it.'

'That's rubbish.'

'See, Phadke and I have been good friends for over ten years. He is a very broad-minded and cooperative person—don't antagonize him unnecessarily.'

'I'm sorry, but I won't change anything in my tally sheet.'

Kamble shrugged and shook his head in despair. 'You need to learn many things,' he said.

There was a long spell of silence, and then both of them walked back inside. Phadke was writing something in the logbook. He looked up as they entered.

'I tried to talk to him, sir, but he's refusing to do it,' Kamble said.

'Oh! I was sure you would convince him,' Phadke said. 'After all, he's also a Jai Bhim-wala.'

'He's a new recruit, sir. He'll take some time to settle down and learn our ways.'

Phadke smiled and moved closer to Avinash. 'You can take away two bottles and a carton of cigarettes,' he whispered.

Avinash stared at him for a moment, controlling his rage. 'No, thank you. I don't want any bottles,' he said, checking his tally sheet. 'I won't write any false remarks in the tally sheet. And if there is a dispute or litigation, I'll tell the truth.'

Kamble and Phadke looked at each other helplessly as Avinash walked out. Mohan was waiting for him outside the shed. As they started walking together, Mohan said, 'You should've taken the bottles and given them to me since you don't drink.'

'Are you crazy?' Avinash snapped.

'I'm just saying that you should not have annoyed them, and I would've also been able to taste imported liquor for free if you'd changed your tally sheet.'

'You mean we should obey whatever they say, even if it's illegal and immoral?'

Mohan shook his head sadly and said nothing. Soon, they went their separate ways.

Later that evening, Avinash narrated the entire episode to his parents at home. Godavari looked worried. 'Don't make enemies at work,' she said. 'I don't want you to lose this job.'

Dagadoo laughed. 'You don't know these things,' he said. 'Avinash has done the right thing.'

'But what if they get offended and create problems for him?'

'Don't worry, he's working for a government agency and is better protected than private sector employees.' Then, he turned to Avinash. 'Honesty and hard work are your shields,' he said. 'But you'll always have to be careful. Don't make any mistakes because you won't be spared.'

Avinash nodded and sat down at his usual spot on the threshold of the house. The piece of the city in front of him was bustling with activity in all its glitz. It had always fascinated him, but the closer he tried to get, the more he discovered how ugly and unscrupulous it was. It had its own rules and regulations, which were not necessarily aligned with morality or legality. It was a make-believe world, boisterous and deceptive.

CHAPTER 13

A week later, some export cargo was being stuffed into containers at the Ballard Pier. The transit shed was full of wooden cases, crates and cartons of different sizes. Avinash verified the shipping bill for each consignment to check if all the necessary permissions from the port authority and the customs department were in order. Then, he examined the cargo for shipping marks and counted the boxes before they were carted into a container. Mohan was monitoring the cargo being stuffed into another container on the other side of the transit shed.

During the lunch break, they decided to go to the canteen in the head office building, which was two blocks away from the dock gate. On reaching the building, they went to the fifth floor, where the canteen was located, and saw that it was getting crowded with the head office staff. Mohan waved at two men sitting at a table and joined them. Avinash followed suit. 'They are our seniors at the docks,' Mohan said to Avinash as he made the introductions.

While eating, Mohan and the two men started discussing 'tricks' to earn extra money from importers, such as finding a mismatch between the shipping documents and the cargo or colluding with them in case the importer wanted to take away someone else's cargo.

Four employees sitting at the adjacent table were clearly amused with the things they were overhearing. One of them finished his lunch quickly, went to the washbasin and then came back to their table, wiping his hands with a handkerchief.

'My name is Chinmay Bapat, and I work in the accounts section here,' he said as they exchanged pleasantries. 'You people are lucky that you are out in the field,' he continued. 'We have to slog it out, sitting in one spot all day.'

'But working outdoors is not easy. It's tiring, and we have to work hard in three shifts,' Mohan said.

Chinmay nodded, adjusting the spectacles on his face. 'Yes, that's right, but some outdoor staff also indulge in malpractices to earn extra money,' he said. 'I think we have to be honest. After all, we get salaries as custodians of all the cargo.'

Mohan looked at Avinash and then at his two friends sitting with them. 'Why don't you apply for an internal transfer whenever there are vacancies in the docks department?' he asked.

Chinmay thought for a moment. 'I'll think over it,' he said, picking up his lunch box and walking away.

'He doesn't know anything about our work,' the bearded senior snapped. 'He's talking like a schoolboy who is the best in the classroom, but doesn't know anything about the world outside.' Mohan and the other man laughed.

Once done with lunch, Mohan and Avinash walked back to the pier. After their shift ended, the duo was walking towards the gate when they saw a new recruit, Chintaman Joshi, walking ahead of them, wearing a bright red woollen jersey with a golden star on the chest.

'You look handsome in this jersey,' Mohan said when they caught up with him.

With his index finger, Joshi pushed his spectacles up on his nose and smiled. Then he looked around and whispered, 'You can also take one. Hundreds have landed at shed number seventeen. I came to know about it from a friend and picked one up for myself.'

'Wow! That's great!' Mohan exclaimed. Then, turning to Avinash, he said, 'Come. Let's go to shed seventeen.'

'Are you crazy? This is theft!' Avinash said. 'I'm not coming with you.'

Mohan shook his head and then hurried back towards the shed. Joshi and Avinash approached the gate, where Kamble stood talking to a policeman. He waved at Avinash, while Joshi went ahead towards the frisking point.

'How are you?' Kamble asked.

'Good,' Avinash replied. The policeman shook hands with Kamble and went away.

Suddenly, there was a shout, and Avinash saw Joshi and a policeman at the gate locked in an argument.

'Isn't he a new recruit like you?' Kamble asked, looking at Joshi.

'Yes, that's Chintaman Joshi from the tally pool.'

Kamble dashed towards the policeman, who greeted him respectfully. 'What happened?' Kamble asked.

'Sir, he's saying this jersey belongs to him, but I suspect it doesn't.'

'Wait,' Kamble said, releasing Joshi's hand from the policeman's grip. He took Joshi aside and said, 'Tell me the truth, and I'll save you. Otherwise, you may lose your job for stealing cargo. You can even end up behind bars for such a petty theft.'

Joshi was shocked and pleaded for help. 'I picked it up from shed number seventeen, where hundreds of bales full of similar jerseys have landed. I just took one for myself.'

Kamble nodded. 'But why didn't you tell the policeman the truth?' he asked.

'Because I was scared that he may take action against me.'

Kamble put his arm around Joshi and began to lead him back to the policeman. 'Remember, always tell the security people the truth. Don't do such things without informing them. Take them into your confidence, or they'll feel cheated.'

At the frisking point, Kamble said to the policeman, 'He brought this from shed number seventeen for himself but was too scared to tell you the truth. He's a new recruit.'

'He shouldn't have lied to me,' the policeman said. Then, eyeing the jersey again, he said, 'I like this jersey.'

'All right,' Kamble said and asked Joshi to take the jersey off. Without a word, Joshi did as told, and Kamble handed the jersey over to the policeman. Then, turning to Joshi, Kamble said, 'Go back to that shed and get another one for yourself.'

The policeman folded the jersey and put it in his bag. 'Yes, get another one for yourself,' he told Joshi, who hesitated.

'I don't want to go back,' he said.

'Don't worry,' the policeman said. 'I'm sitting here. Nobody will stop you.'

Joshi looked at Kamble and then at the policeman for a moment. Then he rushed back to the shed, beaming.

Kamble cursed under his breath, watching Joshi disappear. He smiled sheepishly as he caught Avinash's eye.

'You've just helped him steal,' Avinash said.

Kamble collected himself. 'It's a minor thing. We have to help one another, across castes and religions,' he said. 'Otherwise, we'll be compelled to survive only on our salaries, or land in jail.'

Avinash felt repulsed, but he couldn't stop himself from asking, 'Aren't we supposed to survive only on our salaries?'

Kamble laughed. 'People like you can survive on their salaries,' he said. 'But people like us want to enjoy life, and we have other expenses too.'

Avinash looked at him with contempt and walked out of the gate. The policeman, having seen him talking to Kamble, just nodded instead of frisking him.

❦

Avinash found the job in the docks not just tedious, but mentally taxing too as he had to deal with greedy staff members and security personnel colluding with thieves and unscrupulous businessmen. But it was a secure job with legally defined and quantified increments, promotions and incentives, provident fund and gratuity benefits, access to medical facilities at the port hospital and a pension. So, he stuck it out, and two years later, he graduated from college. As usual, his parents celebrated the event. Dagadoo got the degree certificate framed and displayed it in the house.

'Now you should start sitting for the competitive civil services examinations,' Dagadoo said.

Godavari shook her head. 'Now that he has such a good job, there is no need,' she said.

Avinash looked at his father and then his mother. 'I want to study further and pursue a postgraduate degree,' he said.

Dagadoo thought for a moment. 'If you wish to continue studying, then you should,' he said.

Godavari was annoyed. 'If you're so keen, then continue with your studies, but don't quit this job,' she snapped.

So it was that Avinash took admission in the postgraduate course in the university's English department. He was already a member of the British Council Library which provided him with a steady supply of books. He loved to spend his weekly day off in the library, reading and browsing through the books there.

A few days later, he visited the British Council Library. There was silence inside the room as usual, except for the occasional whispers at the issuing counter and the distant murmur of traffic. Avinash was browsing through a book he had just picked up when he saw a familiar face. It was Vinayak Patwardhan, an assistant docks manager. He was wearing a sky-blue shirt with white stripes and a pair of black trousers. Of average height, and with a paunch and a receding hairline, Patwardhan was looking up at a bookshelf.

Avinash decided to walk up to him. 'Hello, sir,' he whispered.

Patwardhan turned and narrowed his eyes, trying to recollect who Avinash was.

'Avinash Gaikwad. I work in the tally pool,' Avinash whispered.

Patwardhan smiled and nodded. 'Oh! It's surprising to see someone from the docks in the library,' he whispered.

'It's surprising for me too, sir,' Avinash said. Patwardhan smiled and went back to the bookshelf. After some time, he came looking for Avinash, who was reading at a table.

'Are you through?' Patwardhan asked. He was carrying a couple of books.

Avinash nodded and picked up the books on the table. After giving their cards at the issuing counter and getting the due dates stamped on the books, they left the building.

'Do you come here often?' Patwardhan asked.

'Yes, sir. I'm doing my postgraduation in literature.'

'Oh, great,' Patwardhan smiled again. A car stopped in front of them, and Patwardhan opened the door. 'Can I drop you somewhere?'

'No, sir, thank you. I'll walk to the university.'

Nodding, Patwardhan got into the back seat and waved at him as the car drove away.

While returning home that evening, Avinash was waiting for a train at the railway terminal when he heard someone call his name. It was Babu.

When Babu reached him, they shook hands. 'How is your new job?' he asked Avinash.

'It's nice. What about you? How is the factory? Have they absorbed you as a regular worker?'

Babu shook his head. 'They didn't hire me again,' he sighed. 'Joseph told me that the management had decided to not hire you and me again—they thought we were troublemakers. And while being issued fresh contract letters, our colleagues were warned against organizing themselves into any kind of union.'

'Oh no. So, what are you doing now?'

'I've found a job in another factory closer to home. The wages are almost the same.'

'That's good. What about the union we were planning? And how is Chetan?'

'A few of our colleagues tried to organize an agitation to demand that we be reinstated, but there was no response,' he said, his face sullen. 'And the worst thing is that when they approached Chetan, who is now a permanent employee, he told them to give up the idea. How could he do that to *us*?' Babu shook his head sadly.

Avinash smiled. 'Babu, we tried to help a co-worker in distress, that's all,' he said. 'Don't expect anything in return when you help others. In Chetan's case, he's handicapped, and it's obvious that he doesn't want to lose his job.'

Babu didn't say anything for a moment. Then he shook his head again in despair. They parted a little after that as their trains were running from different platforms.

On his way home, Avinash found students from his Sunday class waiting in front of Buddha Vihar. They were all clearly in a jubilant mood as they surrounded him and showed him their annual examination marksheets—they had all passed with good marks.

'My father wants to meet you,' Anil said. 'He's waiting for you.'

All of them walked to Anil's house, where his father offered them sweets and expressed gratitude to Avinash. 'I have a very small request,' Anil's father said to Avinash. 'It would mean a lot if you would accept it.' He took some currency notes from his shirt pocket and held them out to Avinash. 'This is a small token of gratitude for coaching my son.'

Avinash shook his head. 'I don't charge any fee,' he said. 'I already told you that.'

'I know, but I'm following the tradition of giving guru dakshina to the teacher.'

'Thank you, but I can't accept this.'

'But then my son will carry the burden of learning something without compensating his teacher.'

Avinash thought for a while. Then, turning to Anil, he said, 'You don't have to carry any such baggage. Whenever a needy student approaches you, help him without expecting anything in return. That will be my guru dakshina. And please, never discriminate on the basis of caste, gender, class or religion.'

Anil nodded. His father looked a little lost in thought. Then, he collected himself, put the money back in his pocket, folded his hands and thanked Avinash.

Monsoon was the dullest season in the harbour because the handling of break-bulk cargo came to a standstill as the hatches of the ships could not be opened when it was raining. The quay cranes, with their hooks pulled up, stood motionless. Labourers were rendered idle for hours or, sometimes, even for the entire duration of their shift.

It was drizzling when Avinash and Mohan reached berth number sixteen for their second-shift duty. The wharf was full of a greyish-white sludge from the asbestos fibres which had fallen from offloaded bags. A few handcarts had been abandoned in the sludge, and workers were either sitting or lying on the cargo stacked inside the shed. Avinash and Mohan had to walk on their toes through the sludge to reach the shed. They reported for duty to the superintendent and waited for the weather to improve.

About an hour later, they heard the foreman's whistles, signalling the resumption of work. When they came out on the wharf, they saw that the rain had stopped, and the ship's hatches were being opened. The quay crane operator was ascending the narrow iron ladder to his cabin.

As the first sling of asbestos fibre bags was lowered on to the wharf, the workers gathered around it. Most were balancing themselves on their toes as they stood in the ankle-deep asbestos-fibre sludge. One worker even slipped and fell in the sludge while helping to land the sling. Avinash went near the sling, balancing himself in the sludge, to check the shipping marks. He noticed that each bag had a safety instruction printed in bold letters: 'Use No Hooks'. There was also an illustration of a crossed-out hook on each bag. Along with this, there was a warning that inhaling asbestos fibre was dangerous for the respiratory system. But the workers were all using hooks to handle the bags, causing yet more asbestos fibre to spill out and settle on the wharf.

'Why are you using hooks?' he asked the morpia, the leader of the twelve-men strong shore labour crew. He pointed at the illustration and the printed instructions on the bags.

'Can't help it, sir!' the morpia said. 'We've always been using hooks.'

'Have you people informed the authorities or the union?'

The morpia sighed. 'Everybody knows,' he said, 'but who cares?'

Avinash asked the men to wait for a second and went back to the shed. The morpia and Mohan followed him. The supervisor and the superintendent were sitting inside, chatting about work slowing down during the monsoon and the resultant decline in their extra income. Avinash greeted them and told them about the condition of the wharf.

'The work cannot be stopped,' said Superintendent Latif Shaikh, a bulky man in his fifties, with dyed hair and a grey beard.

'Sir, how can they work in these conditions?' Avinash asked the superintendent. 'They are also working without any safety gear and are using hooks.'

'Yes, sir, the workers are also saying that they can't work in such conditions,' the morpia said.

The superintendent frowned. 'Who will pay for this idle period if work is stopped?' he asked.

The supervisor then yelled at the morpia, 'Get back to work!'

'Sir, can we at least ask the stevedore to stop the work and have the wharf cleaned?' Avinash asked.

After mulling over it for a minute, the superintendent summoned the stevedore's supervisor, who shook his head. 'Shaikh sir, we're already behind schedule,' he said. 'There is a lot of cargo to be discharged, and the vessel is due to set sail in two days.' Then, after a pause, he said, 'By the way, keeping the wharf clean is your responsibility. The only thing we can do is pause the work to facilitate the cleaning.'

The superintendent scratched his head. He picked up the telephone and asked the operator to connect him to the assistant docks manager on night duty. After a moment, he described the situation on the wharf to the manager and waited for his response. 'Yes, sir,' he said ultimately and hung up. Then, turning to Avinash, he said, 'Nothing can be done immediately.'

'But, sir, it's not just the issue of the sludge on the wharf. The workers are also using hooks and inhaling the fibre. May I explain the situation to the manager?'

The superintendent narrowed his eyes. 'Are you crazy? Just get back to work.'

'Sir, please allow me to use the phone.'

The superintendent stared at him blankly. Avinash picked up the receiver and asked the operator to connect him to the assistant docks manager.

'Yes, sir,' the operator said. After a few seconds of some music playing, somebody said, 'Hello' in a hoarse voice at the other end of the line.

'May I please speak with the ADM on duty?' Avinash asked.

'Yes, this is Potdar, the ADM on duty. Who is this?'

'Sir, I'm calling from berth number sixteen about the condition of the wharf.'

'I just told you, Shaikh, that nothing can be done till morning. Why are you bothering me again?'

'Sir, this is not Shaikh,' Avinash said. 'My name is Avinash Gaikwad; I'm tallying the asbestos fibre bags.'

'What?' Potdar snapped. 'How dare you presume to talk to me directly! Don't you know the hierarchy and the procedures? I've already spoken to the superintendent.'

'But, sir, the condition of the wharf is terrible.'

'Shut up!' Potdar said and hung up.

'What did he say?' the superintendent asked as Avinash kept the phone down.

'He refused to talk to me, saying that he had already spoken to you.'

The superintendent shook his head. 'I told you—nothing can be done.'

Avinash came out on to the wharf. It had started raining again, and the ship's hatches were being closed. He entered the shed and found Mohan standing at the door.

'It's good that it's started raining,' Mohan remarked. 'I'm in no mood to work.'

They went inside and recorded the time of the rain in their tally sheets to account for the cargo operation remaining idle.

Half an hour later, the headlights of a vehicle lit up the sludge on the wharf. A jeep from the docks department slowly reached the shed, ploughing through the sludge and creating deep tracks in its wake. It stopped close to the door, and a tall, thin, bespectacled, middle-aged man with greying hair got out. It was Potdar.

The superintendent and the supervisor rushed to the door to greet him. 'Sir, this is what I was talking about,' the superintendent said, gesturing to the sludge on the wharf before quickly opening an umbrella and holding it over the manager's head.

Potdar walked into the superintendent's enclosure, with the others in tow. He then sat in the superintendent's chair and checked the logbook. 'Hmm, the condition of the wharf is quite bad,' he said. 'I'll send the sanitation staff to clean it up.' Then he got up and walked back to the jeep. Just as he was about to get in, he stopped and, turning back, asked the superintendent, 'Who was that fellow who called me?'

'Sir, he's our tally clerk, Avinash Gaikwad,' the superintendent said, pointing to Avinash.

'Gaikwad?' Potdar asked, stressing on the word and looking at Avinash from head to toe. 'How do you imagine that you can talk to me directly? And where were you when the dock safety committee visited?'

'Sir, he's a new recruit,' Shaikh intervened.

'Oh,' Potdar said, looking at Avinash with contempt. 'First learn how the system works, young man. Don't act too smart.'

'But, sir, I'm only trying to ensure that the work is done safely and properly,' Avinash said. 'The workers have no safety gear and are using hooks to handle these bags.'

'That is not your lookout,' Potdar said. 'And don't argue—stay within your limits.'

'But, sir, what have I done wrong?'

Potdar ignored him and got into the jeep. 'Don't encourage such people,' he told Shaikh, who nodded.

'But sir—' Avinash tried to defend himself, but Shaikh pulled him back.

'Don't argue with the ADM,' he said.

The jeep drove away slowly, creating new tyre marks in the muck. As soon as it disappeared, Avinash was subjected to a long lecture from Shaikh about how to conduct himself in the docks. Mohan, too, cautioned Avinash against antagonizing the bosses.

After a while, some sanitary workers with spades, wheelbarrows and other cleaning equipment arrived on the wharf. The rain had stopped, but the stevedore preferred to wait till the wharf was cleaned before resuming work.

As the workers got back in position around the sling, the morpia of the shore workers took Avinash aside and, after ensuring that nobody was close to enough to overhear them, thanked him for his efforts.

'Don't thank me,' Avinash replied. 'I didn't do anything extraordinary—the supervisor or the superintendent should've done this as a matter of routine.'

'You are right, but who will tell them?'

'But why do the shore workers use hooks when there are clear instructions to the contrary on each bag?'

'What else can we do? We have always used hooks while handling gunny bags. And with lightweight cargo, we have to struggle to complete the tonnage datum.'

'I understand that you get an incentive for handling weight above the prescribed tonnage datum during a shift, but using hooks on such cargo is harmful to your health.'

'We are helpless—what can we possibly do?'

This turn of events was hard for Avinash to accept. There were enough laws in place to protect the workers, but these laws were kept tightly enclosed within books and manuals by managers who were entirely uninterested in implementing them.

A few days later, Avinash visited Mohan's house. The rain had stopped completely by then, leaving puddles of various sizes everywhere. It was a dull, cloudy evening in congested Girgaum, but the multi-storeyed chawl wore a festive look. A series of tiny coloured bulbs stretched over the length of the common balcony, and devotional music, along with the fragrance of incense sticks and flowers, was wafting out of the decorated rooms. Avinash, Mohan and two of their colleagues alighted from a cab. 'This is where I live,' Mohan said, leading them inside the chawl and climbing up a creaky wooden staircase to the first floor.

The smell of incense and flowers grew stronger as they took off their footwear and entered Mohan's tiny house. There were cabinets on the wall and foldable furniture below. On the wall facing the door was a row of garlanded pictures of various gods. The room was decorated with streamers and tiny bulbs twinkling in different colours. A small idol of Lord Ganesha had been installed under a decorated canopy, with an offering of flowers, fruits and sweets at its feet.

Mohan introduced his parents, brother and sister to his colleagues. His father was a middle-aged man of average build, clad in a white kurta-pyjama. He wore a saffron tilak on his forehead. 'I'm glad you have come to our house,' he said, his hands folded in greeting. 'I work in a post office.'

Mohan's mother was wearing a festive sari in bright red with a golden border. She had a traditional golden nose ring with pearls on her nose. She too, welcomed them with a smile, while Mohan's sister, dressed in a sky-blue salwar kameez, served them water. His teenage brother was wearing a silky golden shirt and brown trousers.

After some small talk, the two colleagues accompanying Avinash got up and quickly performed some rituals before the idol of Lord Ganesha. Avinash did not join them, immediately attracting the family's attention. He merely folded his hands and smiled.

'Avinash is an atheist,' Mohan explained. 'He was reluctant to come here, but I told him that he would not be required to perform any rituals. I wanted him to at least know where I live.'

Mohan's father threw a sharp look at Avinash, while his mother and siblings clearly showed their discomfort. The two colleagues finished paying their respects and sat down, looking at Avinash scornfully.

'I'm sorry about this—I was not willing to come today, but Mohan insisted,' Avinash said.

'You don't install the Ganesha idol in your house?' Mohan's father asked.

'No.'

'Your father never has?'

'Never.'

'But how come? These are our traditions!'

Avinash glanced at the faces around him. 'Uncle, my parents and ancestors were untouchables; they were not allowed to enter temples or worship Hindu gods,' he said. 'Even in a city like Bombay, where my family migrated to, we were not allowed to celebrate Ganesha Chaturthi.'

'Really?'

'Yes. There have been demonstrations by people from my community, demanding participation in the Ganesha celebrations. Prabodhankar Thackeray and Dr B.R. Ambedkar, along with several liberals, had united to demand entry of the so-called untouchables in Hindu temples and festivals. Once, when Dr Ambedkar announced an agitation at a Ganesha festival at Dadar in 1927, he received death threats and had to carry a pistol to the venue as a precautionary measure.'

'Oh! You are a Jai Bhim guy.'

'Yes, my parents embraced Buddhism a year before I was born.'

'So that means you worship the Buddha.'

'No, we don't because he is neither a god nor a prophet. We practise Buddhist principles, without focussing on any meticulous rituals or blind faith.'

'Oh! My family follows the mainstream Indian culture—the Hindu culture.'

'It is true that the Vedic way of life, with its Brahminical traditions, is followed by the majority of the country,' Avinash said, 'but a parallel culture, called the Shraman tradition, also existed in our country since ancient times. This tradition includes Lokayat, Jainism and Buddhism, and it rejected Vedic beliefs, social hierarchy and rituals. Both these traditions have been around since long before Islam or Christianity arrived in India. Now, of course, we have Abrahamic religions, too, and the pluralism is well addressed by our liberal Constitution.'

Mohan's father appeared a little upset, but he collected himself. 'I don't know about these things,' he said. 'I just follow the traditions that have been handed down by my ancestors.'

Avinash smiled. 'Of course, that is certainly your choice,' he said. 'But I can't follow the traditions of my ancestors, who languished in the poverty, illiteracy and servility that was imposed upon them by the caste system. I now live a different life, one that is protected by the Constitution.'

An uneasy silence fell in the room until Mohan's mother brought out some snacks and tea. After they finished eating, they took their leave and descended the creaking staircase with Mohan; his father came along as well. On the road, while Mohan was trying to hail them a cab, his father thanked them for visiting. 'You boys are lucky to have secure and lucrative jobs. Do your work properly and make your parents proud,' he said. Then he took Avinash aside. 'Mohan tells me that the two of you are together almost every day,' he said.

'Yes,' Avinash replied.

'Do you drink regularly?'

'I don't drink at all.'

'No? But these days, Mohan often comes home drunk late in the night!'

'I don't know anything about that—he doesn't drink while on duty.'

'Can you please tell him to reduce his drinking?'

'I can tell him, but I don't know if it will work.'

Mohan's father nodded. 'At least try,' he said.

'All right, don't worry,' Avinash said.

Mohan had, in the meanwhile, found a cab. Avinash and the two others got into it and waved at Mohan as the cab drove away.

A few days later, it was raining again and cargo operations had been paused on the docks. The shore workers were sitting idly at Jetty's End. Avinash was sitting on a wooden case and reading a book. Mohan was wandering around the shed, reading the shipping marks on imported cargo. After some time, Mohan emerged from behind a stack of boxes and sat next to Avinash.

'What were you doing behind the boxes?' Avinash asked.

'Nothing, just looking at the imported cargo.'

'What's there to look at?'

'You don't know the things I've learnt from our seniors,' Mohan said. 'I was tearing off the labels and tags mentioning the consignee's particulars wherever possible.'

'Are you crazy? Why are you doing that?'

'Any discrepancy in the shipping marks comes in handy for us,' Mohan said. 'When the importer or his agent comes to pick up the cargo, we can refuse to issue a gate pass saying the cargo is not his.'

'But in such cases, there is a provision to release the delivery order with a "Nil" marks clarification.'

'Yes, I know that when shipping marks are not visible or the labels are missing, we can release the cargo under "Nil" shipping marks, but getting such an approval from the deputy docks manager involves additional paperwork,' Mohan said. 'So, instead of going through the hassle and paying the higher amount for getting all the permissions, it's more affordable for the consignee to pay us a smaller amount and get the gate pass!' Mohan winked.

'This is illegal and wrong, Mohan,' Avinash said. 'And does nobody complain?'

Mohan laughed. 'This is a common practice,' he said. 'The clearing agents, who usually take the delivery of imported cargo, know the tricks of the trade. They don't complain because they have to deal with us every day. And they also earn some extra money by inflating the amount paid to us without any receipts while billing the consignee.'

Avinash was struck speechless. There was a long pause in the conversation, during which Mohan started humming a Hindi film song.

'The weather is perfect for a drink,' Mohan said after a while. 'I think I'll stop at a bar on my way home.'

'Have you started drinking more liquor?' Avinash asked.

Mohan stared at him suspiciously for a moment. 'Did my father complain to you?' he asked.

'That's beside the point. You just said that you would like to drink today, and you've been saying that you drink from time to time. There is no special occasion today, unless you want to use the weather as a pretext.'

'Well, a small drink does no harm,' Mohan said. 'Also, I've become friends with some seniors who give me tips about how to earn more money while doing my duty. And sometimes, I have to take them out for a drink.'

'You'd better watch your expenses and your health while hobnobbing with these seniors to get tips on earning illicit money.'

'No, no! I drink in moderation, and only after duty hours. You should also join me and mingle with our seniors. Just remember that when we're promoted to the delivery pool, we'll be issuing gate passes for the pick-up of imported cargo, and we'll be making extra money.'

'You know I don't drink, and I don't want any tips to earn money using these dishonest methods. I can manage my family's expenses within my salary.'

Mohan shook his head in despair. 'Think big, Avinash, think big!' he said. 'We need more money to be happy in life.'

Avinash smiled. 'I'm already happy because I'm getting enough,' he said. 'You haven't got enough because your wants have increased. Don't be so obsessed with money that you lose sight of what is legal and moral.'

Mohan narrowed his eyes and said, 'The ends justify the means, Avinash. If you can't scoop ghee out of a jar with a straight finger, you have to bend your finger.'

Avinash simply shook his head. Mohan got up and walked away towards a group of workers playing cards.

The street outside the docks was buzzing with activity as usual. Trucks, multi-axle trailers, cranes and forklifts were everywhere. The multi-storeyed office of the trade union outside the compound wall of the docks, however, wore a deserted look. Only a few workers were chatting at the entrance, while some were standing on the balcony of the first floor. The trade union flag was hanging limply from a pole at the entrance. A jeep and a car with small union flags on their bonnets were parked in the compound.

Avinash and Mohan had walked out of the docks and were near the union office when they saw someone wave at them. Mohan waved back, and said, 'Let me introduce you to a friend. We are going to a bar together.'

They walked towards the union office, and on reaching the man waiting there, Mohan shook hands with him. Then, turning to Avinash, he said, 'Meet Shantaram Kelkar, he's an office-bearer of the union.' As they shook hands, Mohan said, 'This is Avinash Gaikwad, my batchmate.'

Shantaram smiled. 'Tell me if you face any problems, and we'll fix it,' he said. 'By the way, we are planning some demonstrations during lunchtime to demand higher wages, allowances, bonuses and many other things. The dates will be declared soon.'

Avinash remembered the incident with the asbestos fibre bags at berth number sixteen and narrated it to Shantaram. 'Can the union do something about this?' he asked.

Shantaram nodded. 'You're absolutely right. We had raised this issue in the past, but nothing happened. We've included it in our list of demands again,' he said.

By now, they had come out on the street, and Avinash bade the two men goodbye.

'Are you not coming with us to the bar?' Shantaram asked.

'No, he's not,' Mohan said. 'I'll tell you about him later.'

When Avinash reached home a little while later, he found Hari talking to Dagadoo.

'Congratulations!' Hari said when he saw Avinash. 'You've got a job in the port. Now, nobody can stop your family from progressing.'

Avinash smiled and went to change into casual wear.

'Is it true that you got selected just like that?' Hari asked. 'I mean, you didn't take my help, and I was wondering if you found another channel through which to get selected.'

'No, Hari, I told you that he would get the job on his own, without any intermediaries,' Dagadoo said.

'If that's the case, that's good,' Hari said with a broad smile. Then, turning to Avinash, he said, 'Now just go ahead and earn as much as you can without thinking about anything else.'

'Hari, don't misguide him,' Dagadoo said. 'He knows what is good and what isn't.'

Hari narrowed his eyes and looked at Dagadoo. 'Have you forgotten how our ancestors suffered? Have you forgotten how *you* suffered in the village?'

'Not at all, I remember it very clearly,' Dagadoo replied.

'Then what is holding you back?' Hari asked. 'Now it's our turn to take revenge ... to make money and get ahead, like all the others. We can't afford to be honest!'

'What are you saying?' Dagadoo asked in an irritated tone. 'Honesty has nothing to do with a person's financial status. One must be upright, irrespective of whether one is rich or poor. Don't think that everyone is like you, Hari,' he said.

Hari looked at Avinash. 'Why can't you be practical? Do you think people from other castes and religions are performing their duties honestly?'

'There are good and bad people across caste, religion and gender,' Dagadoo said.

'When the government has reposed its faith in us and is paying us for our work, it's anti-national to be corrupt,' Avinash said. 'And the corrupt in the government should be punished more severely than other corrupt people because they represent the government, and as public servants, they are paid salaries from the taxes paid by the public.'

'To hell with morality, ethics, principles and honesty!' Hari shouted. 'These things are good for people who have their tummies, cupboards and bank accounts full—not for people like us. We have a long history of poverty, illiteracy and humiliation. Now is the time to settle the score.'

Dagadoo raised his hand, gesturing for Hari to stop. 'Don't try to impose your ideas on my son,' he warned his cousin.

Hari laughed again. 'Do you think you'll get a medal for being honest, Avinash? Listen to my advice—you'll never regret it. On the contrary, you will prosper, like me.'

'It's not about getting a medal, Hari kaka,' Avinash said. 'It's about doing whatever is legally and morally right.'

Hari sighed. 'If you want to live in a slum for the rest of your life, I can't help it.'

All this while, Godavari listened to the conversation in discomfort, but she did not react. She quietly made some tea and served it to the men.

They sipped the tea in silence, after which Hari left. Avinash noted that this time, apart from the usual gold chain around his neck, he was also wearing gold rings, all proof of his worldly progress, on his fingers.

As he sat on the threshold of the house and watched Hari disappear behind the rows of hutments below, Avinash realized that his uncle had adapted himself to the popular traditions of the city and was racing towards progress. He wondered how many Hari kakas were out there, all of them trying to justify their greed for wealth on the pretext of settling scores because they had experienced poverty, illiteracy, humiliation and injustice, or were simply obsessed with wealth and power.

❁

It was a typical working day in the city. People were hurrying past one another on the pavement as streams of vehicles flowed alongside. At various intersections, traffic signals changed colour to pause the flow of vehicles and pedestrians. When the traffic stopped, Avinash crossed the road. Wiping the sweat from his face with a handkerchief, he entered the gate of a building displaying a large American flag. Between the compound wall and the building was an enclosure for security guards and their gadgets. After passing through a metal detector and emptying his pockets for the guards to check their contents, he entered the building.

Once he was inside the library on the ground floor, the noise, heat and smells from outside ceased to exist. A few people were reading books and magazines in the reading section, while some others were looking through the bookshelves. Avinash picked a book from a shelf and browsed through it. Moments later, he approached the issuing counter.

'My name is Avinash Gaikwad. I applied for membership a month ago and was told that I'd be intimated within a couple of weeks. But I haven't heard anything yet,' he whispered.

The man nodded and opened a drawer in his table, murmuring, 'Avinash Gaikwad.' He checked some papers and said, 'We sent a letter to the address you furnished two weeks ago. You'll have to bring it with you to get your membership activated.'

'But I haven't received any letter!'

The man shook his head. 'We've sent it. So, please get it with you—we need to verify addresses before granting membership.'

Suddenly, Avinash remembered the common letter box nailed to the wall of a local shop in the slum. 'Sir, I live in a slum, and the postman dumps all the letters in a common letter box,' he said. 'The letter box has no lock, and anybody can open it and go through the post inside. Maybe that's why I haven't received the letter.'

The man stared at him for a few seconds and then said curtly, 'Sorry, you can't be admitted as a member of the library unless your residential address has been verified.'

'But, sir, the address I gave is correct. The only problem is that the postman doesn't go door to door to deliver our letters.'

'That's not our problem. Now please don't waste my time,' the man said.

Avinash looked at the bookshelves with longing. He had spotted some books he wanted to borrow. Dejected, he pushed open the glass doors of the library and was instantly overwhelmed by the heat outside. By the time he reached the university campus, he was sweating. The tower clock showed that it was 12.30 p.m. Avinash hurriedly made his way upstairs to the university library. It offered a soothing respite from the heat outside, different from the artificially cooled air-conditioned structures elsewhere. He borrowed some books before going to attend his lectures.

In class, the students were waiting for the lecture to begin. The presence of an unusually large number of students indicated that a lecture by Professor Nimish was scheduled. Avinash found a place to sit, waving at some of the students he was acquainted with.

Professor Nimish taught American literature and was popular among the students. He arrived on time, wearing an oversized, full-sleeved cream shirt and a pair of dark brown trousers. He was tall, fair and bespectacled. He was carrying some papers in his hands. Entering the hall, he peered over his gold-rimmed spectacles at the students and smiled. As usual, he walked between the rows of benches as he taught, speaking about literary trends, pausing only to throw a cursory glance at the notes in his hand. While answering queries, he referred to many authors, including some contemporary ones not included in the syllabus.

After the lecture, he thanked the students before walking out. Avinash followed him down the corridor to his cabin. After waiting for a few moments, he knocked on the door and pushed it open a bit. 'Sir, may I come in?'

Nimish nodded and smiled. Avinash told him about his membership application being rejected by the American Library and the reason behind it.

'These are rather special circumstances,' Nimish said. 'But don't worry, I'll have a word with them. When is it possible for you to go there again?'

'I can go right now, sir.'

'Good. Then go now, and I'll call them up and have a chat with them about your membership.'

Avinash thanked him and headed straight to the library, beaming.

At the library, the same man was sitting behind the counter. Before Avinash could say anything, the man gave him a broad smile. 'Why didn't you tell me that you were Professor Nimish's student?' he asked. 'He just called.'

Without waiting for Avinash to respond, the man quickly completed the membership formalities and issued him a membership card. 'You can borrow books right now, three at a time for three weeks each,' he said. 'I'm sorry about what happened earlier, but we must follow the rules.'

Avinash thanked him and rushed to the bookshelves, spending about half an hour browsing through the collection before finally picking up three titles. He reached home feeling richer, but also a little unnerved. It was clear that he could not have accessed the library without the professor's intervention.

After dinner that night, he reported for night duty at the docks and was posted at the Ballard Pier Extension berth, usually reserved for passenger ships, but where a new container vessel had docked. The ship, the wharf and the transit shed, which also served as a passenger terminal for cruise ships, were all brightly lit up with tiny bulbs glittering in different colours. 'Be careful,' the superintendent told him, Mohan and two others. 'There is a party on board tonight, and our chief manager is going to attend it.'

They nodded and took up their positions on the wharf, where trucks had lined up and containers were being loaded and unloaded by the ship's cranes. Around midnight, the docks manager, dressed in a cream suit and a red tie, arrived on the wharf in a car. With him were two other officials.

The superintendent rushed to open the car door. The manager followed him into the shed after taking a quick look at the ship and the activities on the wharf. He checked the logbook and asked the superintendent some questions. Moments later, the ship's agent came and escorted him to the vessel's gangway on the wharf. They made their way up and were received on the deck by the ship's first mate.

Meanwhile, Avinash and his colleagues were busy tallying containers, and the work continued without a break. A couple of hours later, the docks manager, followed by his companions, slowly staggered down the gangway. The superintendent and the supervisor helped him step down from the gangway onto the wharf. Even as he walked towards his car, the manager swayed and the officers had to lead him by his arms to the car. The superintendent held the door open, and the manager somehow got in, slumping on the back seat, mumbling something. Once the car left, the staff heaved a sigh of relief.

CHAPTER 14

The following day, when Avinash reached the university canteen, it was crowded and the strong smell of boiling tea filled the air. Students were sitting in groups, either talking or sipping tea. Some were also smoking. Avinash spotted his friends Dheeraj and Rita chatting at a table. Dheeraj was a bulky boy with a drooping moustache. He was dressed in a brown kurta and blue jeans. Rita was in a black casual shirt and blue jeans. Avinash joined them.

'Avinash, give me your notes from Nimish sir's lecture,' Dheeraj said, rolling up the sleeves of his kurta. 'I didn't understand some of what he said.'

'I also want your notes,' Rita said, pushing her sunglasses up to the top of her head. 'I'm totally at sea when he talks about obscure literary concepts.'

'I'll give you my notes, but why don't you first read the books in the syllabus?' Avinash asked. 'We're expected to read them and then write our assignments.'

'My God, I have tried to read them! But there are so many books that have been prescribed, and many of the writers are so difficult to understand,' Rita grumbled. 'Can I get study guides that will simplify them and make my life easy?'

'Guides? You must be kidding,' Avinash said. 'Be serious.'

'No, no,' she said, sweeping her silky hair back from her shoulder with her hand. 'Seriously, I don't like reading books.'

Avinash was shocked. 'Then why have you enrolled for a master's degree in literature?' he asked.

She twitched her nose and shook her head. 'My father wants me to get a postgraduate degree to improve my marriage prospects and help me move in elite cultural circles.'

Avinash and Dheeraj looked at her for a moment and then at each other. Without another word, Avinash opened his bag, pulled out his books and gave the notebook to Dheeraj. 'After you're done, pass it on to Rita,' he said.

As he was putting the remaining books back in the bag, Dheeraj asked, 'What is that book?'

Avinash took the book out. 'It's *The Harlem Renaissance*,' he said.

'Why are you reading this when so many other books have already been prescribed for us?' Rita asked.

Avinash smiled. 'I'm curious and I like to read across ideologies, genres and nationalities. It helps me rise above stereotypical thinking and transcend mental barriers to get a better perspective. I can relate to Black literature because it's been written by people marginalized by racism. I belong to a community which was considered untouchable until that practice was outlawed by the Indian Constitution.'

'Oh.'

'In 1972, when I was in school, some Dalit youths and litterateurs had formed a rather short-lived Dalit Panther organization influenced by the Black Panther movement in the US.'

'Is it? But why didn't it last long?'

'Because of an ideological conflict among its leaders—some favoured the Ambedkarite–Buddhist model, while others were inclined towards communism,' Avinash said. 'And after being disbanded, various splinter groups were formed.'

'So, it was a futile exercise.'

'Not really. The Dalit Panthers revitalized the oppressed to counter exploitation and rise up for their constitutional rights at a time when established Dalit leaders had allied with mainstream political parties in return for ministerial berths,' Avinash said.

'Their other major achievement was persuading the Maharashtra government to publish volumes of Babasaheb Ambedkar's writings and speeches, which are now available at nominal prices.'

'Oh! But I heard that the caste system was merely a system of segregation for the sake of hygiene,' Dheeraj said, picking his nose.

'*Hygiene?*' Avinash asked. 'When the highly educated Babasaheb Ambedkar was appointed military secretary in the princely state of Baroda, he could not get a house on rent, and files were thrown at him from a distance by the staff—to say nothing about denying him access to drinking water in the office. You mean all that was for the sake of *hygiene?*'

'I don't know much about these things,' Dheeraj said, trying to force a smile. 'I just told you what I've heard. It's also said that the caste system was just a division of labour.'

Avinash laughed. 'It was not a division of labour but a division of the labourers,' he said. 'It was "divide and rule" on the basis of caste, and there was no freedom to choose what means of livelihood one wanted to pursue as it was imposed by birth into a particular caste.'

'But the caste system is a thing of the past,' Rita said. 'It doesn't exist anymore.'

'It's still alive and kicking in forms both obvious and subtle. You don't feel it because you belong to a privileged family and have been brought up in a controlled urban environment, oblivious to lived reality,' he said. 'Have you ever read the matrimonial columns of a newspaper?'

Rita narrowed her eyes. 'Yes, what about that?' she asked.

'Have you seen how prospective brides and grooms are classified according to caste and religion?'

'Oh, yeah, that,' she said in a low tone. 'But one has to follow traditions, no?' she asked.

'But have you ever realized that traditions are created by men to subjugate women?' Avinash asked. 'Social evils don't have to be followed simply because they are part of outdated traditions or religious practices.'

'Come on! Don't be upset—we're all free to make choices,' she said.

'That is only because of the efforts made by social reformers and because of the provisions of the Indian Constitution, which provides equality of opportunity,' he said. 'Otherwise, as per ancient holy books like the Manusmriti, as a woman, you had no right to education or property. The Constitution changed it. Do you know who Jyotiba Phule and Savitribai Phule were?'

'Yes, I've seen their pictures. They were a rustic looking couple from Pune, right?' she asked.

'Yes, that rustic looking couple opened the first school for girls in Pune, braving grave opposition from orthodox Hindus, and it's because of the Phules that you are sitting here now as a postgraduate student.'

There was a long moment of silence, during which Rita seemed to struggle with her thoughts, making faces to express embarrassment, pain and, finally, joy. 'But now things have changed,' she said gleefully. 'Women have been empowered and promoted. They have access to education and employment—even the corporate world and political parties are in favour of women having greater opportunities.'

'Yes, but I don't think that's because they are genuinely concerned about gender equality,' Avinash pointed out. 'The politicians are only concerned with garnering votes, while industry wants to make profits from the emerging pool of economically independent women.'

No one said anything for a while. Then, Rita shrugged and said, 'I'm sorry about your family history. You must feel ashamed of being born in such a family.'

'I'm neither proud nor ashamed. Nobody should be either, as my caste is an accident of birth,' he said. After a pause, Avinash asked, 'Are you proud of your lineage?'

Rita narrowed her eyes and then nodded with a smile. 'Well, I'm tempted to be because my father is rich,' she said. 'And I'm also proud of my looks because they make me resemble a film star.'

Avinash laughed. 'You take pride in things you have done nothing to achieve as an individual,' he said. 'Your lineage, wealth and appearance are not accomplishments.'

Rita looked up at the ceiling, lost in thought as she mulled over what he had said.

'Avinash, what's the problem if someone inherits good looks or wealth?' Dheeraj intervened. 'These things would naturally make him or her proud.'

'There's nothing wrong as long as the person doesn't flaunt these as achievements or take pride in them. And going by your logic, a person with average looks or one living in poverty must feel ashamed,' Avinash said. 'In truth, a person should neither be ashamed nor proud of his or her lineage or looks because he or she has simply inherited them without any individual effort. The corporate world induces shame in such people and sells them cosmetics and other products, most of which are unnecessary and bought out of artificial needs created by the market and amplified by peer pressure. The value of a person should be determined not by birth but by merit. And everyone should have equal opportunity to prove one's worth.'

'You have such weird ideas,' Dheeraj said. 'You mean people who inherit huge properties and live a life of luxury are worthless?'

'To the best of my knowledge, it's only among humans that you can find living beings who inherit property and don't slog to earn a livelihood. Their supreme achievement is that they were born into a particular family,' Avinash said. 'Have you seen an animal or a bird being protected and mentored by its parents once it grows up?'

'You're being judgemental.'

'I'm just expressing my opinion based on what I've learnt from the experiences of my family and after reading books. You may have a different opinion,' Avinash said. 'I'm just acquainting you with things you are oblivious about. The intention is to induce empathy for the marginalized. Also, to assert that the same accidental factor of being born in a particular family is what lies behind the pride of the privileged and the woes of the marginalized, not individual merit.'

The three of them sat in silence as they waited for their tea to arrive. Once it came, they sipped it quietly. When they got up to leave a little later, Rita said, 'Avinash, you're a nice guy. You're honest and hardworking, but you have too many demerits, like being born in a poor Dalit family.'

Avinash laughed. 'Yes, I have limitations, like being born in an erstwhile untouchable family. But I believe in overcoming these limitations with hard work and honesty instead of whining about what others possess and I don't,' he said. 'An adverse situation is also an opportunity to prove one's mettle.'

Avinash completed his night shift and, in the morning, when he reached home, he saw the residents of the slum standing in groups outside Buddha Vihar.

'What happened?' he asked Raja, who was standing with one of the groups on the road.

'Sudhir's sister lost her two-year-old son,' Raja said. 'He had been admitted to the Maharajawadi Hospital a few days ago.'

Avinash could hear women wailing as he went up the crude stairs in the gully towards where the sound was coming from. Sudhir was standing outside his sister's house. Avinash saw that it was crowded with women trying to pacify the bereaved mother. The dead boy lay in front of her, wrapped in a white cloth.

'The boy was suffering from gastroenteritis and was being treated at Maharajawadi Hospital,' Sudhir told him. 'He died this morning. We found that the intravenous fluid administered to him was contaminated. We've complained to the hospital authorities; they are conducting an inquiry.'

'Did you file a police complaint?' Avinash asked.

'We went to the police station, and they said they'll look into it.'

'Maharajawadi is a municipal hospital. Did you contact the local corporator?'

'Not yet.'

'Let's go meet him immediately,' said Avinash. A few minutes later, the two of them set off for the corporator's home, which was in another locality at the base of the hill.

When they got there, a group of bearded young men, standing at the door of the corporator's house, stopped them. They all had long hair and sported red tilaks on their foreheads. A single car and a few bikes were parked nearby. 'Sudhir?' one of them called out, recognizing him. 'What brings you here?'

Sudhir told him what had happened, and the young man nodded. 'So, you finally felt the need to seek our leader's help,' he said sarcastically.

'He is the local corporator,' Sudhir pointed out.

The corporator came to the door just then and looked at them. He was in his twenties and like the rest of the men, he also had a beard and a red tilak on his forehead. He was dressed in a spotless white shirt and trousers, and had a thick gold chain hanging around his neck.

Turning to his acolytes, he asked, 'They are from the slum on the hill, isn't it?'

'Yes, Bhai,' the youth said. 'They need your help.'

Once again, Sudhir narrated the tragedy that had befallen his family.

'Oh, convey my condolences to your family,' the corporator said. 'But remember, the people from your slum didn't vote for me.'

'Sir, you represent the entire constituency, irrespective of whether or not they voted for you,' Avinash said.

'Who are you to teach Bhai about his job?' one of the youths shouted as his friends surrounded Avinash.

'Wait, boys. What he says is true,' the corporator said, smiling at them. 'Don't worry, in the next election, the voters on the hill are going to re-elect me by a huge margin.' The young men burst into laughter and began shouting slogans in his support. Turning to Sudhir, the corporator said, 'You may leave.'

'Saheb, can you please take this issue up with the concerned officials or raise it with the municipal corporation?' Avinash asked.

The corporator shook his head and without another word, went inside the house, leaving his henchmen laughing.

Sudhir and Avinash retreated.

'He won't do anything,' Sudhir said.

'I think we should inform some newspaper,' Avinash said.

The minute they reached Avinash's home, he pulled out an old copy of the *City News* to look for its telephone number. Once he found it, they went to the telephone booth at the local grocery shop and called the newspaper's office. The lady who answered the phone transferred their call to the editorial department. A male voice answered, and Avinash quickly told him about the child's death. The man on the other side asked some questions, which he answered after consulting Sudhir.

'I'll send a reporter, but you'll need to help him find the house. Where can he meet you?' the man asked.

'Sir, I'll wait at the Ghatkopar station on platform number one. I'll stand right below the clock,' Avinash said.

'How will he identify you?'

'I'm wearing a blue shirt and black trousers, and my name is Avinash.'

'All right, he'll be there in an hour or so.'

Avinash told Sudhir about the reporter's impending visit and, after a while, he left for the railway station. An hour later, a young man wearing a white shirt over blue jeans, with a satchel slung over his shoulder, approached him.

'Are you Avinash?' he asked, even as Avinash nodded.

'My name is Kiran, and I'm from *City News*.'

They shook hands and Avinash escorted him to the slum, where Kiran spoke to Sudhir's sister and her husband. Then he took some photographs and looked at some documents from the hospital before leaving. 'I'll go to the hospital and talk to the authorities now,' he said.

By this time, the crowd outside Sudhir's sister's house had swelled, and some furious voices called for retaliation against the medical staff and the corporator. Several youngsters volunteered to ransack the hospital, but Avinash, Sudhir and some elders managed to pacify them. A little while later, the last rites were conducted at the local cemetery.

The next morning, while on his way back home from the night shift, Avinash saw a photograph of Sudhir's nephew on the front page of *City News* with the headline, 'Adulterated drug kills boy'. He bought a copy and read the full story. Then he went to Sudhir's house to show him the article. But someone had already told Sudhir and his sister about it, and they had bought a copy of the newspaper. Besides, a police officer and a couple of constables had visited them and recorded their statements earlier in the morning.

Before heading home, Avinash called up the newspaper office from the telephone booth to thank Kiran.

'The story has had a good impact,' Kiran said. 'A doctor and two nurses have been suspended and a case has been filed against the pharmaceutical company.'

Avinash immediately went back and informed Sudhir and his sister's family about the development. A sense of fulfilment came over him, and in that moment, he started to toy with the idea of becoming a journalist.

A few days later, Avinash's shift at the dock changed and he was posted at shed number five for the day shift. He was standing at the main entrance of the shed and Kamble was restlessly pacing up and down outside when a swanky black sedan appeared on the wharf.

Kamble ran towards it. The car stopped near Avinash, emitting heat all around. The doors opened a second later and two men in suits and a fat middle-aged man in a silky white kurta-pyjama alighted. They were escorted inside the shed by Kamble. About ten minutes later, the trio, along with Kamble and the superintendent Phadke, came out wearing broad smiles.

After the visitors departed, Avinash asked, 'Who were they?'

Kamble grinned. 'An importer had come for some log entry formalities. His consignment of expensive chemical drums has gone missing,' he said.

'Chemical drums?' Avinash asked.

'Very rare and expensive chemicals,' Kamble said and smiled. He led Avinash to a corner of the shed and, looking in both directions to make sure nobody was within earshot, whispered, 'Don't tell anyone. It was ordered by the importer himself—we just helped him.'

'What? You mean the same importer who imported the consignment, stole it?'

'Yes.'

'I don't believe this! Why would anyone steal one's own cargo?'

Kamble pursed his lips and closed his eyes for a moment before explaining, 'This particular chemical is very expensive, and the quantity of its import is controlled by the government through fixed quotas and import licences. After stealing the consignment, the importer can declare that it was stolen and claim insurance. Besides, he can get a fresh licence issued to import another identical consignment again. He can either use it himself or sell it on the black market.'

Avinash was stunned. 'How can this happen so easily when there are multiple law enforcement agencies deployed to implement the law?' he asked. 'This is illegal! And immoral!'

'That is just the way it is,' Kamble grinned. 'Anything is possible when there is a consensus about mutually beneficial deals.'

'This is like being in a dystopian world.'

Kamble laughed. 'Your dystopia is our paradise,' he said and winked.

Speechless, Avinash turned to leave when he spotted Shantaram nearby and waved at him. Shantaram waved back and approached them.

'Kamble saheb, where were you yesterday?' he asked. 'I didn't see you at Phadke saheb's ceremony.'

Kamble smiled. 'I was busy with something else. That's why I couldn't attend,' he said.

'Oh, I thought as much. After all, you two are such good friends,' Shantaram said. 'Anyway, I must go now—someone is waiting for me.'

'Did Phadke organize some ceremony?' Avinash asked Kamble after Shantaram had left.

'It was some religious ritual,' Kamble said.

'Why didn't you go?'

Kamble looked around and then whispered, 'I wasn't invited.'

'What? But you both are good friends.'

'We are. But in matters such as these, they prefer to invite only select people.'

'Oh. So, your friendship and cooperation here don't level everything after all.'

'You're right,' Kamble said, his face sullen. 'In all other things, we are buddies, but not in such matters.'

Avinash shook his head. Corruption was not a unifier after all. Caste happened to be more important and eternal than the 'practical' adjustments people made to make money.

Over time, Avinash settled down in his job in the tally pool, although there were intermittent arguments with his seniors, much to the chagrin of his colleagues, who were happy with the work culture. Meanwhile, Mohan was eagerly waiting for a promotion in the delivery pool, which handled the delivery of imported cargoes. The news came during their lunch break on a particularly hot day. The loading and unloading of cargo had paused, and the timekeeper's office was crowded. Fresh notices detailing the promotions were displayed on the noticeboard inside.

Avinash and Mohan were walking towards the canteen when they saw members of the field staff jostling with one another anxiously to get a look at the notices and find out about their new positions. Mohan rushed forward and elbowed his way to the noticeboard. Moments later, he emerged with a broad smile on his face.

'Our seniors in the delivery pool have been promoted and transferred to different dock offices for fixed, three-year tenures. The good news is that we've been promoted to the delivery pool, and fresh recruits will take our place.'

'All right,' Avinash said. 'That means our salaries will increase.'

'Yes, but not by much,' Mohan said. 'But who cares about the salary now?'

Avinash narrowed his eyes and looked at him.

Mohan stood with his hands on his hips. 'Do you know what this change means?' he asked.

'Yes. Now we'll be delivering imported cargo by issuing gate passes to the importers' trucks,' Avinash said.

'And we'll have ample opportunities every day to earn extra money while issuing these gate passes!' Mohan said cheerfully. 'We've hit the jackpot. Because as per the tradition here, to issue each gate pass, we get some money, even if it's a routine, clean delivery. So, we won't go home empty-handed, ever. And, of course, if there is a shady deal, it's a windfall for us as we get more money!'

'I'm not interested in any illegal income,' Avinash said.

Mohan chuckled. 'But I am,' he said, beaming.

'Don't you think it's wrong? And what if you get caught?'

Mohan laughed. 'What world are you living in?' he asked. 'It's not wrong because everyone is doing it. The importer manages all the law enforcement authorities involved in the chain of procedures, right up to the dock gate. And since it's a chain linking different government agencies, there is no risk. If at all, one gets caught accepting a bribe, one can also get out of it by bribing the investigating officer.'

'Is it that simple? What if the officer is honest?'

Mohan scoffed. 'No chance. Honest people have disappeared from this planet, like the dinosaurs, and if we do come across one, we can always seek help from the various politicians involved.'

Avinash shook his head sadly as they walked to the canteen. They found it crowded and noisy with the conversations of people and the clattering of dishes. Almost everyone was talking about the promotions and the transfers.

'Let's go to the central data processing office,' Mohan said after they finished eating lunch. 'I have a few friends there; we'll have to go there frequently now to arm ourselves with additional information.'

The data office was bustling with activity even though it was the lunch break. At the entrance, a huge blackboard displayed a chart detailing the names of ships, their berths, tonnage, import general manifest number, type of cargo and the last free date of delivery from each shed, after which importers would have to pay additional charges for storage.

At the counters, employees were still working in haste. Importers and clearing agents were everywhere with their documents in hand. A female employee, seated behind a counter, was haggling with an importer, who had thrust some documents towards her through the window. He was a bald, middle-aged, pot-bellied man wearing a beige safari suit. On his forehead he sported a long red tilak, and his mouth was red from constantly chewing betel leaf.

'Jyotiben, please hurry up,' he said, gulping the betel leaf juice in his mouth.

Jyoti was a fair and plump middle-aged lady dressed in a grey sari with a black border. She stared at the documents in the importer's hand. 'I won't touch your papers,' she said firmly, 'unless you clear my previous dues.'

'Don't trust him,' a young woman sitting at the next counter told Jyoti. 'He had promised me a gold chain, but he hasn't kept his word.'

'Madam, I remember,' the importer said to the young woman. 'Don't worry, ladies, I'll make both of you happy.' Then he turned to Jyoti and grinned, revealing a gold-capped tooth. 'I know, Jyotiben, that some previous hisaab is pending,' he said. 'I'll meet you before you leave in the evening and settle everything.'

Jyoti looked at him suspiciously for a moment, her eyes glinting. 'I'll trust you for the last time today—but you'll have to pay a penalty for that,' she said finally.

'All right,' he said, still grinning. She took the documents and began to verify them. Then, she promptly prepared the delivery order, applied the rubber stamp, signed it and handed it to him. He left, smiling broadly.

Other staff and port users went about their business as usual; only some threw a casual glance towards Jyoti and the importer but even they didn't react to the conversation. Mohan waved to a person sitting behind one of the counters and went up to him. They talked for a couple of minutes, after which Mohan came out. 'He's one of my mentors who gives me tips on making more money,' he said. 'Let's go to our shed.'

As they left the data office, Avinash asked Mohan, 'Did you see the women employees behaving like corrupt men and demanding favours to perform their work, for which they receive a salary?'

Mohan broke into laughter. 'Even I was a bit shocked when I saw them for the first time,' he said. 'But there is nothing wrong with it—they are simply following tradition.'

'It's illegal and immoral, Mohan,' Avinash said. 'I'm surprised because I didn't expect women to be corrupt like men.'

'Give up your stereotypical thinking, my friend—they are also human beings with ambitions, lifestyles and families.'

Avinash sighed. 'They are educated, modern women who have been empowered by the Constitution after thousands of years of patriarchal servitude,' he said. 'And yet, they behave like crooked men.'

'What about Kamble?' Mohan asked. 'He's Dalit, but he's among the most sought-after people when it comes to fixing shady deals.'

'You're right,' Avinash said, shaking his head in despair. 'I don't understand why the oppressed start behaving like their oppressors when they are empowered.'

'What do you expect, Avinash?'

'Well, I think they should outshine their oppressors in efficiency and sincerity, and set an example to cleanse the system.'

'You must've heard the proverb that a newly appointed cleric shouts louder than his seniors while praying. Well, so does a newly empowered person. You always praise the Constitution for ushering in liberal values like equality. Well, *this* is equality. These women and men are just enjoying the equality of opportunity to make money because equality means equality in everything, be it good or bad. They have made their choice, just as you have made yours.'

There was a pause in the conversation as they stopped walking and stood looking at each other.

Avinash wondered why the historically marginalized emulated their mainstream oppressors and aspired to become like them, instead of paving a different path for themselves, one that was more efficient and ethical. And what prevented the untouchables (including the former Shudra communities, now known as the Other Backward Classes or the OBCs) and women from coming together to usher in a social democracy? While untouchables were in a minority, women comprised half the population. But even after India became a republic and started governing itself through its egalitarian constitution, organizations representing women and former untouchables mostly functioned separately, without uniting on core issues. Ambedkarite organizations were dominated by men who were self-centred, dynastic and servile to some or the other mainstream political party—usually the party in power. Women's organizations, on the other hand, were usually led by upper-caste women, and most were female wings of mainstream political parties.

Was this lack of solidarity because of one or several compartmentalizing factors like caste, gender, ideology, class, region, religion and language?

Suddenly, someone tapped Avinash's shoulder, breaking his chain of thoughts.

It was Chinmay. 'Hello, do you remember me? I'm Chinmay. We met in the head office canteen some months ago,' he said, introducing himself with a broad smile.

'Yes.' Avinash nodded.

'Yes, of course,' Mohan said.

'I wanted to work in the docks and appeared for a test. Now I've joined the tally pool,' Chinmay said. 'But I'm nervous because I don't know anything about working outdoors.'

'Don't worry, you'll be trained by your seniors,' Avinash said, smiling. 'And there is nothing very difficult about the job—just go by the book.'

Chinmay smiled back. 'I know that, but I don't have any practical knowledge,' he said. 'Like how to deal with imports, exports, warehousing and delivery.'

'Just remember—enforce the law and do your work honestly and efficiently,' Avinash said.

Chinmay looked at him blankly for a moment. 'I know,' he said, sniggering. 'But how do people make extra money?'

Avinash sneered. 'Well, there are some employees who indulge in malpractices,' he said. 'But I don't think you want to join them.'

The smile on Chinmay's face vanished and he quickly walked away. Moments later, he halted abruptly and turned back to follow Avinash and Mohan as they walked towards the shed.

Addressing Mohan, he asked, 'May I talk with you for a minute?' Mohan stopped and Chinmay took him aside for a quick chat.

Leaving the two talking, Avinash resumed walking towards the shed. Moments later, Mohan caught up with him; he looked like he was trying to stifle his laughter. 'Chinmay wanted to know the tricks to make extra money and the standard rates of hisaab in various cargo operations,' he said.

'What?' Avinash was shocked. 'Do you remember what he had told us in the canteen?'

Mohan burst into laughter. Avinash looked at Chinmay walking away, and hollered his name. Chinmay came running towards them.

'Were you asking Mohan about hisaab?' Avinash asked.

Chinmay avoided his gaze and said, 'Well, I was just curious.'

'Your ideas were completely different when we met in the canteen.'

Chinmay took a deep breath. 'Actually, I've always envied people working in the docks for making extra money while I was surviving only on my salary,' he said in a low voice. 'Now that I have the opportunity, why should I let it go? Everyone else is doing it with impunity.'

'Then deal with Mohan in the future,' Avinash said firmly.

Chinmay tried to smile, but the look on Avinash's face forced him to quickly walk away.

'I'm really surprised by this,' Avinash said. 'Are the people who portray themselves as being honest just people who've had no chance of being corrupt?'

Mohan chuckled. 'Yes, my friend. Most people who speak against bribery and corruption are those who haven't had the opportunity to indulge in such things. Given the chance, even the so-called angels will not hesitate, not even for a moment, to become devils. Their adherence to the law is largely out of their fear of punishment or the lack of opportunity to sin.'

'But all people are not like that.'

'Of course, there are some idiots like you, who actually believe these things and don't make hay while the sun shines.'

Avinash looked at him with contempt. 'How can you possibly justify this dishonest and illicit behaviour?'

'I'm just saying that it makes sense in following the majority. It's easy, safe and beneficial to everyone.'

As they walked in silence, the incident with some bystanders stealing apples from a hawker's cart outside the railway station flashed through Avinash's memory. Apparently, people were mostly the same everywhere, infested with fear and greed.

❦

A week after the promotion announcements, Avinash and Mohan started work at their new postings. On his first day as a delivery clerk, Avinash was posted at berth number fifteen. When he reached the wharf, the sky was overcast and the cargo handling operations for the day were still to begin. There was no movement of trucks, cranes or other vehicles on the wharf. But operations at berth number fifteen, designated for ships unloading raw fertilizers like urea and sulphur in bulk, were in full swing, and the smell of both chemicals hung heavy in the air. From a distance, Avinash could see quay cranes directly loading the urea into the trucks lined up on the wharf. As he approached the berth, the smell, reminiscent of the putrid odour in unclean public urinals, became overwhelming and irritated his eyes.

Earlier that morning, when Avinash had been assigned the dry bulk terminal for the day, many of his colleagues in the delivery pool had heaved a sigh of relief. They abhorred being posted for dry bulk cargo delivery as it meant gruelling work that was not lucrative and required spending the whole shift in the stinking atmosphere, issuing one gate pass after the other for the endless line of loaded trucks. There was no scope for making extra money.

By the time Avinash reported for work, about a dozen truck drivers and cleaners were standing in queue in front of the delivery counter at the back of the shed. As soon as Avinash took his seat, the first person in the line thrust his hand in through the window with the challan invoice, which included the particulars of the truck, the ship and the payload tonnage certified by the weighbridge. Avinash checked the documents and issued a gate pass. The driver picked up the challan and the gate pass and left a note at the counter before turning away.

Avinash called him back. 'What is this?' he asked, pointing at the note.

'Saheb, this is the hisaab for the gate pass,' the driver said.

'Take it away at once.'

The driver looked at him and then at the note, but he didn't touch it. 'Saheb, I can't give more than this,' he pleaded, looking at the others in the queue behind him.

'Saheb, we usually give this much for a local truck and double for a truck going out of the city,' the next person said as the others nodded.

Avinash raised his hand. 'Please try to understand, I get a salary for doing this work. I don't want your money. I'm neither angry nor interested in making extra money like this.'

There were confused murmurs in the queue. Someone standing at the very end of the queue shouted, 'Saheb, we've been waiting for a long time, please hurry.'

Someone then called the consignee's supervisor, who was out on the wharf, issuing the challans. He came rushing to the counter with his files. 'What happened?' he asked. The driver told him what Avinash had said.

The supervisor scratched his head. 'Sir, these are the standard rates followed by everyone. Usually, more than a hundred trucks are loaded per shift, and at the end of the shift, I'll pay you a token amount per gate pass. Neither I nor the drivers can afford to give you more. But you won't go home empty-handed.'

Avinash repeated himself and only after a great deal of persuasion did the supervisor finally go away, looking suspiciously at him as he left. Avinash told those in the queue that they did not have to pay him anything for the gate pass. Some laughed and some refused to believe him. The first driver picked up the note, thanked him and left. Avinash soon got busy issuing gate passes for the entire duration of his shift, taking only a small break for lunch. By the end of the shift, over a hundred trucks had been loaded.

The following day, he was posted at shed number four. He was sitting at the delivery counter when Rustom, a customs house clearing agent, approached him with a delivery order. Avinash checked the documents and verified them against a consignment of a hundred wooden cases lying in the shed. Everything was in order. He counted the cases while they were being loaded into two trucks and issued the gate pass. Rustom collected the gate pass and placed some money on the counter.

'Wait, what is this?' Avinash asked.

'Saheb, this is your hisaab,' Rustom said. 'It's a reasonable amount.'

'I don't want it. Please take it away.'

Rustom scratched his head and pleaded. 'But I can't give you any more than this,' he said. 'And my cargo and my documents are all in order.'

'Yes, I've seen them. So why are you paying for the gate passes?'

Rustom paused for a moment and then said, 'This is the tradition, sir. Whether everything is in order or not, we have to pay. If there is a discrepancy, we pay more.'

'Please take the money away. I get a salary for issuing gate passes.'

'But, sir, everybody takes hisaab.'

'I don't.'

Rustom thanked him and took back the money, eyeing him disbelievingly as he did so.

About an hour later, a fat young man dressed in a golden silk shirt, brown trousers and white footwear, and carrying a briefcase, approached the delivery counter. He pushed some documents towards Avinash through the counter window. The diamond rings on his fingers sparkled. 'Sahebji, namaste,' he said with a broad smile. 'I am Umerji. Your seniors know me very well.'

The name rang a bell as Avinash remembered it being mentioned by many of his colleagues, including Mohan. Umerji was one of the favourite importers of the dock employees because he paid generous bribes for facilitating shady deals.

'Namaste,' he replied. He examined the documents and came out of the delivery enclosure. A consignment of 2,000 bags of moulding powder was stacked against the shed wall. Several other consignments of moulding powder were also stacked nearby.

'This consignment is yours,' he said, pointing at the bags near the shed wall.

Umerji nodded and left the shed, returning a few minutes later with two loaders. Standing near his consignment, he instructed the men, 'Load a thousand bags from this lot and'—pointing at the neighbouring consignment—'a thousand from this other lot.'

'Wait,' Avinash said. 'That is not your consignment. Take your consignment only.'

'Both are moulding powder consignments, Sahebji.'

Avinash pointed to the shipping marks and said, 'The consignees are different, as are the grades of the contents inside.'

Umerji wrapped his hand around Avinash's shoulders and took him aside. 'Sahebji, I'll make you happy,' he said. 'I'll pay you five thousand rupees for the gate pass.'

'No.'

Umerji grinned. 'All right, I'll make it seven thousand rupees.'

'Are you crazy?'

Umerji closed his eyes and smiled. 'My last offer is eight

thousand rupees—I can't afford any more. I have to pay the shed superintendent and the gate staff also.'

Avinash controlled the anger building up inside him. 'I'm not stopping you for the sake of money. You are taking a cross-delivery, which amounts to theft.'

'Sahebji, this is how things work here. You know it. I know it. Everyone knows it. All right, the maximum I can pay is ten thousand rupees, and not more than that.'

'You're not getting my point. I don't accept such money, and I won't allow cross-delivery.'

'Really?' Umerji laughed. 'Sahebji, in this world, money is everything. You just throw money and people lick your feet.'

'Don't take that for granted. Not everyone is up for sale, and money is not everything.'

Umerji left in a huff with the two men in tow, and Avinash returned to the delivery counter. Moments later, Superintendent Shaikh arrived. 'Gaikwad, what happened?' he asked, and Avinash told him about the incident.

The superintendent took him aside. 'See, we have to ignore such minor things like cross-delivery. After all, Umerji is paying you a reasonable amount. He has the reputation of being a good paymaster. Issue the gate passes.'

'No, sir, I won't do it. This amounts to theft on his part and connivance on ours—he's cheating the government.'

The superintendent got very angry. 'What do you think of yourself?' he shouted. 'I'm your senior and this is my order.'

Avinash smiled. 'All right, sir. Please issue a written order then,' he said.

'What written order? I'm telling you in person.'

'No, sir. An oral order won't do. Please give it to me in writing.'

Shaikh stared at him for a moment and said, 'No. I can't.'

'Then you can counter-sign the gate pass, and I'll write in the remarks section that this cross-delivery has been released on your orders.'

Shaikh stared at him in disbelief and rage. 'You are so mean that you won't even find a place in hell,' he said.

'Sir, I don't believe in heaven or hell,' Avinash said.

Shaikh walked away angrily, with Umerji following him, mumbling, 'I'll see you later. I'll call the assistant docks manager in charge of this section.'

'Please do, sir,' Avinash said. 'I have not committed a crime—I'm only following the rules.'

Minutes later, Umerji came back to the counter. 'I won't take the delivery today,' he said, collecting the delivery order and walking away, a sullen expression on his face, muttering, 'weird' as he left.

Avinash could feel the power of morality and the law. A sense of accomplishment engulfed him, for having done his duty well.

After a while, Shaikh came to the delivery enclosure. 'What have you done?' he asked. 'You missed an opportunity to earn some extra income.'

'I don't want such money,' Avinash said firmly.

'Do you think you can stop these things from happening at all?' Shaikh asked.

'Sir, I know I'm a speck of dust,' Avinash said. 'I don't have the power to change the world, but whatever little I can do within my power, I want to do it.'

'Umerji will come for the delivery tomorrow when you're posted elsewhere. He'll have to spend more money on the gatekeepers, the shed staff and the person in your place, who will readily cooperate with him. Your principles don't matter and they don't make a difference.'

'My principles may make little or no difference to the world, but they make a world of difference to me. Whatever work I do and in whatever areas I have jurisdiction over, I can set an example for others to follow. At the least, I can send out a message that not everyone is up for sale, and corrupt people can't have their way all the time.'

'I don't think you'll last long in the docks,' the superintendent said, shaking his head and walking back to his enclosure.

Two days later, Avinash was waiting at the dock office for his day's posting when Mohan arrived, wearing a wide smile and waving at various colleagues. He shook hands with Avinash, who noticed a black thread with a tiny rectangular piece of black cloth tied around his arm.

'What's that?' Avinash asked.

Mohan raised his arm and kissed the piece of black cloth. 'It's a tabeez I got from a very powerful tantrik,' he said. 'It will ensure prosperity and save me from evil eyes.'

A few colleagues overheard this and immediately surrounded Mohan, requesting him to bring them similar charms. In the meantime, two of their seniors, Gulam Khan and Akash Deshmukh, approached Avinash.

'Are you A.D. Gaikwad?' Deshmukh asked. He was a dark-skinned, hefty pot-bellied man, and he wore his thick moustache twirled up.

'Yes,' Avinash replied.

'Come here,' Gulam said, and they walked a few paces away from the crowd and stopped. Gulam was a tall and lanky bearded man with several rings on his fingers and a gold chain around his neck. 'You were posted at berth number fifteen the day before, right?' he asked.

Avinash got a whiff of alcohol as the man spoke. 'Yes,' he answered.

Gulam frowned. 'You did not accept any money from the drivers,' he said. 'And yesterday, when I was posted there, the truckers refused to pay me. It took me and the clearing staff several hours to convince them that they have to pay as per tradition. Even the superintendent had to intervene!'

Avinash smiled. 'I haven't done anything wrong,' he said.

'Do you realize that you're setting a bad precedent?' Gulam asked. 'If you don't want to earn extra money, we don't care. But don't meddle with our income.'

'Gaikwad, keep your lofty, bookish ideas to yourself,' Deshmukh said curtly, raising a finger. 'If you want to remain hungry, we don't mind, but don't spoil our meal.'

A few colleagues overheard the conversation and eyed Avinash with contempt.

'Friends, if you think I've committed a crime or made a mistake, you're free to complain against me,' Avinash said. 'But I'm just following the rules.'

'The rules are good to read or discuss. The actual work is performed differently, with unwritten rules in play,' Deshmukh said.

Gulam clenched his teeth and said, 'This is our last warning. If you create problems for us, you'll face dire consequences.'

Mohan spotted the trio and came over. 'Gulam bhai, Deshmukh bhau, what happened?' he asked.

'Tell your batchmate to behave himself, or you know what will happen,' Gulam said and then walked away with Deshmukh.

'What happened?' Mohan asked, and Avinash told him about the whole episode.

'Why are you doing this?' Mohan asked. 'If you feel ashamed about demanding money, just accept whatever comes to you without asking for it. But don't break these traditions.'

'I can't, Mohan—it's illegal, unethical.'

'Everyone is doing it.'

'You mean if everyone is doing something wrong, it becomes right?'

'Yes!' Mohan laughed as Avinash shook his head in disgust.

After the day's posting was assigned, Avinash and Mohan walked towards the wharves where they saw Shantaram talking to someone. Mohan waved at him, and Shantaram approached them. He looked at Avinash and asked, 'You are A.D. Gaikwad, isn't it?'

'Yes,' Avinash replied.

'Do you know what he did at the dry bulk terminal?' he asked Mohan.

'Yes, and I'm trying to convince him to refrain from doing such things,' Mohan said.

Shantaram wrapped his hand around Avinash's shoulder. 'Don't do this,' he said. 'Just wash your hands in the flowing river.'

'You talk as if I've committed a crime,' Avinash said.

Shantaram laughed. 'No, not at all,' he said. 'You're following the rules. But the question is, why become enemies with the fish when you live in water as well?'

Avinash controlled his anger and said, 'I'm just doing my job the way it's supposed to be done.'

'Are you scared of being caught? If you are, then my advice is don't indulge in shady deals, but at least accept whatever comes to you without your demanding it. There's nothing wrong with that. The money is merely to encourage us to work more efficiently—it's speed money.'

'Sir, I'm not scared—it takes courage to be honest. And what you call "speed money" is bribery. Real speed money is a legal incentive for extra work, like handling more tonnage of cargo than usual.'

Shantaram sighed. 'It appears that you come from a rich family and are not interested in earning more money,' he said.

'No, I actually live in a slum.'

'Oh really? In any case, my advice as your friend is this: you have a secure and lucrative job. Don't stick your neck out. Work like the others, make extra money, buy a decent house, enjoy your life and retire as a happy pensioner.'

Avinash looked at him with disbelief. 'Thank you, but my conscience doesn't permit me to behave like others.'

Shantaram nodded with a smirk. 'Then I wish you the best of luck,' he said and walked away.

Moments later, as Avinash and Mohan were passing by the dock office, a jeep from the docks department stopped near them. The door opened and Patwardhan alighted. He looked around and saw Avinash.

'Hello, sir,' Avinash said.

Patwardhan smiled. 'Gaikwad, come with me,' he said and walked into the dock office. Avinash followed him upstairs to his cabin. 'Sit down,' Patwardhan said, pointing to a chair.

Avinash thanked him and sat down as Patwardhan occupied his own chair behind the table.

'We are sending some employees for civil defence training at the state government's facilities. Are you interested in going?' he asked.

'Yes, sir.'

'That's good. From next Monday, you'll be relieved of your duties at the docks for a few weeks. You'll get the necessary instructions about this change tomorrow.'

'Thank you, sir.'

When Avinash came out of the office, he saw that Mohan was still waiting.

'What did he say?' Mohan asked.

'I'm going for civil defence training for some weeks,' Avinash said. 'If you're interested, I can request him to include your name too.'

Mohan laughed. 'No, no! I don't want to go anywhere, especially when my job has become so lucrative,' he said.

A few days later, as instructed, Avinash joined a group of employees from different departments of the port authority to undergo training at the Directorate of Civil Defence. The course consisted of classroom instructions as well as practical training in first aid, firefighting and rescue operations, which included climbing ladders and jumping from the second floor of a structure into a safety net and holding the net secure to rescue victims jumping from a building.

At home, Avinash's parents were glad that he had learnt some new skills, and as always, Dagadoo had the training certificate framed and added it to the row of certificates in the house.

Months later, Avinash was at Mohan's residence. This was his second visit, and the old chawl and its surroundings remained more or less unchanged. There were some boys playing cricket with a rubber ball, while a few elderly people were sitting and talking in the veranda. The air was filled with the sound of both devotional and film songs emanating from different houses, making it a riot of surreal music, with different rhythms cutting one another.

Everything was the same—except Mohan's house. Avinash saw that it had undergone a complete metamorphosis, with freshly painted walls and new furniture. Besides, it was now crowded with domestic appliances. Mohan was lying on a cushioned couch, watching something on a television set that appeared to be too large for the small room.

Avinash made himself comfortable in a chair. Mohan's mother came out of the kitchen to give him some water, and he saw that she was now wearing gold jewellery.

'Have you noticed the changes?' Mohan asked, looking around the house.

Avinash smiled. 'Yes, many things are new,' he said.

Mohan's mother came back from the kitchen, this time with tea in expensive crockery.

'My son is an achiever, and God has blessed him,' she said, her face beaming.

Avinash smiled and nodded politely. He was sipping the tea in silence when Mohan's father came in, carrying some shopping bags.

He greeted Avinash and handed over the bags to Mohan's mother. 'Be careful,' he told her. 'There's a glass bottle inside.'

Avinash noticed the difference in Mohan's father as well. He was wearing a gold chain around his neck and there were two gold rings on his fingers.

'I've bought the brand of whiskey you asked for,' he told Mohan after freshening up and sitting down with them.

Avinash was startled. 'Whiskey?' he asked. 'But you were concerned about his drinking.'

Mohan's father smiled sheepishly and seemed at a loss for words. 'Well, yes, I'm still concerned about his drinking,' he said finally. 'I want him to consume less, but when he does drink, it should only be good quality stuff.'

Mohan threw a victorious glance at Avinash and smiled.

'He should drink at home instead of spending time and money in a bar,' Mohan's father added, avoiding eye contact with Avinash, who was speechless.

'We're planning to get him married; we've received many proposals,' Mohan's mother said.

'Congratulations,' Avinash said.

'No, no, not so soon,' Mohan said. 'I want to buy a flat before I marry. This house is too small to accommodate a growing family.'

'Yes, that's true, and with God's grace, it will happen soon,' his father said. 'Because of Mohan, we've started making progress.'

'I must leave now,' Avinash said, getting up. Mohan accompanied him to the bus stop.

'Your father has changed,' Avinash said when they were outside the chawl. 'There was a time when he wanted to stop you from drinking.'

Mohan laughed. 'Money has the power to change anything, stupid!' he exclaimed. 'I'm earning many times more than him, and the extra money has no limit.'

'So, now everyone must be happy.'

'Yes, but there is a small thing that irritates me.'

'What is it?'

'Every day when I return home from duty, my parents ask me how much my extra income for the day is.'

'Oh.'

'The problem is that it's not a fixed amount, and there's also no minimum amount that I get every day. There are days when it's a really meagre amount, and sometimes, it's nothing.'

'Hmm.'

'On such days, they think I'm lying. Can you imagine?' he asked, spreading his hands. Then, after a pause, he added, 'It breaks my heart to see that they don't trust me. It makes me restless. I spend nights lying awake, thinking of how to earn more the next day. And to ensure that I fall asleep as soon as I hit the bed, I must drink more.'

Avinash was flabbergasted. The usual vivacity on Mohan's face had vanished, making him look like a helpless victim. He didn't know what to say to him.

The bus arrived soon after and Avinash boarded it. He was aghast at how things in Mohan's family had changed so drastically.

A few days later, Avinash was at a warehouse outside the docks where uncleared imported cargo was stored. There was also some export cargo being loaded into containers for a shipment there. The superintendent sat behind his desk, signing some documents. There was a row of pictures of various gods on the wall behind him.

The labour supervisor was a clean-shaven middle-aged man with a paunch. He was wearing a spotless white uniform and a pair of gold-rimmed sunglasses. A locket hung from a chain around his neck, and gold rings studded with precious stones twinkled on his index, middle and ring fingers.

'I'm ordering some chicken biryani,' the superintendent said. 'Do you want anything?'

The supervisor smiled and approached the superintendent's table. 'No, don't order anything for me. I'm going to have some home-cooked seafood from a private mess. And I've asked for something extra today,' he said, winking at the superintendent. 'My favourite cook is going to deliver my lunch!'

'Wow!' the superintendent exclaimed, and they both laughed.

'What about you?' the superintendent asked Avinash. 'Shall I order something for you?'

'No, sir, I've brought my lunchbox,' he said.

Moments later, a peon left on a bike to fetch food for the superintendent.

By the time he came back with the food, a young woman in her twenties arrived at the door of the warehouse with a tiffin box inside a bag. She was fair and had a round face and large black eyes. The bright red kumkum on her forehead and the mangalsutra around her neck indicated that she was married. She wore her hair in a bun with a gajra of white jasmine flowers around it. She was wearing a lemon-yellow sari with a green border. She widened her smile as she handed the tiffin box to the supervisor.

'Why didn't you wear the new sari I gave you?' he asked, looking at her from head to toe.

The smile vanished from the woman's face. 'Sir, I washed it today,' she said apologetically. 'I'll wear it the next time.'

He nodded. 'Don't worry, I'll get you another one,' he said.

The woman left the warehouse and Avinash saw her walk outside and wait under the shade of a tree. The superintendent and the supervisor went upstairs to the cargo receiver's office to have their lunch. Avinash opened his tiffin and had lunch at his desk.

Once they finished their meal, the superintendent and the supervisor came downstairs. The supervisor went out with the bag in which the woman had brought him the tiffin and handed it to her. After a brief chat with him, the woman walked away towards a deserted spot where some empty containers were placed. The supervisor, meanwhile, came into the warehouse, whispered something in the superintendent's ear and then quickly went out again, following the woman. Most of the labourers were resting inside the warehouse after their lunch break and there was nobody outside.

A little later, the supervisor hurriedly walked back to the warehouse, heading up the stairs to the cargo receiver's cabin. As he ascended the stairs, he told the superintendent, 'I'm going upstairs for a nap.' The superintendent just grinned and nodded in response.

Avinash was taking a walk around the warehouse when he saw the young woman emerge from behind the empty containers and walk towards a tree. She sat down under the tree with the tiffin box in front of her. She looked exhausted and dishevelled, as if someone had mauled her. The knot of her hair had come loose, and the string of jasmine flowers was hanging down her back with some flowers missing. The kumkum on her forehead had been partly wiped off.

'Is there a problem?' Avinash asked her. 'Shall I fetch you some water?'

The woman looked at him with tired eyes. 'No,' she said curtly and, getting up hurriedly, started walking towards the warehouse gate.

Avinash caught a whiff of talcum powder as she crossed him. 'Are you all right?' he asked. 'Do you need any help?'

She stopped for a moment and glanced at him. 'No, I'm just tired,' she said. 'I have two hungry kids to feed at home, and my husband is jobless.'

He thought she would break down, but she didn't. Instead, she collected herself, arranged her clothes and wiped her face with the pallu of her sari. Then she took a deep breath and walked away without another word. Avinash watched her leave the warehouse compound and walk down the road till she disappeared around the corner.

CHAPTER 15

The master's degree exams were announced by the university, and Avinash decided to take leave for a couple of weeks to study. When he visited the dock office during the lunch break and filled the leave form, he learned that Patwardhan was on leave and Narendra Oswal was in charge of the staff. He knocked on Oswal's door and asked if he could come in. Inside, he found Oswal seated behind his desk. Somewhere in his forties, Oswal was fair-skinned, tall and hefty. He had dyed hair and was wearing a spotless white shirt and grey trousers. He looked up at Avinash from the file he was reading.

'Sir, I have applied for leave,' Avinash said, handing over his application.

Quickly going through it, Oswal asked, 'You want leave for your exams?'

'Yes, sir. I'm studying for a master's degree,' Avinash said.

'In which subject?'

'English, sir.'

Oswal's face lit up. 'Oh! Sit down,' he said.

Avinash dropped into a chair, thanking him.

'I'm also a postgraduate in English. I was a lecturer in a college before joining here,' Oswal said, smiling. 'I love teaching.'

'But then why did you leave teaching and come here?'

Oswal leaned back in his swivel chair and rotated to his left and then to his right, enjoying the movement. 'Simple,' he said. 'Money—money is everything. It's not God, but it's not less powerful than God either.'

Avinash was surprised. 'But teaching is a noble profession, with a reasonable salary, that too,' he said.

Oswal stopped moving his chair and leaned forward on the table. 'Not the kind of money I earn here. You know what I mean,' he said, winking and snapping his fingers. 'On sensitive positions, I can earn a professor's monthly salary just like that, in a single day. Right now, I'm stuck in this non-lucrative chair, but not for long. Don't you think I did the right thing?'

Avinash was shocked. He looked at Oswal, smiling and nodding eagerly, waiting for his endorsement, and remembered Hari, his father's cousin, a semi-literate crane driver who had boisterously argued on similar lines. He also remembered Kamble, who had no qualms about engaging in theft or bribery.

'Sir, I think you did the right thing by giving up teaching,' Avinash said, getting up and walking towards the door. 'Otherwise, you would've taught your students the same thing and made them run after money at the cost of everything else in life.'

The smile on Oswal's face vanished instantly. 'How dare you talk to me like this?' he yelled, standing up. 'I'm your boss.'

'Yes, sir, you are. I only expressed my opinion because you asked for it.'

'Get out!' Oswal shouted.

Avinash left the cabin, and Oswal immediately pressed the call bell and summoned the office superintendent sitting in the hall outside. The superintendent promptly got up from his chair and entered the cabin.

'Is there a problem?' a peon asked Avinash. 'I heard saheb yelling.'

Avinash shook his head. 'Nothing much,' he said.

The superintendent came out a moment later with some papers in his hand. When he saw Avinash, he approached him.

'Your leave application has been rejected,' he said curtly. 'If you still go on leave, it'll be leave without pay.'

Avinash nodded and left.

As the day shift concluded, Avinash wound up his paperwork. While walking towards the main gate, he saw groups of sari-clad women exiting the docks without being frisked. All of them appeared pregnant and were walking slowly, chatting loudly as they passed the gatekeepers. Some of them waved at the security personnel, who reciprocated the greeting.

Just as Avinash came out of the gate and turned towards the railway station, a motorcycle roared past him. The rider looked in his side-view mirror and stopped, the tail light of the bike blazing red. He looked over his shoulder and took off his helmet as Avinash caught up with him.

'Avinash, right?' he asked.

Avinash looked at the rider. 'Kiran? How are you?' he asked as they shook hands.

After exchanging pleasantries, Kiran pointed at the women and asked, 'Who are these women, and why do all of them look pregnant?'

'Ah, it's got to do with the import of woollen garments and their pilferage,' Avinash said. He then told Kiran how hordes of women entering the docks was a common enough sight every morning. The women, all of them dressed in saris, worked in transit sheds stuffed with bales of garments imported as 'woollen rags'. In the evening, the women hid some of these woollen or synthetic garments under their saris before leaving the transit shed. Once outside the dock limits, they went to a secluded spot or a public toilet to pull out the stolen garments and stuff them into their bags. The garments were then sold to agents, who channelled them ahead to hawkers and small shops for sale at throwaway prices. It was an open secret, known to everyone working in the docks.

'Wow! This is a fantastic story!' Kiran exclaimed. 'I'll work on it, but in the meanwhile, see if you can get me some more details.'

As Avinash nodded, Kiran put on his helmet and kick-started his bike. 'May I drop you somewhere?' he asked.

'No, I'll walk to the railway station, but thanks.'

Kiran's bike roared away and disappeared in the traffic ahead.

After that meeting, Avinash started collecting bits of information whenever possible and conveyed everything to Kiran over the phone. On one occasion, Kiran took Avinash with him to the customs office to meet a senior customs officer he was acquainted with. He introduced Avinash as a friend and a dock employee.

The officer, wearing a crisp white uniform and sporting black epaulettes with the national emblem and golden stripes on it, smiled. The name tag on his chest read 'Ramachandran'. As the three got talking, Kiran raised the issue of woollen rags.

'The import of woollen rags is permitted as raw material for manufacturers of woollen blankets and garments. The bills of entry describe the cargo as "woollen rags", but sometimes even new and reusable garments arrive in these consignments. So, before delivery, each piece has to be manually torn apart into four pieces to render it useless,' Ramachandran said. 'But there are some unscrupulous traders who've made this a lucrative business. Women are engaged through contractors to mutilate the garments in the docks, but you've seen what happens.'

'But this is happening despite the presence of several law enforcement agencies,' Avinash pointed out.

'You're right,' Ramachandran said.

'When will this stop?' Avinash asked.

Ramachandran smiled. 'Do you know why criminal systems work so efficiently?' he asked. 'It's because the implementation of law depends on a chain of people at different stages. It's like a supply chain, to use corporate parlance. Since the number of dishonest people is greater, the chain of dishonesty works smoothly. Honest people, on the other hand, are very few and scattered, often not linked in the same chain. Justice can only be served when all the links in a chain, from the bottom to the top, function in unison.

For instance, if you detect a malpractice and complain, your boss, then his boss, then the investigating officer and everyone in the hierarchy has to go by the book and take the matter forward to its logical end without fear or favour. The problem is that the chain of lawbreakers is far stronger than that of honest people.'

'Yes, you're right,' Kiran said.

'And the number of dishonest people is greater because there is no incentive for being honest,' Ramachandran said. 'So, it's easy for a gullible person to fall in line with the crooks. It's difficult to expand the network of good people or expect morality from the impoverished masses.'

Kiran thought about this for a moment. 'But there are people from impoverished backgrounds who are honest—like him,' he said, pointing at Avinash.

Ramachandran nodded, and Kiran told him about Avinash's background.

The customs officer smiled. 'I'm also a marginalized person, but in a different sense. I'm marginalized in my department because of my honesty,' he said. Then he looked at Avinash and nodded again. 'But I must admit that you are doubly marginalized because of your caste.'

While they were still talking, Ramachandran was summoned by his senior officer. Avinash and Kiran thanked him and left the office.

'Tomorrow, I'll talk to some people engaged in this work in the docks,' Kiran said. 'Try not to be around. But if we come face to face, act like we don't know each other so that people won't suspect that you're my source and create any problems for you.'

A couple of days later, on his weekly day off, Avinash was standing under a tree in front of Buddha Vihar and talking to Sudhir when

Raja approached them, wearing a blue jersey with a golden coat of arms on the chest.

'Whose jersey is this?' Sudhir asked Raja.

'It's mine,' Raja said. 'My mother is now working in the docks, and she brought it home.'

'Oh, it's beautiful. Ask her to get me one too,' Sudhir said. 'I'll pay for it.'

'There are other imported garments like this lying at home. Come and take a look.'

'All right,' Sudhir said, and the three of them walked up the steps to the narrow gully where Raja's house was.

Once they reached his house, Raja's mother, Narmada, showed them some jerseys lying around. 'A couple of women working in the docks asked me to join them. It's a good job. We sell some garments and keep some for personal use,' she said, smiling.

Then, turning to Avinash, she said, 'I've seen you in the docks a few times.'

'So, you're among the women who walk out of the docks every evening with these garments stuffed under their saris?' Avinash asked.

'Yes,' she nodded with embarrassment.

'This amounts to theft.'

She laughed. 'Everyone does it; it's no big deal.'

'But when you get paid for your work, why indulge in such things?'

She sneered at him. 'Wages?' she asked sarcastically. 'We don't get any wages. Our contractor, Sohan Babu, has asked us to take away garments instead.'

'But this is wrong. He has to pay you proper wages,' Avinash said. 'You should talk to your co-workers and organize them.'

Narmada stared at him blankly for a moment and then shook her head. 'Leave it, Avinash,' she said. 'I don't think anyone will be ready to do it. We're happy with this arrangement. We simply tear a few garments for the customs officer to examine and select some of the intact pieces for ourselves. Everyone knows it.'

'But if you get paid well, would you stop this?'

She stared at him, then looked up at the roof. 'Err ... I don't know,' she said. 'All I know is that I'm making more money than I used to as a maid.'

Avinash looked at her, and then at Raja and Sudhir.

'What she's saying is right,' Sudhir said. 'She's a poor woman struggling for the most basic of things.'

Raja nodded and said, 'You know my father is an alcoholic who works as a mason whenever he gets a chance. I don't have any regular employment, and am doing all kinds of odd jobs to survive.'

'I'm the only person in this family with a regular income, and this job is lucrative,' Narmada said. 'I'm happy.'

'But this is illegal,' Avinash pointed out. 'What if you get caught?'

She sighed. 'When a person is poor, hungry and helpless, things like morality or law are unaffordable,' she said. After a moment, she smiled broadly and added, 'But in our case, there is no fear of getting caught because everyone is involved.'

Sudhir pulled out a couple of clothes from a pile and selected one. 'I'll pay you tomorrow,' he told Raja's mother. Then, turning to Avinash, he said, 'Let's go.'

The next day, when Avinash was passing by a warehouse with bales full of woollen rags stacked inside, he peered in. Some women were sitting on the floor, with piles of garments all around them. A few port employees were rummaging through these heaps, looking for the right size and colour of garments to pick. Boxes stuffed with yet more garments were stacked against a wall. Some were open, with garments spilling out. A couple of men were standing at the door, talking with Superintendent Shaikh, who smiled at Avinash.

'Want a synthetic jersey or a woollen coat?' he asked.

'No, sir, I was just passing by,' Avinash said.

'Go inside and pick up whatever you like.'

'No, thank you. I'm looking for a contractor named Sohan Babu.'

'Sohan Babu?' Shaikh asked. Then he pointed at a short man with curly hair standing nearby. 'There he is.'

Sohan Babu was a middle-aged man dressed in a pair of white trousers and a silky white shirt with a thick gold chain around his neck and a gold bracelet on his right wrist.

'Are you Sohan Babu?' Avinash asked, walking up to him.

The man peered over his gold-rimmed goggles. 'Yes, what can I do for you, sir?' he asked.

'I'm told that some contractors don't pay wages and instead ask these women workers to steal garments.'

Sohan Babu laughed and Shaikh grinned.

'No, sir,' Sohan Babu said. 'Some women may be taking away a few garments, but we overlook it because it's a minor thing; even the security personnel don't object. But your information about the wages is wrong. Who told you this? Can you bring even a single complainant before me?'

Avinash looked at Shaikh, who took him aside. 'Don't get into all this,' Shaikh said. 'You're already notorious as a rabble-rouser.'

'But I just want the law to be implemented properly.'

Shaikh shook his head. 'That's not your lookout,' he said. 'Just stick to your role in this system. There are other agencies to look after labour laws.'

As Avinash turned to leave, Sohan Babu approached him. 'Sir, there are some very high-quality jerseys in this lot. You can choose some for yourself and your friends and family,' he said.

Avinash stared at him for a couple of seconds and left, shaking his head in disgust.

A couple of days later, there was a commotion in the docks as senior officials from several law enforcement agencies visited many of the transit sheds where bales of woollen garments were stacked. Later, they held discussions with some of the officers involved while the women who worked in these sheds waited outside the dock gate. Some were haggling with the security staff to let them enter the docks.

'Do you know that the whole process of mutilating woollen rags has been suspended and the malpractices in the system are being investigated?' Mohan asked Avinash when he met him near the dock office.

'Is it?'

'Yes, some newspaper has published a report on it.'

'Which newspaper?'

'I don't know—some English paper.'

Avinash went outside the docks and bought a copy of the *City News*. The story had been published with a picture of a group of women coming out of the dock gate. They were all wearing saris and appeared pregnant. Later in the evening, he telephoned Kiran and told him about what had happened in the docks.

The next day, after his shift ended, Avinash was walking out of the main gate after being frisked when Mohan followed him.

'I want to tell you something important,' Mohan said. 'I've heard that some people are very angry with you. Be careful.'

'Is it?' Avinash asked. 'Why?'

Mohan shook his head. 'Many people think that you create problems. The latest one being the newspaper report on the woollen rags. People believe that you leaked out the information,' he said. 'You're a marked man.'

'But I'm just an ordinary delivery clerk. Why would they spend their time and energy on me?'

'Because you create unnecessary hurdles for them. Some shady people have even started checking the location of your posting at the timekeeper's office before scheduling their cargo delivery in order to avoid you.'

Avinash had been expecting this. 'My conscience is clear,' he said. 'If my action leads to some rectifications in the system, that's good.'

Mohan simply shrugged.

Avinash pondered over it. The newspaper report had most likely annoyed the powers that be. He was not sure whether the subsequent investigation would result in any punitive action and systemic rectification or not. It could fizzle out, considering the nexus between the security personnel and rogue elements. But there was a glimmer of hope that it could result in some systemic corrections if, as Ramachandran had said, all the links in the law enforcement chain were united.

Avinash had kept his parents in the dark about the development as he felt they would get worried about his safety. They were satisfied with his salary and were happy he was studying simultaneously. They were particularly thrilled that they could renovate the house—the crude staircase was repaired with cement and the floor was concreted over. Besides, the walls of the house were cemented till about four feet from the ground, with tin sheets making up the remaining height. It was a much-awaited luxury.

After Avinash finished his master's degree, Dagadoo suggested that he should prepare for the civil services' competitive examinations. But as his friendship with Kiran developed, Avinash got increasingly attracted to journalism.

'How does one become a journalist?' he once asked Kiran.

'Why don't you enrol yourself in a journalism course?' Kiran asked. 'You're already a post-graduate. But you'll have to read a lot, develop contacts and keep abreast of current affairs.'

'I'll do it,' Avinash said. 'I would love to be a watchdog of society.'

However, when he actually enrolled himself for a journalism course, his parents were jittery. Dagadoo was apprehensive about whether he would be able to get a job and be allowed to write what he wanted to. 'It's a noble profession, but it's dominated by the elite castes and is in private hands, son,' he said.

'So what?' Avinash asked. 'I'm currently working in a government entity in the open category.'

'True, but your current job is secure. Your salary, allowances, promotions and everything else is protected. Even after retirement, you'll get a pension and have access to government medical facilities.'

Avinash grew agitated. 'You mean we should only work as government employees, generation after generation?' he asked. 'As such, most of our community is in government service on reserved seats. There are other vital sectors in which we need to get a foothold. Reservation is not going to last forever, and government job opportunities are shrinking.'

Dagadoo sighed. 'I wish for our boys and girls to shine in all fields, but there are limitations,' he said. 'Getting a government job is comparatively easy because of reservation. The private sector, however, is either monopolized or dominated by historically privileged communities.'

Godavari had been listening to them silently, but she got up now and stood in front of Avinash with her hands on her hips. 'You are not quitting your port job,' she said firmly. 'If you don't want to make extra money, that's fine. But don't give up a secure job. Remember, I gave up working as a maid because of your port job. Don't make me go back to washing dishes for other people again.'

'Don't worry,' Avinash said. 'I won't leave my job until I get regular employment in a reputed media house.'

'Have you gone mad?' she screamed. 'People *yearn* for a government job.'

Avinash looked at his father helplessly.

Dagadoo scratched his head and looked at them. 'A government job is indeed most secure,' he said, 'but if you want to make a career in journalism, I won't stop you.'

Godavari banged a vessel on the floor in protest. 'Nobody listens to me in this house,' she shouted.

Avinash went and sat on the threshold of the house with his feet on the steps below. A plane with a white bird painted on its red tailfin flew overhead. The metropolitan habitat in front of him appeared as vibrant and fascinating as ever. He wanted to be a part of it, but the more he wanted to join it, the more it appeared to be a captivating labyrinth, seducing him deeper and deeper.

A few days later, when he returned home in the evening, there were several pairs of slippers on the steps outside his house and loud voices were emanating from within. He found his parents discussing something seriously with Narmada and two other women, who were strangers to him. As he entered the house, the conversation stopped abruptly.

'How are you, Narmada maushi?' he asked with a smile, but she threw him an angry look and left in a huff with the other women following her, eyeing him sharply.

'What happened?' he asked.

'Narmada and many other women have lost their jobs in the docks,' Godavari said. 'And they all believe that it's because of you. I never expected that you would make people jobless.'

'How can I be responsible for this?' he asked. 'I'm neither their employer nor an authority with decision-making powers. I'm just a junior employee without any say in such things.'

'They think that you leaked information to a newspaper, because of which their work has been stopped,' Dagadoo said.

'They are all poor women trying to earn a livelihood,' Godavari said. 'How could you do this?'

'Do you know that some of the contractors were not paying them wages and had asked the women to steal clothes instead?' Avinash asked. 'They should've paid them proper wages. And these women should've united to fight for legal wages instead of indulging in theft.'

Godavari looked up at the roof, folded her hands and closed her eyes. 'God, please enlighten my son,' she muttered. Then, turning to Avinash, she said, 'I don't understand what you are saying. Just do something and get them to restart their work.'

'Who am I to do this?' Avinash asked. 'I don't have the authority. An investigation is in progress now, after which the authorities will take a decision.'

'Don't misunderstand him, Godavari,' Dagadoo said. 'He has not made a mistake.'

'How can you snatch away the livelihood of these poor women?' she shouted. 'They must be cursing you, and I don't want my son to be cursed.'

'Mother, we're also poor, but we're making a sincere effort to overcome it,' Avinash said. 'Poverty is not a licence to commit crimes or to play the victim and beg for sympathy or blame everything on fate.'

'What you're saying is true, but it's very difficult to reason with impoverished people,' Dagadoo said. 'Poverty and greed can easily sweep away your ethics.'

'I understand the plight of these women, but Kiran and I thought it was our duty to expose the racket.'

'But what is the alternative? What will these women do now?'

'I don't know,' Avinash said and paused for a moment, wondering what the poor women could possibly do. 'Yes, it is a calamity for them. Perhaps, they'll return to their old jobs as domestic workers,' he said. 'But I hope the authorities rectify the system by punishing the contractors and ensuring proper wages for these women so that they can earn a dignified livelihood.'

'Why are you even dabbling in such things?' Godavari shouted.

'I've just helped a journalist expose a racket.'

She stared at him angrily. 'Why did you help him? Has he paid you for this?' she asked.

Avinash shook his head. 'No. He didn't pay me anything. It was my duty to help him in a good cause,' he said. 'And remember, he's the same journalist who helped us in exposing the racket at Maharajawadi Hospital when Sudhir's nephew died. Neither had I paid him at that time to publish the news nor has he paid me now. These things are beyond monetary considerations. It's our social duty.'

'Why meddle in things at all when everything was going smoothly and nobody was complaining? Why change anything?' Godavari demanded.

'Because change is necessary, especially when things are going wrong and nobody is complaining. Didn't you experience the change after migrating here and giving up the traditional work you'd done in the village?' Avinash asked. 'And our basis for determining what is wrong or right, is the Constitution. This is an attempt to ensure that the law is enforced for the welfare of all.'

'For me, the disgraceful thing is that you have trampled upon the livelihood of these women,' she said.

Avinash was speechless. He stood at the threshold of his house and looked down at the city below, which was part of the world spinning around him. He felt trapped and demonized for something he considered was legal and moral. He was tormented by the thought that the very people for whom he was seeking justice had turned against him and branded him a villain. Was it really that difficult to be ethical when you were poor? Did the women join the racket simply because they had no other option to ensure their survival, or were they lured by the opportunity to earn easy money, even if it meant committing a crime? Were they not afraid of getting caught because there was a chain of corrupt men protecting them? Did people become corrupt because it was, unfortunately, the norm? Can the traditions followed by the majority be allowed to continue even if they are immoral, illegal and oppressive? Did people jettison the tenets of morality because they offered no immediate material incentives? Should a criminal act be condoned simply because a poor person had committed it? Going by that logic, could a poor person's crime be pardoned? What if a gangster from an impoverished background justified his crime on the basis of his poverty? Why did the voice of reason always rest with a minuscule minority? Avinash thought that it was possible to inculcate values in the minds of the masses to usher in a collective thought process that could counter those few unscrupulous elites who had clandestinely designed a template of socio-economic, religious and political practices which were against the principles of natural justice—wasn't it?

Later that night, around midnight, there was a knock on the door. Godavari was asleep, Dagadoo was away on night duty, and Avinash was reading. He got up and opened the door as quietly as possible, but the sound woke up Godavari.

'Who is it?' she asked.

Sudhir was standing on the steps, panting.

'Sudhir,' Avinash said.

'Sudhir? At this hour? Is there a problem?' she asked.

'No, it's nothing. I just wanted to talk to Avinash,' Sudhir said, gesturing to Avinash to come out of the house.

Avinash slipped into a casual shirt and closed the door behind him. 'What happened?' he asked Sudhir as he climbed down the stairs.

'Come,' Sudhir said and walked in silence as Avinash followed him. When they reached Buddha Vihar, it was closed and nobody was in sight. A few stray dogs sleeping near the vihar stood up, raised their ears and then sat down again.

Sudhir sat on the steps of the vihar with Avinash beside him. 'Have you noticed anything strange these days?' he asked Avinash. 'Like someone following you or staring at you?'

'Following me? I don't know,' Avinash said. 'Why would anyone follow me?'

Sudhir shook his head. 'I was contacted by a thug who lives on the other side of the hill,' he said. 'He was asking whether anyone named Avinash Gaikwad resides here. He has been asked by someone to track your movements.'

Avinash looked at Sudhir in shock. 'Track my movements? Why would anyone do that?' he asked.

'A supari is probably being circulated.'

'Supari?'

'Yes, it looks like someone wants to hire goons to hurt you. Have you harmed the interests of any rogues lately?'

'I'm just doing my job honestly, which may be indirectly annoying some rogue elements.'

'Your intentions are good, but have you thought about what your parents will do if something happens to you? How will they manage?'

'But I've not committed a crime or done something wrong!'

'I know. But you are doing something unaffordable.'

'Unaffordable?'

'Yes. Don't think that the whole responsibility of implementing the law rests only on your shoulders. There are several government agencies to do it. Don't step beyond your area of jurisdiction. And remember, you're a junior government servant with little or no power to change things.'

Avinash thought about it for a moment. 'I know that. But who wants to hire goons to hurt me?'

'You never know. But don't worry. I told the guy that you are the pride of our locality, and anyone touching you will face severe repercussions.'

'Oh! But will it end there?'

Sudhir patted his shoulder. 'Don't worry—to ensure that the supari is neutralized, I also went with him to the person who had sent out these feelers. I've told him also that if anything happens to you, he will face the consequences.'

'Who is he?'

'I don't know—some shady character operating in the docks.'

Avinash felt uneasy. 'What did he say?' he asked.

Sudhir looked up at the sky for a moment and sighed. 'He asked me to persuade you to stay within your limits,' he said. 'I don't think he'll cause you any harm because the miscreant told him about the strength of our boys and the possible repercussions of messing with you.'

There was a long silence as Avinash thought about what Sudhir had told him. 'I want to meet him,' he said.

'No, there is no need,' Sudhir said. 'Just be extra careful everywhere.'

'All right.'

'I'll ask two of our boys to follow you closely for some days, just in case …'

'No, Sudhir, there's no need.'

Sudhir paused for a moment. 'I don't think this rascal will go ahead with his plan,' he said. 'But there may be someone else we don't know about, who wants to teach you a lesson. At least allow me to accompany you tomorrow to the main gate of the docks and show you how to be vigilant.'

'All right.'

'And don't tell your parents about this.'

'Of course not.'

They parted ways after that and Avinash went home. Godavari woke up when he opened the door.

'Why had Sudhir come at this hour?'

'He just wanted some advice on a personal matter. Don't worry; go back to sleep.' But for the next several hours, Avinash could not sleep himself.

The next morning, when he was getting dressed for work, Sudhir appeared at the door.

'Sudhir, what is the problem?' Godavari asked, offering him a cup of tea.

'Nothing, Godavari kaki. I'm just going to the docks with Avinash,' Sudhir said, sipping the tea.

When they left a little later, Sudhir explained to Avinash how to be alert in public places. As they walked down the main road, he showed Avinash how to look around constantly for suspicious movements, how to face the traffic, avoid tight corners, sit facing the door or sit in a safe spot in public places. He told him to be careful while talking to strangers and to change his timings and routes regularly.

From that day on, Avinash's life changed completely. He was vigilant all the time and looked with suspicion at everyone around him on the road and while travelling in the local train. It was at once thrilling and terrifying.

A couple of days later, when he visited the dock office block, he found Patwardhan talking to someone at the entrance. He waited till the conversation was over before greeting him.

Patwardhan smiled. 'I was just thinking about you. Come with me,' he said, walking upstairs to his cabin. Avinash followed him.

When they were seated, Patwardhan said, 'Your name was brought up at a meeting of officers and port users at the head office. They wanted some punitive action to be taken against you for overstepping your limits and poking your nose in things beyond your jurisdiction. Their allegation is that you leaked the story of the woollen rags to the newspaper and maligned the image of our port. But the legal department made it clear that there are no grounds for taking any action against you.'

'But sir—' Avinash tried to say something, but Patwardhan stopped him.

'I know you are honest and hardworking, but as you know, there are rules in place, there is a hierarchy and a compartmentalization of authority,' he said. 'As of now, the import licences of two importers have been suspended, and further investigations are in progress.'

Avinash nodded as Patwardhan pulled out a bunch of papers from a file lying on his table. 'By the way, the central government has asked us to depute some employees for census work. The job includes enumerating crew members of ships visiting our port. I was thinking of including your name in the list. As such, we are short of volunteers.'

'As you wish, sir.'

'Good. You'll join the census commissioner's team. It will be a new experience for you, and you'll be away from this madhouse for a while.'

'Thank you, sir.' Avinash got up and walked towards the door.

'But be careful, Avinash. People are just waiting to pounce on you.'

Avinash nodded and left the cabin.

A few clusters of fluffy white clouds were scattered across an otherwise clear blue sky. A tugboat moored to the harbour wall was bobbing in the water, its radar scanner rotating on the mast and the engine running. Captain Mark Fernandez welcomed the volunteers aboard. A stout man in his thirties, Fernandez was wearing a spotless white uniform with anchors embroidered on the black epaulettes on his shoulders. He instructed the crew to untie the mooring lines.

'Today, we are visiting some ships at the offshore anchorages,' he told the volunteers as the tugboat rumbled out of the harbour, propelling a steady stream of frothing water behind it. 'I'll drop each one of you on a different vessel and pick you up after an hour or so. Then we'll go for a second round on other ships.'

Avinash had travelled in a passenger ferry for a joyride in the harbour in the past. But venturing out into the open sea was a new experience. As the tugboat surged full throttle ahead, the harbour and the city's skyline receded rapidly, shrinking till it appeared to be swallowed up by the waves.

With no coastline in sight, it was just water all around. They were at the centre of a circular horizon, and it felt like they were floating in a giant bowl of water. The tugboat continued to hurl masses of water behind it in a steady stream that spread out like a peacock's feathers, indicating movement ahead, but appearing to be stuck in the middle of a giant bowl of water in the absence of any other object to show its forward movement. The sea was choppy, with huge waves breaking on its bow, occasionally raising a spray as high as the bridge where the helmsman had activated the windscreen wipers. The breeze whistled through the windows of the helmsman's cabin on both sides. The wireless set crackled with the communication between the control tower and the ships—Fernandez was in touch with the control tower and was coordinating with the ships waiting at the offshore anchorages.

For Avinash, it was a feeling of being detached from the congested man-made world, as if he were one with the elements. The journey seemed endless as the tugboat appeared to be stuck at the centre of the horizon with its engine running, till the hazy silhouette of a cargo ship appeared in the distance, followed by another. The ships gradually became larger as they approached closer. Soon, more ships became visible against the hazy background.

The nearest cargo ship, standing with its anchor dropped, was coloured a deep blue with a line of red running along its sides. Its name, *Ocean Glory*, was painted on both sides of the bow. A Liberian flag, with red and white horizontal stripes and a white star in a blue canton, was fluttering on its astern mast. After a brief radio conversation between the tugboat and the ship, a gangway was lowered from the ship's starboard side as the tugboat pulled up along its side. The upper deck of the ship towered nearly thirty feet above the tugboat.

'Would you like to be the first to go?' Fernandez asked Avinash.

Avinash nodded and was assisted by the crew in getting to the gangway that heaved a couple of feet above the tugboat's deck.

As he made his way up to the ship's deck, the tugboat left on its onward journey.

On the deck, he was received by a sailor, who shook his hand and escorted him into the ship. In a meeting room, the ship's first mate and a couple of sailors were waiting for him. After exchanging pleasantries, he was provided with the crew list, the cargo manifest and other documents. While going through the list, he found that the crew comprised sailors from different nations.

'You have crew from India and Pakistan on board,' he said.

'That's right, we have crew from various nations on board,' the first mate said, instructing a crew member, who rushed out and then returned a few minutes later with two sailors, both dressed in orange boiler suits.

'He's Indian,' the first mate said, pointing at a clean-shaven sailor. Then, pointing at the bearded one, he said, 'And he's from Pakistan.'

Avinash exchanged pleasantries with them and then asked, 'Do the hostile relations between your countries create any problems for you while working on the same ship?'

The two sailors looked at each other with smiles on their faces and then turned to Avinash. 'No,' they said together.

'We don't discuss politics or things that can create any kind of hostility between us,' the Indian sailor said.

'Yes, after all, we're sailing in the same boat,' the Pakistani sailor said, laughing. 'We are colleagues.'

The first mate nodded. 'We're all at sea here,' he said with a smile. 'And we also have international maritime rules to follow.'

Avinash completed the paperwork, after which they offered him a drink that he declined. A casual conversation on mundane matters followed till the tugboat returned to pick him up.

On reaching the tugboat, Avinash found that there was nobody onboard except the crew as the other enumerators had been dropped off on different ships.

'You can take a break for some time before we go on our second round,' Fernandez said.

'No, sir. No need for a break—I'm ready,' Avinash said.

Fernandez nodded and instructed the helmsman to steer the tugboat towards a yellow cargo ship flying the Chinese flag, with its name, *Orient Star*, written in Chinese and English letters along the bow. After a radio conversation, the ship's gangway was once again lowered and as Avinash climbed onto it, the tugboat heaved on the waves and left.

On the deck, he was escorted by an officer into the ship. They entered a conference room with a huge table with chairs around it. Several maps were hanging on the walls of the room. A uniformed officer, sitting at the head of the table, rose and shook hands with Avinash. Two other crew members were standing behind him.

'I ... first mate,' the man said.

Avinash introduced himself and told the first mate about the purpose of his visit. The officer pulled out some documents from a file and placed them on the table. Avinash wrote down the particulars, asking some questions. The officer replied, pausing in between as he searched for the right English words.

After the task was over, a sailor brought big bowls of steaming noodles and soup, along with a plate containing large chunks of roasted meat with the bones sticking out.

'What is this?' Avinash asked, pointing at the meat. The crew said something in Chinese that he did not understand.

The man curved his index fingers and placed them above his head, like horns. 'Cow,' he said, smiling.

'Oh, I don't eat this,' Avinash said.

'You ... no ... eat ... cow?' the officer asked.

'No.'

The officer spoke to the crew in Chinese; then, turning to Avinash, asked, 'You ... eat ... fish?'

'No, I'm vegetarian.'

'Oh,' the officer nodded and spoke to the crew again. A plate full of fruits, including bananas and apples, arrived a few minutes later.

'I'm sorry, sir, but I'm not hungry,' Avinash said. He had lost his appetite at the sight of the huge chunks of meat and bones.

'Drink?' the officer asked. Avinash refused the offer and left the room to stand on the deck near the gangway. There were about a dozen ships at the offshore anchorages, with the closest ones clearly visible and those further away appearing blurry in the haze. When the tugboat announced its arrival with a honk, Avinash shook the officer's hand and then carefully descended the gangway. The tugboat surged ahead, increasing the spread of water streaming behind it.

The deputation for census work continued for several weeks, during which period the enumerators visited many vessels berthed in the docks. For the tugboat crew, visiting the offshore anchorages was a regular matter, but for the dock staff, it was a rare experience. On one occasion, Avinash had the opportunity to interview the captain of a ship, with the crew of the government's Films Division recording the interview for the *Indian News Review* series that was usually screened in cinema theatres before the feature film began.

There were also several meetings with census officials from Delhi to review the work. After the census, when Avinash resumed his duty in the docks, he sensed that something was not quite right. He was not only being eyed strangely by people, but he was also being actively avoided by those around him. He could see people stealing glances at him and maintaining a distance from him.

Mohan was as ostentatious as ever. He had gradually become a connoisseur of perfumes, liquor and food, all a result of his negotiating extremely favourable deals with importers and their agents, especially in murky transactions. Some colleagues had even started seeking his help in fixing up shady deals. Initially, Mohan negotiated for his colleagues for free, but eventually, he started demanding a commission and they happily paid him.

'I feel like I'm on top of the world,' Mohan told Avinash when they were at the dock office. 'Marriage proposals are pouring in, and I'm a suitable, much sought-after boy.'

'That's expected,' Avinash said. 'But remember, the proposals may be coming more for your money than you.'

Mohan thought about this for a while. 'Perhaps so, but I don't care,' he said. 'This is my moment, and I'm enjoying it. If my wealth is going to get me a beautiful girl, so be it.'

A week later, Mohan distributed invitation cards for his wedding and showed Avinash a photograph of his fiancée. 'Among all the proposals we received, she is the fairest,' he said. 'Much fairer than me.'

Avinash looked at the photograph. 'Did you select her only because of the colour of her skin?' he asked.

'Yes, she looks so beautiful,' Mohan said, looking at the photograph with dreamy eyes.

'You're being racist.'

'No, I'm not. I'm just following popular aesthetics—everyone wants a fair bride.'

'These popular aesthetics have been formulated by an elite and racist patriarchy that imposes the supremacy of fair skin over darker skin tones, and by corporates interested in peddling products that promise fair skin,' Avinash said.

'I don't care,' Mohan said.

'What happened to your plan of marrying only after buying a new house?'

Mohan nodded. 'There was too much pressure from my parents,' he said. 'But I've booked a flat, and we'll shift as soon as it's ready.'

Mohan and his family had already waited for months to move into the flat, but there were some glitches and the builder could not complete the work within the promised deadline. With the project delayed, Mohan's parents rented a room in the same building as theirs for the prospective couple and decided to go ahead with the wedding. Mohan invited his colleagues and seniors to the wedding ceremony which was held in the air-conditioned hall of a hotel. Avinash contributed his share for a gift bought collectively by their colleagues.

The wedding was lavish—all the invitees were sprayed with perfume; there were abundant flowers for decoration and a series of glowing multi-coloured bulbs lit up the space. Revellers were dancing to high-decibel music. Mohan's entire family was dressed in its wealthiest best, displaying their choicest attires, accessories and jewellery. The women wore heavy make-up. After the rituals and the photo session, a multi-course dinner followed. There was a special treat for some guests in a separate room. Deshmukh was standing at the door and letting in people. When Avinash saw some known faces enter the room, he became curious, but as he approached the door, Deshmukh stopped him.

'You can't enter,' he said. 'This is not for people like you.'

Avinash was shocked. 'What?' he asked. 'What do you mean?'

Deshmukh grinned. 'This special treat is only for those who drink,' he said, opening the door a bit. Avinash peeped inside and immediately got a strong whiff of alcohol. He could see several men either sitting or standing with glasses of liquor in their hands. Some were smoking, while others were talking.

'I told you, this is not for you,' Deshmukh said. Then he winked and said, 'But it's never too late to amend your ways. You can start drinking from today and enjoy life like us.'

'You don't have to drink to enjoy life,' Avinash said. 'There are numerous other ways to do so.' But Deshmukh only folded his hands and nodded.

After the ceremony, Mohan went on a week-long leave for his honeymoon at a holiday resort in Shimla. On his return, his colleagues congratulated him and some even teased him about the novelty in his life. He acknowledged the comments with his face glowing, and wore the proud expression of an achiever.

'What did you think of the wedding arrangements?' he asked Avinash as they walked towards the dock basin on the day he resumed duty.

'They were good, but too extravagant,' Avinash said. 'It could've been simpler. It was as if you were desperately trying to impress people with your wealth.'

Mohan burst into laughter. 'What's wrong with that?' he asked. 'If you have it, flaunt it.'

'You're right. After all, it's your money, your choice.'

'I have a lot of money, and it will continue to flow. After all, it's easy money. Easy come, easy go. I've not earned it through blood and sweat.'

'That's true.'

'Everyone was impressed. And a lot of people—friends, colleagues and relatives—were shocked and jealous,' Mohan said, grinning. 'I enjoyed their heartburn.'

'Does that make you happy?'

'Yes. I have so many things which they don't possess and can't afford.'

'But I think this is the wrong way to seek happiness. It only evokes destructive and negative feelings like jealousy, hatred and anger. There are positive things from which one can derive pleasure. I was not impressed.'

Mohan sneered at him. 'That's because you are weird. You live in a different world, of which I don't want to be a part of. Ever.'

Avinash smiled.

'There is one development in my life which you'll be happy about, though,' Mohan said. 'I've stopped drinking.'

'Wow. That's good.'

'My wife doesn't like the smell. And now, I don't need liquor to sleep peacefully.'

'I'm glad that you've given up drinking,' Avinash said.

However, the change in Mohan's life eventually turned out to be ephemeral. A couple of weeks later, Avinash found Mohan in a depressed mood, turning down an offer from a colleague to strike a deal with an importer for a commission. When the astonished colleague went away with a shrug, Mohan sat on a chair inside the shed, shaking his head. 'People think I'm a money-minting machine,' he said.

'What happened?' Avinash asked.

Mohan looked at him in despair. 'I had a sleepless night,' he said, widening his eyes. 'Problems at home.'

'What is it now?'

'My parents, my brother and my sister were so proud of me for making their lives happy. But now they suspect that I'm pampering my wife at their cost.'

'Really?'

'Yes … Whenever I buy something for my wife, my sister expects me to buy the same thing for her. And my parents and my brother support her.'

'Don't you buy anything for your sister?'

'I do, but sometimes I buy some things only for my wife.'

'Hmm.'

'My wife confronted my sister about quarrelling with me and asserted that as my wife, she was entitled to get priority over others.'

'Don't worry. Everything will be all right if you handle it properly and pacify both sides.'

Mohan laughed. 'You think it's so simple?' he asked. 'I'm trying my best.'

'I hope everything gets sorted out soon.'

Mohan shook his head. 'Yesterday was a lean day, and my extra income was meagre. When I handed over the money to my mother, she looked at me with suspicion and asked why I had earned so little.'

'Oh!'

'You know this kind of extra income varies from day to day. My mother now suspects that I'm hiding my income from her and giving the money to my wife.'

Avinash was stunned.

The following day, Mohan turned up for duty in an inebriated state, stinking of booze.

'Have you started drinking again?' Avinash asked. 'And that too while on duty?'

Mohan looked at him with drowsy eyes. 'Sorry, I had no other option,' he said, barely pushing the words out through his stiff tongue.

'What happened?'

'My honeymoon is over, and I'm doomed,' Mohan said. 'My family life has turned into a battleground.'

'Battleground?'

'All these years, I used to hand over my salary and even my extra income to my mother, and everything was fine. Now my wife says I should hand over my extra earnings to her, and not to my mother.'

'Oh.'

'I've continued with my old practice, but my wife is getting more and more aggressive. She's now demanding that I leave my parents and live separately with her in a bigger place in another locality.'

Avinash shook his head in despair.

Mohan attempted to say something in a choked voice, but stopped because his eyes welled up.

PART FOUR

The Newspaper

CHAPTER 16

On Kiran's suggestion, Avinash had enrolled himself for a journalism course. It was interesting to learn about the various aspects of journalism, from its history to the nuances of news reporting, editing and feature-writing. He continued with his job in the docks even though he wanted to quit it as soon as possible.

A couple of years later, armed with his degree in journalism, he started looking for a job in a newspaper and also enrolled for a degree in law. He approached Kiran's newspaper as well, but was told that there was no vacancy. As he continued his search for a job, he visited the office of *People's Power*, a popular newspaper, located in an upmarket locality of the city. Avinash entered the building and went up a flight of stairs to reach the editorial department. The large hall was almost deserted, and only a couple of peons were arranging some files in one corner. A row of small cabins skirted the walls. At the farthest end was a closed cabin, with a nameplate on the door that read 'Editor'. Below it was another nameplate that read 'Kaustubh Godbole'. A lady was sitting at a desk outside the cabin. There were files full of newspapers, letters and documents lying around. She looked up when Avinash stood in front of her. A strong smell of perfume hung in the air around her.

'I would like to meet the editor, please,' he said. 'Is that possible?'

She raised her eyebrows. 'Do you have an appointment?' she asked.

'No, I just want to talk to him for a minute.'

'And you are from?'

'I'm a student.'

'Wait here,' she said. Then she got up, pushed open the door and vanished behind it. A few seconds later, she came out. 'Go in, you can meet him now,' she said.

'Thanks,' he said and pushed the door open slowly.

A bald, bespectacled man was sitting behind a table. He had a saffron tilak on his forehead. There was a bookshelf behind him, and on the table in front of him was an idol of a god, a plastic globe and a pile of neatly folded newspapers. Another newspaper was spread open in front of him.

'May I come in, sir?' Avinash asked.

The editor looked up from the newspaper and nodded.

'Sir, I've finished my postgraduation in literature with a diploma in journalism, and I'm currently studying law. I'm looking for a job as a reporter,' Avinash said, standing by the table. 'Is there any opening in your newspaper?'

The editor waved at him to have a seat. Avinash handed over the file he was carrying and occupied a chair.

'What is your name?' the editor asked.

'Avinash Gaikwad, sir.'

The editor narrowed his eyes and muttered, 'Gaikwad.' Then he started leafing through the file. Suddenly, he stopped after reading something and then looked up at Avinash.

'You are from a backward caste, is it?'

'Sir, my ancestors were untouchables, but now we are Buddhists,' Avinash said.

'Hmm. What does your father do?'

'He's a watchman.'

'Oh! Then why don't you try for a government job?'

'Sir, I'm already working for the port authority.'

'So, you already have a cushy permanent job with the privilege of getting promoted out of turn!' The editor smirked. 'That's great. Why do you want to leave such a job?'

'Sir, I want to become a journalist,' Avinash said. 'And for my current job, I competed in the open category and did not use the reservation quota. Thus, there is no question of me getting an out-of-turn promotion.'

The editor stared at him for a few seconds and then collected himself. He closed the file and threw it in front of Avinash. 'You may leave,' he said curtly. 'We don't have any openings.'

'Sir, please give me a chance to prove my worth,' Avinash said. 'Just try me out for some time.'

The editor laughed. 'You think anyone can become a journalist?' he asked sarcastically, flaring his nostrils. 'This is a specialized job that requires a lot of intelligence, knowledge and an analytical mind. This profession is not for you people. Just be content with government jobs.'

Avinash was stunned. Being slighted for his caste was nothing new, but a remark like this one, coming from the editor of a reputed newspaper was entirely unexpected. 'Do you mean that people like me can't become journalists?'

'Don't argue with me,' the editor said, reclining in his chair. Then he leaned forward, resting his elbows on the table. 'Continue with your current job; it has ample scope for making extra money,' he said with a wink and a grin.

Avinash felt anger building up inside him. 'I'm really surprised that the editor of a mainstream newspaper has such notions,' he said. 'For your kind information, sir, I don't indulge in malpractices to make extra money.'

The smile on the editor's face faded away. Before he could say anything, however, the telephone on his desk rang, and he picked it up. 'Yes? Oh, I'm fine, thanks! I reached home around two last night,' he replied with a sheepish smile. 'It was great being at your home. No wonder people call you the perfect host!' He cupped his hand over the mouthpiece and, glaring at Avinash, said, 'Leave.'

Avinash collected his file and left the cabin. The lady at the desk outside was talking on the telephone in whispers. She spared him a glance and continued with her conversation. Avinash came out of the building feeling dejected. He not only had a postgraduate degree but also one in journalism—he only needed an opportunity to demonstrate his skills.

When he reached home, Godavari had gone to the market and Dagadoo was reading some papers. Sitting down, Avinash narrated the entire incident to his father, and Dagadoo shook his head sadly.

'I'm not surprised,' he said. 'This is why majority of our people are employed in government jobs, where we have reserved seats. Newspapers are privately owned, and they are usually out of bounds for us.'

'I'm just looking for an opportunity—on merit.'

'You are right, but the media is dominated and controlled by the upper castes. They prefer to employ someone like them, someone from their caste, religion or region, someone who speaks the same language or has the same ideology. But don't give up, son. Don't get weighed down by their prejudices; keep trying. You'll find someone who will give you an opportunity. There are still some sensible people around.'

Just then, Godavari returned home and overheard the last of their conversation. 'I have told you already,' she said, looking straight at Avinash. 'Continue with your secure government job and forget about leaving it. It's all right if you don't want to accept bribes. We can survive comfortably on your salary.'

Avinash remained silent. The city below the hill was pulsating with life as always. He wanted to be a part of it, but somehow, those in the city were repulsed by him. His background and his sincerity were becoming a dangerous combination, a double jeopardy.

Avinash went back to the docks heartbroken. It appeared as if he would never become a journalist in a reputed mainstream newspaper. A couple of weeks later, he was returning home in a local train. It was the evening rush hour, and the suburban train was packed well past its capacity. Avinash was clutching a handrail above his head. Some commuters were dozing, and some were looking out of the windows. A couple of them were reading newspapers, holding them close to their faces. One man was reading *Everyday*. Avinash glanced at the headlines and then saw an advertisement recruiting reporters. He tried to get a better view of the page but couldn't manage it. At the next station, the man folded the newspaper and got off the train. When Avinash reached Ghatkopar, he bought a copy of the newspaper and read the advertisement properly.

The next day, he prepared his application and visited the *Everyday* office with his documents. The receptionist directed him to the editorial department, where several people were frantically typing on their machines, with papers and notes lying scattered on their desks.

'I'm looking for a job as a reporter. Who should I meet?' he asked a lady sitting close to the door.

She stopped typing for a moment to look at him and then pointed at a man sitting behind a table a little distance away from them. 'Meet Madhav,' she said, her fingers flying back to hammer the keyboard again.

Behind the table, a grey-haired man sat talking on the telephone. Several documents and a pile of newspapers were lying in front of him. He was wearing a cream-coloured shirt with white stripes and a pair of brown trousers. He looked like he was in his fifties.

As Avinash approached his table, Madhav looked up at him.

'Sir, I'm here in response to your advertisement for recruiting reporters,' Avinash said, handing over his file.

Madhav opened the file and gestured for him to sit. Avinash sat down and waited, trying to gauge the expression on Madhav's face.

'Hmm, your qualifications seem all right. Have you worked in a newspaper before?' Madhav asked.

'No, sir, I'm a dock worker.'

'Come with me,' Madhav said, getting up and walking towards the door. Avinash followed him as they left the room and took the elevator to the seventh floor. Entering through a glass door, on which the word *Everyday* was painted in big letters, they went into another hall where several employees were working at their desks. At the end of the hall was a cabin that had the word 'Editor' painted on its door. The nameplate below it read 'Abdul Ahmed'. Madhav knocked on the door and entered with Avinash. The cabin had a cool and trendy look. There were many pictures of sportspeople, especially cricketers, on the walls, and trophies and books were scattered on the shelves. Piles of newspapers, magazines and papers were lying on a table. A tall and clean-shaven middle-aged man with greying hair sat facing them. Madhav sat down in a chair and waved at Avinash to sit next to him before handing over the file to the editor.

The editor flipped through the documents carefully as Avinash waited anxiously. He asked Avinash some questions about his background, which Avinash replied to.

'Your qualifications are all right, and I'm not concerned with your caste but with your performance,' he said curtly, closing the file and putting it on the table. 'However, there is one problem—you have no experience.'

'That's true, sir,' Avinash said, 'but I'm willing to learn.'

'We don't know how you write. Have you written anything at all for a newspaper or a magazine before?'

'No, sir.'

The editor and Madhav looked at each other.

'Remember, we need reporters badly,' Madhav said to him.

'We can try you out,' the editor said. 'We'll hire you as a trainee reporter for three months. But if we don't find you up to the mark, you'll have to leave. If your performance is satisfactory, we'll put you on probation for another three months, after which, we'll confirm your position as a reporter.'

Avinash thought about it for a moment. It was a big risk to quit a secure government job and take up an insecure one in a private company and then prove his worth in three months. He thought of his parents, his house, the docks and all the difficulties he had faced while trying to find a job as a journalist.

'Sir, I'm willing to work as a trainee. Thank you very much for this opportunity.'

'Good,' the editor said.

'Are you sure?' Madhav asked. 'You'll be leaving a secure job in the docks for a temporary job in a field where you have no experience. Think about it carefully.'

'I'm sure,' Avinash replied.

The editor picked up the phone on his desk and briefly spoke to someone before instructing Madhav to send Avinash to meet the personnel manager for some administrative formalities.

At the personnel department, the manager asked Avinash to submit copies of his certificates and about half an hour later, he issued Avinash a letter offering him a job as a trainee reporter.

Avinash was at once jittery and exhilarated. He would have to quit his job in the docks, about which he had no regrets, but the newspaper job was a risky affair. The editor had been very clear that if he did not perform well in the first three months, he would be thrown out. In that case, he would be jobless. He was, however, confident of fulfilling the editor's expectations and so, he decided to take the plunge. The stipend the newspaper was offering was meagre and much lower than his current salary, but he had made up his mind.

When he told his parents about his decision, his mother burst into tears.

'Are you mad?' she screamed. 'Oh God! Now I'll have to start working as a maid again.'

'No, no, please don't worry. I'll manage things,' Avinash said. 'It's just a matter of three months.'

'You want to quit a secure job and work in a position that you don't know if you'll get confirmed in, at a salary which doesn't even match your existing job?' she demanded.

Dagadoo stared blankly at his son. 'Hmm, I never thought this would happen so soon,' he said finally. 'I have confidence in you, but I'm also worried about whether your employers will judge you purely on merit or not. This is unknown territory for us.'

'I understand your concerns, but you always say that not everyone is bad,' Avinash said. 'The editor told me that he doesn't care about my background, only my performance.'

'Hmm, but with our background and history, it's difficult to trust the world, especially in the private sector, where employees don't have the protection that their counterparts in government entities do,' Dagadoo said. 'But still, that doesn't mean we should never try to prove ourselves in professions unknown to our forefathers.'

And thus, the next day, Avinash submitted his resignation to the port authority. It was accepted with great alacrity, and the leaves that were due to him were adjusted against his notice period.

At first, Avinash found it thrilling to work as a newspaper reporter. To have a ringside view of critical current events and write the first draft of history made Avinash feel important. But right from the first day, he understood that working as a field reporter was different from doing his class assignments. As part of his journalism course, he had interned for a month at *City News* and covered some press conferences, including those organized by unions of textile workers' on strike to demand higher wages and bonuses. The strike was already in its third year, with no end in sight.

He had seen hectic activity start in the newsroom every evening and last beyond midnight. He had seen the importance of exercising economy of words, of verifying information and using words with care to avoid libel. Working with speed and accuracy within the deadline were a must. But it wasn't enough. Newsgathering in the field required you to stay up to date with current affairs, know how various systems worked and how to back up reliable sources. In these matters, he started from scratch.

Racing against time, he made up a list of the telephone numbers of people in positions of authority and of news sources, making courtesy calls whenever possible. Besides, he stayed back after filing his stories to watch senior reporters and sub-editors putting the newspaper to bed. He made constant efforts to find exclusive stories, and it was exhilarating to go around interacting with people from a cross section of society. But it was equally heartbreaking to cover fire incidents, riots, accidents and crime scenes. The work was laborious but rewarding as he could see his name in print.

Getting acquainted with his fellow journalists while working on different beats, like crime and civic affairs, came with its own challenges. When Avinash visited the press room in the police commissioner's office to collect the daily crime sheet issued by the control room, it turned out to be a cross-examination of sorts.

He found two senior reporters chatting with each other in the press room. They turned to look at him curiously, and one of them asked him what he wanted. When he told them he was there for the crime sheet, they asked for his identity card, which he promptly showed them. One of the reporters, a bulky man wearing a wig, looked at the card and asked, 'Gaikwad? Who are you?'

'A reporter, a trainee actually.'

The man looked at the other reporter and smirked. 'Stupid, I mean, are you a Maratha or an OBC?'

'Neither.'

'Then?'

'I'm a Buddhist,' Avinash said.

'Oh,' the man nodded, his eyebrows raised. 'A Jai Bhim guy.'

'Is that a problem?'

'No, not at all.'

Avinash picked up a crime sheet from the pile kept on a table near the door and was reading it when someone knocked on the door. A bearded young man in his twenties, dressed in a green shirt and blue jeans, poked his head in and asked, 'Can I meet Kundan, sir?'

'Kundan?' Avinash asked.

'Yes, the journalist Kundan.'

The two reporters sitting inside heard the young man, and the one wearing the wig said, 'Come in, I'm Kundan.'

The man entered the room, his hands folded.

'Do you want to give me some news?' Kundan asked.

'No, sir. I need your help,' he said. 'Yusuf bhai has sent me to you. My brother has been absconding after committing a crime, but now he wants to surrender to the police. Yusuf bhai said you are the right person to sort it out.'

Kundan nodded, a twinkle in his eyes. 'Don't worry, just give me the details of the case, and I'll tell you what to do and how much it will cost.'

The man sat down in a chair and produced some papers. Kundan read them and the duo went into a huddle. Then, Kundan made several phone calls, after which he went out with the young man. The other reporter, too, left the room.

After a few minutes, Kundan returned with a smile on his face. 'Come here,' Kundan beckoned Avinash. 'Do you want to learn the tricks of the trade?'

'Tricks?'

'Yes, I can tell you how to develop contacts and make some extra money.'

Avinash looked at him suspiciously. 'I'll develop the contacts myself,' he said. 'And I'm not interested in doing non-journalistic things—even if they bring extra money.'

Kundan laughed. 'Well, you'll understand what I mean in due course.'

Avinash shook his head, pushed his chair back and rose to leave.

'Wait! Have you been to any dance bar, massage parlour, brothel or rave party in the city?'

'No.'

Kundan came near him. 'I can arrange it for you. When the cops raid such places, they first send in a bogus customer, and only when this bogus customer sends them a signal, do they enter and conduct their raid,' he said.

'So?'

'You can be the bogus customer!' Kundan exclaimed, winking at Avinash. 'If you want, I can fix things up for you.'

Avinash looked at him in disbelief. 'No,' he said.

'Think it over,' Kundan said. 'The police are going to raid a posh massage parlour, that's also a brothel, in an upmarket area next week. You can have a clean, good-looking girl for free. Enjoy life a little.'

Avinash grimaced. 'Is this what you call journalism?' he asked.

Kundan broke into laughter. 'These are the perks for those who become part of the system and learn how to enjoy it,' he said.

Avinash shook his head in despair and left the press room.

When he reached the office, he told Madhav about his encounter with Kundan.

Madhav burst out laughing. 'Why are you telling me these things?' he asked. 'If you want to go, you don't need official permission, and if you don't want to, then forget Kundan ever said anything.'

Avinash was appalled. 'I find it unethical and illegal, Madhav,' he said. 'Can we do a story on this?'

Madhav shook his head. 'How are you going to prove anything?' he asked. 'And by the way, always remember—dog doesn't eat dog.'

Avinash was speechless. He realized that it was probably stupid for him to assume that all journalists were upright. After all, they too belonged to the same society in which he had encountered lots of dishonest people, irrespective of their backgrounds. The only solace was that there were still some ethical and altruist people around, even though they were a miniscule minority functioning without a network.

A week passed and Avinash worked with as much fervour as before. He was covering the municipal corporation on his regular beat now. Whenever an exclusive story with his byline appeared in the newspaper, he showed it to his parents and friends in the neighbourhood. They were all proud of him. But his parents were still apprehensive about the security of his new job and its meagre salary. The real test, though, came when he went home with his monthly earning.

'What are we going to do with such a paltry sum?' Godavari shouted. 'You were getting thrice this amount in the port!'

'Yes, but this is only a phase,' Avinash said. 'Things will improve.'

'Improve? How? What will happen after three months?' she asked. 'I'm sure you'll be roaming the streets, jobless.'

'Certainly not. I'm sure they'll absorb me as a regular employee.'

'What if they don't?'

For a moment, Avinash visualized himself wandering the streets, jobless, visiting offices and factories to look for a job. But then he reminded himself of the confidence he was gaining every day at work.

With anguish writ large on her face, Godavari closed her eyes, folded her hands and muttered something inaudibly, seeking divine support. Dagadoo was caught in a dilemma. Neither did he want to discourage his son, nor could he ignore his wife's concerns.

However, two weeks later, the editor summoned Avinash to his office. As Avinash entered the cabin, the editor looked up from a glossy magazine and smiled. 'I have something for you,' he said, opening a drawer in his table and pulling out some papers. 'From next week onwards, we're putting you on probation for three months, after which you'll be confirmed.' He placed the papers on the table. 'This is your probation letter. Sign a copy as acknowledgement, please,' he said.

Avinash could hardly believe it. He was being put on probation even before his three-month training period was over. 'Thank you,' he said.

'We are delighted with your performance, Avinash. You've picked up the ropes very fast. Keep it up!' the editor said.

Avinash thanked him again and left the cabin beaming.

That evening, when he broke the news to his parents, Dagadoo was very happy. 'I knew it!' he said. 'You are on the right track, son.'

Godavari merely stared at him blankly for a moment and then asked, 'Are they going to increase your wages?'

'Of course.'

'Will it be on par with your salary at the port?'

'No, it's still a little less.'

'Oh. Are they making you a permanent employee?'

'Not right now, but once my three-month probation is over, they will,' he said.

She looked at Avinash with suspicion and continued with her daily chores.

Three months later, Avinash got his confirmation letter as a reporter.

When he told his parents about it, Godavari asked sarcastically, 'Have they raised your salary?'

'Yes, it's a little higher than my port salary now,' he said.

Godavari's face lit up. It was the first time since he had resigned from the port that she had smiled while discussing his new job.

Dagadoo was elated. 'I knew it!' he said. 'Keep up your hard work.'

Being confirmed was a major boost for Avinash, and he gradually settled down in the profession of his choice and liking. He was given a free hand to write a weekly column on civic affairs, and he also had the opportunity to cover several beats. Eventually, his mother also made peace with his choice, which made him happy.

CHAPTER 17

Avinash had been working for *Everyday* for a couple of years when an opening in another newspaper, the *National News,* was advertised. It was an opportunity to work in a mainstream national daily, and Avinash didn't want to forego it. But he could also not forget that when he had been struggling to enter journalism, *Everyday* had given him the opportunity to build and showcase his skills. He was in a dilemma as he did not want to do anything to offend either the editor or Madhav, both of whom were good to him.

He eventually brought up the subject with Madhav, expecting him to get annoyed, but the opposite happened.

'It's a good opportunity,' Madhav said. 'You'll get a wider canvas and a national platform.'

'But I feel guilty,' Avinash said. 'I'm in this profession because of *Everyday*—I just don't want to ditch you all.'

'No, no! Please don't get emotional. It's perfectly all right to switch jobs for better prospects. And though I'll lose a good reporter, I won't stop you.'

'But our editor may feel bad.'

'No, he won't.'

Feeling slightly relieved, Avinash submitted his application to the *National News* and after a meeting with its editor, he was issued an offer letter.

The next day, he resigned. Madhav took him to Abdul Ahmed.

'Congratulations!' Ahmed said, shaking hands with Avinash.

'I feel guilty about leaving the newspaper which helped me enter this profession without caring about my background,' Avinash said.

'No, don't think that way. We're happy that we groomed a good reporter, one who has been picked up by a national newspaper,' Ahmed said. 'We'll waive your notice period so that you can join *National News* immediately.'

Then Ahmed picked up the phone and spoke to someone in the personnel department, asking them to waive Avinash's notice period. Avinash completed the exit formalities soon and was relieved of his duties.

At *National News*, the editor, Jai Singh, welcomed Avinash to their team. A tall man with a fair complexion and greying hair, he was sitting in his cabin and talking to a man when Avinash entered. He introduced Avinash to the man sitting in front of him. 'Meet Digambar Gaokar, the city editor,' he said as they exchanged pleasantries. Gaokar was a short and plump man with a round face. His hair was heavily dyed, and he was wearing a grey shirt and black trousers.

'Avinash is in your team,' Singh told Gaokar. 'Now, let's get to work and print some exclusive stories!'

'Hmm, let me think about which beat to assign him to,' Gaokar said.

After some time, Avinash and Gaokar left the editor's cabin and walked towards the latter's cabin. Once inside, Gaokar asked Avinash, 'How do you know the editor?'

'I don't know him personally. I've only met him once before, when I came to hand over my documents.'

'Really? I usually recommend new recruits,' Gaokar said. 'But that's not a problem—we'll work together.'

'Sure.'

Gaokar smiled and began explaining the daily routine of the newsroom, the shift duties and the primary writing style of the paper. 'To begin with, you'll be in the office on reserve and rewrite duty, rehashing press releases,' he said. 'You'll also be assisting beat reporters in case something big happens, or you might have to fill in for an absent reporter.'

'Sure, no problem.'

Right away, Avinash was given a desk, from which he started monitoring the perennially overflowing tray of incoming press releases, invitations and other documents. A little later, Gaokar came out of his cabin and handed him a bunch of stapled sheets. 'Go through this and condense it to four paragraphs,' he said.

Avinash nodded and had barely started reading it when he found someone standing near him.

'Hi, my name is Sanjeev. I cover politics,' the man said.

'I'm Avinash.'

'Where were you before this?'

'At *Everyday*.'

'Oh! Are you Avinash Gaikwad? I've read your bylines.'

Avinash smiled.

'Gaikwads are found in several communities. Which one do you belong to?'

'If you're asking about my caste, I'm a Buddhist convert from an erstwhile untouchable family.'

'Oh! You are a Jai Bhim guy. That's surprising—how did you find your way into this profession?' He listened quietly as Avinash briefly described his background.

'If I were you, I would've stuck to the government job rather than plunge into this high-risk job,' Sanjeev said.

'I'm here by choice,' Avinash said.

'I hope it works out well for you,' Sanjeev said with a smile. 'By the way, many political leaders from your community are my friends, and they are always very cooperative.'

'Most of them are more concerned with aligning themselves with the ruling party for crumbs of power than implementing Babasaheb's vision.'

Sanjeev narrowed his eyes. 'What do you mean?'

'Babasaheb was aware that the untouchables were a scattered minority without the numbers required to get their representatives elected on their own. So, his idea was to forge a solidarity between the Scheduled Castes, Scheduled Tribes and Other Backward Classes, making them the largest chunk of voters belonging to the historically marginalized people,' Avinash said. 'But he died before the Republican Party of India could be floated. And his lieutenants, none of whom had his intellectual prowess, confined it only to our community, shutting out the others.'

Sanjeev nodded. 'Yes, I do find that they are too gullible,' he said. 'But they seem happy with the crumbs of power thrown at them.'

'Well, mainstream parties create an impression of social integration, albeit a superficial and symbolic one. On the contrary, Babasaheb's idea was to turn the social majority into a political one through democratic methods to ensure that elite castes and classes don't exploit the masses by using wealth, power or religion.'

Sanjeev smirked. 'You mean everything is messed up?' he asked.

'Yes. The traditionally privileged communities, which are actually a minority, dominate all vital sectors of life, from agriculture, trade and industry to bureaucracy, politics and media. The presence of marginalized communities in government agencies and educational institutions is mainly because of the reservation policy. Business as well as arts, media and cultural affairs, which are all with the private sector, are dominated by dynasties of traditionally privileged communities.'

Sanjeev cleared his throat. 'You speak as if being born in a privileged community is a crime,' he said.

'No, I'm just saying that the traditional compartmentalization of society worked in the favour of the privileged communities, depriving the masses of equality of opportunity and determining the status of a person only on the basis of his or her birth.'

'That's a thing of the past,' Sanjeev said, shaking his head. 'The fact that a person like you is here proves it.'

'That's an exception,' Avinash said. 'I'm here only because the Constitution changed the rules by criminalizing caste and gender discrimination. And I had to struggle to enter this profession despite being qualified.'

'Yes,' Sanjeev nodded. 'But you must admit, most of the beneficiaries of reservation are all corrupt,' he said.

'See, there are good and bad people in all communities,' Avinash said. 'But for argument's sake, the number of people holding key positions in government employment as beneficiaries of the reservation policy is negligible. In lucrative professions, like in the corporate sector and in arts, they are almost non-existent. So, if corruption is rampant, the majority of people involved in it are from the upper-caste communities, not Dalits.'

Sanjeev closed his eyes for a few seconds and then shook his head. 'I never thought of it this way,' he said. 'You have a different angle of looking at things.'

Avinash smiled. 'Naturally, we come from different worlds after all,' he said.

A week later, Gaokar called Avinash into his cabin. 'You have worked in the port, and we don't have a reporter on the shipping beat. Can you get some good, exclusive stories?'

'Yes, I'll do it,' Avinash replied with a broad smile.

Going out into the field was a big relief for Avinash. He visited the offices of the director general of shipping, the port authorities and associations of shipping companies, importers, shippers and seafarers. He was curious about a new port being developed across the harbour, and after talking to various stakeholders, he visited the site. The new jetties had been constructed and the quay cranes were being installed. While going through the port's financial records, he found a story and submitted it.

The first thing he did when he woke up the next morning was to check whether the story had been used or not. It had, that too on the front page. He had written about the financial lapses that had been committed while importing quay cranes for the new port. Substandard and used cranes had been imported as new ones at a higher cost than the market price of new cranes. There were audit objections, and a probe had been ordered. Before he filed the story, Avinash had called the chairperson of the port, Ariana Kapoor, for her comments. She had claimed that all was well, and that the crane story was just a minor thing not worth reporting.

The day started off well, and after completing his chores at home, he reached the office to find Gaokar waiting for him.

'Your story has created a problem,' he said. 'The editor wants to see you immediately.'

'Problem?'

'Yes, come with me.'

The editor was waiting for them in his cabin. 'Your exclusive is a good one, but there's a problem,' Jai Singh said slowly when they were all seated.

'What problem, sir?' Avinash asked.

'Do you know that the port chairperson is the wife of one of the top officials of the Reserve Bank of India?'

'No, sir,' Avinash said. 'But how does that matter?'

'Ideally, it should not. But she has contacted our chief editor in Delhi and accused us of tarnishing her image,' Singh said. 'Moreover, her husband has contacted the owners of our paper to express his displeasure.'

'But, sir, what we have published is based on facts,' Avinash said.

'We know that,' he replied. 'But our proprietors are worried that her husband may create problems for us.'

'What problems?' Avinash asked.

'You don't understand,' Gaokar said. 'He may go to any lengths to find fault with our company's financial transactions.'

Avinash looked at Gaokar and then at Singh. 'But why should we fear such things? I presume our company has not violated any law.'

The editor smiled again. 'You are right,' he said. Then, leaning forward, he whispered, 'But you never know. We live in a country where litigation continues for years and the process itself becomes the punishment, whether you've committed an offence or not.'

'Yes, sir.'

'The head of our marketing department, Ashutosh, wants to meet you,' the editor said.

'All right, but I want to tell you again that I don't think I've committed a crime.'

'Of course not, Avinash. You've only done your job. Talk to him and see what he has to say.'

Gaokar and Avinash thanked the editor and left the cabin.

'Go and meet Ashutosh right away,' Gaokar said. 'And be polite; he's from the owner's family.'

When Avinash reached the marketing department, he found Ashutosh surrounded by a group of employees who were all clearly in an upbeat mood. Ashutosh was wearing a dark grey suit with a blue tie on a white shirt. He was tall and lanky, sported a thin moustache and was probably in his thirties.

'My name is Avinash. I'm from the editorial department,' Avinash said when he caught Ashutosh's eye.

'I've been waiting for you. Come,' Ashutosh said and walked towards his cabin, pushing the door open. He asked Avinash to sit down and then went and sat in his heavily cushioned swivel chair. There were piles of newspapers, glossy magazines, charts and files scattered everywhere.

'Good story,' Ashutosh said, pointing at a copy of the *National News* lying on the table.

'Thank you, sir,' Avinash said.

There was a long moment of silence as Ashutosh flipped through a file lying on his table. Then, he looked Avinash straight in the eye. 'Look at this,' he said, pointing at some charts in the file. 'The new port is a fresh opportunity for us to enhance our advertising revenue. My team had already drawn up a plan to explore this revenue potential. But before we could do something, your story was published. Now the chairperson of the port is mad at us, and her husband is also upset.'

'I'm just doing my job,' Avinash said. 'Whatever we've published is based on facts.'

'I know that!' Ashutosh said. 'But besides losing revenue, we also don't want the government breathing down our necks, looking for something to haul us up for.'

'If there is anything wrong with our story, they can send us a clarification or sue us.'

Ashutosh shook his head and then looked up at the ceiling for a few seconds. 'Can we undo this?' he asked.

'Undo what?'

'Can we do something to undo the damage done by your story?'

'They have to undo it by punishing those responsible for the lapses.'

Ashutosh slumped in his chair. 'No, what I mean is can we do something that will make them happy?' he asked.

'I think we should wait till the enquiry is over and some action is taken against the guilty. We can publish that.'

Ashutosh pursed his lips and shook his head again as an uncomfortable silence followed. Then he sighed and said, 'Okay, you may leave. Let me see what can be done.'

Avinash thanked him and left the cabin. There was silence in the office outside, and some of the more voluble employees frowned as he passed by. On reaching the editorial department, he told Gaokar about his conversation with Ashutosh.

'It's all right. Don't worry,' Gaokar said and rushed to the editor's cabin.

CHAPTER 18

The old harbour was buzzing with activity as usual when Avinash entered the docks a few days later. Heads turned when he walked into the dock office. Some employees were pointing at him, while some were pretending to be too busy to notice him. He waved at some familiar faces, and they waved back.

The superintendent at the dock office smiled formally when Avinash met him. He enquired about Mohan's whereabouts and was told that he was on leave. Avinash then went to the office block to meet Patwardhan. The manager looked up and smiled when Avinash entered the cabin. 'Just give me two minutes,' he said, flipping through some papers and signing them. When he finished going through the pile, he pressed the call bell. A peon entered the cabin, and he asked him to take the files away.

'It's good that you are out of this muck,' Patwardhan said when they were alone. 'I'm sure you are comfortable in your new profession.'

Avinash smiled. 'Well, I'm settling down,' he said.

'I think that people like us are always on the margins because we don't gel with the majority, irrespective of our lineage,' Patwardhan said. 'But you are doubly marginalized because of your background ... I've requested my seniors to keep me in this "unproductive" personnel management section forever, instead of rotating me on "sensitive" posts,' he said.

'I'm sure this arrangement will make officers like Oswal happier.'

'Of course, but Oswal is not alone. There is an army of such people, right from the labourer on the wharf to the chairperson and the chief manager,' Patwardhan said. 'Do you know the latest news?'

Avinash raised his eyebrows. 'No, tell me, sir.'

'The new chairperson is related to a senior minister in the central government,' Patwardhan whispered. 'And he has asked all our officers to collect money for the party in power at the centre—each officer has been given a target.'

Avinash was shocked. 'It's that blatant now, is it? I wish I could write about this. Would it be possible to gather some evidence that he has done this?' he asked.

Patwardhan shook his head. 'It was an oral order given informally, in person, in his cabin, after an official meeting, and the money is to be collected in cash,' he said. 'Many officers have promised to surpass the targets in return for appointments to lucrative posts.'

'But we need something concrete to run the story.'

Patwardhan sighed. 'I don't have any proof. And more than that, I don't want to stick my neck out,' he said.

'But, sir, can't something be done?'

'Yes, but who'll do it when the majority wants this?' Patwardhan asked. 'As such, our laws don't punish economic offenders seriously and promptly enough to make an example of them. Sometimes, I think there should be capital punishment for the corrupt, especially those entrusted with running the government.'

'I agree. It's also ironical that after amassing wealth through illegal means, they usually get away with paying fines,' Avinash said. 'All the more reason to do something to overcome the increasing deficit of honesty.'

Patwardhan shook his head in despair. 'I'm not that brave,' he said. 'I want to retire in peace. All these years, I've never demanded money. I've accepted whatever I was given instead of taking punitive action, and my honesty ends there. Yet, the staff and the port users speak highly of me because they think I'm a shred better than my colleagues in not being greedy. Honesty has various shades, Avinash, and your shade is different from mine.'

Avinash was struck speechless. He took his leave soon after and headed back to his office. On the way, he thought about Patwardhan's confession. All these years, he'd been told by his colleagues and the port users that Patwardhan was an honest officer. Avinash had presumed that he did not accept bribes. After the confession, however, it was clear that he did, but without being greedy.

A couple of years passed. The central government created a new category of reservation for the Other Backward Classes (OBCs) and also extended reservation in the Scheduled Castes category to include former untouchables who had converted to Buddhism.

Dagadoo was happy with both the developments. 'So far, only the Maharashtra government had extended reservation to our community, now it's available across the country,' he said. 'And the good thing is that those who declared themselves as "Hindu-Mahar" in official documents but who strut around as Buddhists, will not have to do it while seeking central government quota for education and government employment.'

'But what is the point,' Godavari asked, 'when we are not using reservation anyway? We've not even obtained a caste certificate.'

'It's all right,' Dagadoo said. 'Avinash won't need it anyway, now that he's in the private sector.'

'I hope our future generations become so capable that they won't need reservation,' Avinash said.

'I hope so too.'

One evening, when Avinash was winding work up at the office, a tall, thin, bespectacled man with long hair approached him.

'My name is Jalindar Patil,' he said. 'I'm from the OBC organization, and I want to give you a press release.' He handed Avinash a small write-up about an agitation being planned by the organization.

'May I know your name?' Patil asked.

'Avinash Gaikwad.'

'Gaikwad,' Patil said softly. 'Are you from an OBC community?'

Avinash smiled. 'How does it matter?' he asked. 'But since you wanted to know, I'm a Buddhist.'

'Jai Bhim?'

'Yes.'

'Oh, that's a pleasant surprise,' Patil said. 'You people mostly take up government jobs. And now, your community is also eligible for central government quota.'

'That's right.'

'Things are improving,' Patil said with a broad smile. 'Now, with the OBCs also eligible for reservation as per the Mandal Commission's recommendations, I hope it will promote solidarity among all marginalized people.'

'It should, but it's very difficult,' Avinash said. 'The OBCs are still aligned with the privileged communities and are the foot soldiers of the majoritarian discourse. The fact is, only Ambedkar's followers have been at the forefront, demanding implementation of the Mandal Commission's recommendations so that reservation could be extended to the OBCs.'

Patil nodded. 'Yes, but gradually, the OBCs have started discovering Babasaheb Ambedkar through his books and speeches,' he said.

'Let's hope so. Most of the OBCs still consider themselves superior to us. Sometimes, they are also involved in caste atrocities, acting as henchmen of the upper castes. Look at what happened at Khairlanji, for instance, where four members of a Dalit family were massacred,' Avinash said. 'Even a large section of the OBCs and Hindu Dalits, who take advantage of reservation, end up as crusaders for the fanatics by othering Buddhist Dalits. They presume that the Vedic discourse is the only ancient mainstream Indian culture and are oblivious of parallel non-Vedic ancient discourses like those of Charvak, Lokayat, Jainism and Buddhism in the Shraman tradition.'

'That's true, and it will take time to change things. The problem is that until the OBCs were granted reservation, they were not even aware that they were traditionally classified as Shudras, which placed them at the lowest rung of the four-tiered caste system. But there is hope for better representation as political reservation has now been extended for the OBCs in local panchayats.'

Avinash nodded. 'Yes, now the Maharashtra government has reserved seats in the local panchayats for OBCs and women,' he said, 'but our experience with political reservation in the assemblies and in the Parliament is that most of the MLAs and MPs elected on reserved seats usually end up blindly toeing the line of the mainstream political party they belong to, instead of serving their communities. Perhaps that's the reason why even though political reservation was provided only for ten years, every party ruling the country has extended it every decade.'

'True, but don't lose heart. Things will improve,' Patil said.

After chatting some more, Patil left and Avinash put the press release in the tray for the night reporter.

Several days later, Avinash was walking towards his office after getting off the local train when somebody tapped on his shoulder and asked, 'Are you going to office?'

He turned around to see Jalindar Patil walking alongside him.

'Yes,' he said.

'I want to tell you something very important.'

Patil took him aside, away from the rush of commuters pouring out of the railway station. 'I've heard that a Dalit officer from the Indian Shipping Company, a government entity, has been wrongly arrested for running a job racket and is being tortured by the investigating officers,' he said. 'Apparently, he's being framed by some upper-caste officers.'

Avinash recollected having read the story about some officers being suspended after the issue was raised in Parliament. 'I'll check,' he said.

They parted ways after that and later in the afternoon, Avinash visited the shipping company's office. After speaking to several officers, he was asked to meet the personnel manager, Prabhakar Nadkarni.

Avinash sent in his visiting card with the peon and waited outside the manager's cabin. A few minutes later, he was ushered inside. With a pile of files on his table and one open in front of him, Nadkarni looked at Avinash with a questioning expression on his face. He was fair, light-eyed and tall.

'What do you want?' he asked.

Avinash asked him about the case of the shipping officer, and Nadkarni glanced at his visiting card again.

'Oh, you're Avinash Gaikwad,' he said. 'You wrote about the fraud in the new port.'

Avinash nodded and remained quiet.

'Nice report. I liked it,' Nadkarni said with a broad smile as he put aside the file in his hand. 'It's true that some officers involved in the job racket have been suspended. They lured some youths by conducting mock interviews, collecting money from them and asking them to wait for their appointment letters. When nothing happened for over a year, the issue was raised in Parliament. The investigation is in progress.'

'I heard that a Dalit officer is among those arrested.'

'Yes, one Arjun Pagare,' Nadkarni smirked. 'You know how these people are. They are all going berserk because they now have the privilege of good education and employment.'

'Sir, there are good and bad people in every caste and religion,' Avinash replied. 'Please don't single out any one community. I'm also from the same community.'

'Oh, is it?' Nadkarni asked, looking a little embarrassed. Then, after a brief pause, he said, 'I have nothing against any community.' He opened a file and put it in front of Avinash. It contained detailed information about the case, including correspondence between the company and the central investigating agency. Nadkarni pointed at a paper. 'This is a call letter issued by Pagare. It's the main piece of evidence.'

Avinash looked at the letter and browsed through the other documents, taking notes.

'Will you publish this?' Nadkarni asked.

'I don't see why not.'

'That's great, but don't quote me,' Nadkarni said. 'I'll ask our public relations officer to give you a statement that the investigation is in progress.'

'Sure, no problem.'

'If you want, I can take you to the central agency's office—I have a meeting regarding this case in half an hour.'

Avinash nodded and after obtaining the official statement from the company's public relations officer, he left with Nadkarni.

A tall middle-aged man received them in his cabin in the investigating agency's office. There were many wooden shelves stuffed with files in the room. On a huge table was a stack of files flagged with red labels. A discoloured white fan rotated overhead, making some papers flutter under a paperweight on the table. On one wall was the agency's insignia engraved on a brass plate. After exchanging pleasantries, Nadkarni pulled out some papers from his bag and handed them over to the officer. Then, he introduced Avinash, and the three discussed the case. Avinash had some queries, which the officer answered. After a while, the officer picked up the phone and said, 'Bring Pagare here.'

Minutes later, two officers escorted Pagare into the room. Pagare was short, dark and plump. He had a horrified look etched on his face. On seeing the officer, he folded his hands and pleaded, 'Sir, this is not just about me, there are many others involved in this case. Please spare me! I come from a poor family and am the only earning member. I made a mistake in using the company's letterhead. Please show me mercy.'

'Yes, of course, you definitely deserve mercy,' the officer said sarcastically. 'You're from a backward community which benefits from reservation.'

As Pagare kept pleading for mercy, Avinash felt rage and anguish building up inside him, but he held his silence. Nadkarni was clearly enjoying the scene and kept throwing glances at him.

The questioning continued for some time, after which Pagare was escorted out. Avinash and Nadkarni also left after that.

On reaching his office, Avinash spoke to Gaokar and filed a story about the case, which was published the next day. A couple of days later, Avinash was waiting for the local train at the station when Jalindar met him.

'What have you done?' Jalindar asked. 'I thought you would take Pagare's side, but you've written against him.'

Avinash explained what he had seen. 'Please don't believe anything at face value,' Avinash said. 'We need to break stereotypes. Good and evil people exist across communities and genders. Let us not get carried away by our emotions.'

Jalindar shook his head in despair. 'But I still feel that while others can do anything and get away with it, those from marginalized backgrounds are being victimized,' he said.

'I think we need to be extra careful and work with honesty to show that we are better than the best. People are only waiting for us to slip.'

A couple of days later, Gaokar called Avinash to his cabin. 'Avinash, you're doing a fine job, but ...' Gaokar trailed off. Then, clearing his throat and avoiding eye contact with Avinash, he said, 'For the time being, you will remain in the office and rewrite important press releases. I'll put you on some beat soon.'

Avinash was surprised. 'But we don't have anyone covering the shipping beat,' he said.

Gaokar nodded. 'We're going to depute another reporter to cover the beat,' he said. 'Rupesh Tripathi will handle it for now. He will also continue to cover his existing aviation beat.'

'Oh, okay. But I had just started covering the beat,' Avinash said. 'Is something wrong?'

'No, no! This is a temporary arrangement. You'll soon be assigned another beat.'

Avinash was quite upset. He thought he had probably stepped on the toes of some powerful people. And he was right.

Two days later, Rupesh Tripathi published an interview with the chairperson of the new port, talking about how the administrative machinery was functioning efficiently and overcoming various hurdles to meet the deadlines. On the lapses committed while procuring quay cranes, the official version was that some corrupt officers involved in the matter had been suspended, and an inquiry had been ordered. A few days later, there was a special supplement on the new port with advertisements from the port authority, associations of port users, transporters, shippers and importers.

A couple of weeks later, Gaokar summoned Avinash to his cabin. 'Our regular reporter for the municipal corporation beat has gone on leave. I want you to cover the civic beat. You used to cover it for your previous newspaper, so you are familiar with it,' he said.

'No problem,' Avinash said. He was relieved that he would now be out in the field and could focus on a particular beat. He was already acquainted with many officials and elected members of the civic body as well as citizens' groups.

That day, he reached the municipal corporation's headquarters before noon and met some of the people he was familiar with. The press room was deserted as reporters were yet to arrive. In the corridor, he bumped into an old acquaintance, Virendra Pathak, who was a reporter for a reputed Marathi newspaper. They shook hands and Avinash told him that he would be on the civic beat for some time.

'Wow! Great!' Virendra exclaimed. 'Now we can meet every day. By the way, I'm working on an exclusive story about a water supply project. I can share it with you.'

'No, don't,' Avinash said. 'It's your exclusive. We can share only routine information.'

Virendra nodded. 'All right. Let's go for some tea,' he said, and they walked to the canteen.

'Have some snacks before you drink tea,' Avinash said.

'No, I'll just have the tea,' Virendra said. 'I'm fasting today.'

'Oh, then eat something that's permitted during a fast? Or at least drink milk?'

'I can't. I have to refrain from eating the whole day. It's a practice I've inherited from my parents. I can't give up fasting. I do it twice a week, sometimes thrice, depending on the religious calendar.'

'I'm not saying that you should give it up. I'm just saying that it shouldn't be at the cost of your health. Don't starve yourself.'

Virendra smiled. 'You've told me this earlier as well,' he said. Then, he pointed at the ceiling and said, 'He will take care of my health.'

After they had their tea, they left the canteen and Virendra lit a cigarette outside.

'It's a deadly combination, tea and cigarettes on an empty stomach,' Avinash pointed out. Virendra laughed and pointed to the sky.

Soon after, there was a meeting of the standing committee, which was well attended by the reporters. The committee members discussed the issues listed on the agenda, with the members of the opposition and the treasury benches largely favouring the financial allocation for the proposals. Tea and snacks were served, after which most of the reporters left.

The meeting concluded in a couple of hours. Avinash and Virendra went to the press room where the reporters were chatting and busy copying the notes scribbled by those who had sat through the entire meeting. Some of them greeted Avinash. One of them, a man named Chandan, looked at Avinash and then at Virendra, and said, 'You two are always after exclusive stories. Our bosses shout at us for being lazy. Don't increase our workload.'

'Just doing our jobs,' Virendra said. 'We're simply exposing the misdeeds of the officials and elected representatives who are the custodians of public money.'

Chandan laughed. 'You take your role too seriously. Just relax and enjoy life. Cover routine meetings, file reports and earn your salary,' he said.

'Chandan, while we get a salary for the work we do, we are also the watchdogs of society.'

Chandan laughed again and shook his head.

A couple of days later, Virendra took Avinash aside when they met at the municipal corporation. 'I've been asked not to move around with you and to maintain my distance,' he said.

'Who told you this? And why?'

'My boss has asked me not to befriend you,' Virendra whispered. 'I don't know why—he probably thinks that people with your background should not be encouraged in our profession.'

'I can understand that. But how does he even know that we are friends?'

'Come on, Avinash! Some of our friends in the press room here have friends in my office, and they are all birds of a feather.'

Avinash shook his head in disgust. 'So?'

Virendra laughed. 'So what? We continue to be friends as before. It's our personal choice,' he said. 'Let's go to the canteen for some tea.'

While they were sipping tea, Virendra invited Avinash to his house. 'I've bought a house and I'm having a house-warming function this Sunday, around noon,' he said. 'I want you to come.'

Avinash thought about the offer for a while before saying, 'I'd be happy to, but my presence should not create any problem for you.'

'I know that. You can come a bit late if you want, but please come.'

That Sunday, Avinash deliberately reached Virendra's house more than an hour late, presuming that the rituals would be over by then. But when he approached the house, he found the place crowded with people. A priest was still performing some rites. He saw some known faces from his fraternity among the crowd. They smiled formally at him but said nothing. He waited outside till the rituals were concluded and the crowd had dispersed after the meal, making sure to keep himself out of Virendra's sight.

'Why are you standing outside?' Virendra asked when he finally spotted Avinash and hurried over to his side.

Avinash smiled. 'Just waiting for the rituals to get over.'

'I'm glad that you came.'

'I hope my presence has not caused any problems,' Avinash said.

Virendra laughed. 'Some of the invitees whispered in my ear about you and asked why I'd invited you.'

'See, Virendra! This is the reason I was reluctant to come.'

'Don't worry. I told them that for me, your presence is as important as theirs, if not more.'

'They must've been offended.'

'A couple of them left in a huff, but I don't care.'

After all the guests left, Virendra introduced Avinash to his wife and son. They exchanged pleasantries, and then she cleared the clutter in the room so they could all sit down. While having lunch together, Virendra told his wife, 'He's the one who keeps lecturing me about fasting several days a week.'

'Oh, is it?' She looked at Avinash. 'Why? Don't you observe a fast on any day?'

'No.'

'Forget fasting, he doesn't even believe in God!' Virendra intervened.

'Oh my God! But how can anyone survive like that?' she asked. 'How can a person defying the existence of God be good?'

'Well, he is—he's just like me ... a vegetarian, a teetotaller, and honest and hardworking,' Virendra said.

'But why is he against you fasting?' she asked.

'Don't misunderstand me, I'm not against his religious practice. The only thing I'm saying is that on the days he fasts, he doesn't eat anything at all, just keeps smoking and drinking tea the whole day, which is harmful to his health,' Avinash said.

She smiled, folded her hands and looked up at the ceiling. 'He is there to take care of us,' she said.

'Don't worry,' Virendra said, 'an astrologer has told me that I will live more than eighty years.'

Avinash did not want to get into an argument that would spoil the couple's special day. And so, he smiled and said, 'I wish you a healthy, peaceful and content life.'

Avinash settled down on the civic beat, filing exclusive stories that exposed lapses in governance. The consistent flow of stories boosted his confidence, until one day, Gaokar called him to his cabin.

'You are doing a good job, and some of your stories are outstanding,' he said, avoiding Avinash's gaze.

Avinash sensed that something was amiss. 'Is anything wrong?' he asked.

Gaokar cleared his throat and smiled. 'No, no, not at all,' he said. 'It's just that we need to groom more people to cover the civic beat.'

'Good idea. So, what do we do?'

Gaokar looked him straight in the eye. 'I want to assign the civic beat to someone else,' he said.

Avinash nodded. 'No problem. But is anything wrong?' he asked again.

Gaokar tried to smile, but failed. 'Nothing much, it's just that the fire department has refused to approve the renovation we have done in our office building,' he said. 'Yesterday, when one of our managers visited the municipal headquarters to expedite the approval, the municipal commissioner and the mayor vented their anger about the stories we're constantly publishing that expose lapses in the civic body's functioning.'

'But we're just reporting facts that expose the maladministration of civic affairs. It's our job,' Avinash said.

'Yes, of course, it is.'

There was a long silence in the room. 'Have we violated any rules while renovating our office?' Avinash asked.

'I don't know, but there are some issues. I've been told to hold our horses. Since I can't ask you to stop doing exclusive, hard-hitting stories, the easiest way is to pull you off the beat.'

Avinash smirked.

'From tomorrow, you'll be in the office as the reserve and rewrite reporter. And remember, from next week, you're on night duty.'

Avinash nodded and got up from his chair. 'I have a request,' he said. 'Will you permit me to go out of the city for stories after my night shift week?'

Gaokar thought for a moment. Then he said, 'Of course, especially if you can get some interesting stories from rural or tribal areas.'

A couple of days later, Rupesh interviewed the mayor, the municipal commissioner and the chairperson of the municipal standing committee. In these interviews, which were published prominently, they spoke about their untiring efforts to manage the city's civic affairs despite all the odds.

Avinash reported for the night shift later that day and was clearing the tray overflowing with incoming press releases when Rupesh approached him.

'Did you see the interviews of the municipal authorities?' Rupesh asked.

Avinash looked up and smiled. 'Yes, a clean job,' he said.

Rupesh dragged a chair and sat down near Avinash. 'I found out that you've been taken off the civic beat,' he said. 'I don't know why, but they asked me to do the interviews.'

Avinash nodded. 'I'm not holding it against you,' he said, throwing some papers into the dustbin near his chair.

Rupesh smiled. 'Yes, but I thought that I should clarify my actions because this is the second time that I've had to do the firefighting for the bosses because of your stories. Ultimately, my career matters to me.'

'That's not an issue. Please go ahead and build your career,' Avinash said. 'I'm happy with what I'm doing.'

'That is old-school journalism, friend,' Rupesh said. 'It's not relevant anymore. If you don't change, you'll remain a beast of burden. Honesty and hard work may help you survive, but you'll never reach the top. And you already have other things holding you back.' Then he rose from his chair and walked towards the editor's cabin, winking at Avinash.

CHAPTER 19

There was a commotion in the office as Chandrashekhar, the chief editor from Delhi, arrived in the newsroom. He was a tall and lean man, wearing a green cotton kurta with the sleeves rolled up and a white pyjama. He went into a huddle with a couple of managers, the resident editor and the heads of various departments in the conference room.

In the evening, when most of the field reporters returned from their respective beats, there was a meeting of the editorial staff. Chandrashekhar sat at the head of the oblong table, with the others either sitting around the table or standing behind it.

Chandrashekhar began by pointing out errors in the recently published headlines and stories. Then he turned to Gaokar and said, 'I need some good exclusive stories from your team.'

Gaokar cleared his throat, looked around and smiled. 'We're already doing some good exclusives,' he said.

Chandrashekar shook his head. 'Very few,' he said. 'We need more hard-hitting stories.'

'All right,' Gaokar nodded.

Chandrashekhar turned to some senior reporters and asked, 'What are you working on?'

They told him about some of the ideas they were working on, and he suggested some new ones. A few other reporters also spoke about their ideas.

When Avinash's turn came, he said, 'I'm thinking of doing a story on defunct textile mills. It appears that the workers are getting a raw deal because the government and the mill owners seem to

"

have colluded against them while formulating the plan for the redevelopment of the mills' lands.'

The expression on Chandrashekhar's face changed as if he had tasted something bitter. 'No, no, don't bother about downmarket issues. Focus on something upmarket ... south of Mahim. Interview the sons and daughters of politicians, celebrities, businessmen and high-society people,' he said. 'And if at all you want to write about mill workers, say that they should leave the city at once. They are not required here anymore.'

Avinash was shocked. 'The textile industry, like any other business, stands on the shoulders of the masses, be they workers or consumers.'

A visibly annoyed Chandrashekhar knitted his eyebrows. 'Are you a communist?' he asked.

'No, sir, but I started my professional life as a factory worker and can relate to mill workers better. I feel they deserve fair compensation and rehabilitation,' Avinash said. 'I can't write what you say under my byline.'

'We are not activists here,' Chandrashekhar snapped.

'Yes, but as journalists, we are the watchdogs of society.'

'Not anymore,' Chandrashekhar retorted contemptuously. 'No more arguments.'

'We'll drop this topic,' Gaokar intervened, gesturing for Avinash to stop.

'All right,' Chandrashekhar said and turned to the staff from the features department.

'We're not doing enough stories on the lifestyle of celebrities,' he said. 'Do something so that we get advertisements from top multinational brands.'

'Yes, sure,' a girl from the features section said. 'The last time we did get a couple of advertisements, but the corporates complained about the quality of our newsprint.'

Chandrashekhar nodded. 'I know. They want their advertisements to be printed on glossy paper,' he said. 'We're now ready to do it.'

A discussion about people to be interviewed for the special features pages followed. Later, the heads of departments complained about having inadequate staff, and Chandrashekhar just nodded. The meeting lasted over an hour, during which period he cracked jokes, triggering loud laughter, with many pretending to laugh just to please him.

After the meeting, the reporters and sub-editors walked out of the conference room, while their bosses stayed back for another round of discussion.

Avinash was walking to his desk when Sanjeev joined him. 'Don't argue with the big boss,' Sanjeev said. 'Stay in his good books. He can make or break your career.'

'I'm here to do my job sincerely,' Avinash said. 'And if I can't, I'd rather leave the profession than deceive myself.'

'You're impossible,' Sanjeev said. 'Don't make your own life miserable. As such, you don't have anyone to fall back upon.'

'This is indeed uncharted territory for me, but I can't compromise on certain things.'

Giving up, Sanjeev said, 'Let's go drink some tea.' Avinash nodded and they walked to the canteen. The usual smell of overboiled tea and cigarettes filled the air in the canteen as the employees sat drinking tea and chatting.

'It must be heartbreaking for you to see the issues that interest you being ignored,' Sanjeev said as they settled down at a table with their tea.

Avinash stared at him for a moment and then said, 'Yes, it is.'

Sanjeev grinned. 'But don't you ever feel that there should be a bloody revolution in this country to radically change things?' he asked.

'No,' Avinash said. 'Violence is never the solution to settle disputes or bring about change. Those who wave red flags are oblivious to caste realities. They classify people only on the basis of economic criteria and want a dictatorship, even if it involves violence. But both violence and dictatorships of any kind are undesirable. Change can be brought about in a peaceful and civilized manner, like the social transformation our country underwent after the Constitution came into force.'

'But has it succeeded?'

'Well, to a large extent it has. For instance, access to education and employment have changed the lives of most marginalized communities and women,' Avinash said. 'But on the flip side, traditionally privileged communities have appropriated the Constitution to ensure their dominance in several vital sectors of life, including education, health, administration, arts, culture, trade and industry. They have turned even noble professions like education and healthcare into businesses of dynasties and corporates.'

Sanjeev frowned. 'It's no use blaming well-established communities who have sharpened their skills for generations and are serving society,' he said.

'You're not understanding my point. The worth of a person should be determined by individual merit, not by their birth in a particular family, caste, religion or gender. There has to be equality of opportunity.'

Sanjeev nodded. 'Yes, now you shouldn't have any complaints.'

Avinash shook his head. 'The problem is that the constitutional provisions have never been properly implemented by the ruling parties,' he said. 'They are only obsessed with capturing or retaining power by any and all means.'

'Yes, that's true. Politics is all about power and wealth.'

'It has become one of the most lucrative professions that doesn't require any academic excellence or technical skills, only elective merit,' Avinash said. 'And the swiftness and nonchalance with which politicians switch loyalties between different parties reveal their mercenary attitude. We are witnessing the flipside of democracy in the absence of political maturity among voters.'

Sanjeev took the last sip of tea from his cup and put it down, smiling. 'So be it. Can we change the world?' he asked. 'The wise thing to do is to fall in line and take advantage of the situation. Have you heard the saying, "Wash your hands in the river flowing by"?'

Avinash shook his head. 'We may not be able to change the world, but we can at least make a small attempt at building up collective strength,' he said. 'At the very least, we can do our duty sincerely and see that the Constitution is implemented properly. Light a lamp, albeit a tiny one, so that others are motivated to do it and there is enough brightness to start dispelling the darkness around.'

Sanjeev frowned. 'You're living in a fool's paradise,' he said. 'Ultimately, what matters is wealth and power. You can't succeed in life without them.'

'It all depends on how you think and what you mean by a successful life. Even underworld dons have power and wealth,' Avinash said, finishing his tea.

That night, after he reached home and freshened up, he sat on the threshold of his house.

'I'm glad you're settling down in journalism,' Dagadoo said. 'We should make a mark in all sectors of life, leaving the comfort of government employment behind.'

'Of course we should,' Avinash said, narrating the events of the day. 'I find that those who have no issue with caste expect me to become servile and help the powers that be make money, even if it's unethical. It's as if the sole aim of journalism is to make profits, like a soap factory. In the process, our integrity is compromised, and rogues are empowered.'

Dagadoo sighed. 'Yes, journalism is changing.'

'The free-market economy has reduced the world to a marketplace. The concept of a welfare state has been jettisoned as governments are reducing budgetary allocations for health and education and promoting privatization instead.'

'Yes, our rulers, irrespective of their political colour, are focussing only on the nationalization of losses at the cost of the public sector and the privatization of profits at the cost of public welfare,' Dagadoo said.

Avinash looked at the city below his house. It was throbbing with human activity as usual, thriving on the template prescribed by the powerful. The city, with all its noise and dust rising above the traffic corridors, was enjoying the evening. He wondered whether it really epitomized the ultimate civilizational progress.

A few days later, when Avinash entered the state headquarters of the National Party, he found himself surrounded by people in white clothes. The office staff, the office-bearers and almost all the visitors were in white, and some of them sported white Gandhi caps as well. Gaokar had asked him to cover a press conference as Sanjeev was on leave. The conference hall was vacant, and a few visitors were waiting outside the cabin of the state president. Avinash sent his visiting card in through the peon. Moments later, as four people came out of the cabin, the peon held the door open for him and ushered him in.

The state president was sitting behind a glass table, wearing a spotless white kurta. A pile of newspapers and some documents lay in front of him. He looked like he was in his sixties, and his thinning hair was dyed black. On the television mounted on the wall in front of him, a Marathi news channel was running with its audio switched off. On the wall behind him were photographs of national leaders, and across the room was a cushioned couch. Several bouquets of flowers were also lying around in the room. A split air conditioner was keeping the cabin nicely cooled.

A middle-aged visitor in a plain blue shirt and black trousers was talking to the state president. When Avinash entered the cabin, the president got up from his chair and shook hands with him. Then he pressed the call bell, and the peon came in.

'What will you have? Tea, coffee or a cold drink?' the president asked Avinash.

'No, I don't want anything,' Avinash replied. 'Thank you.'

'Have some juice at least.'

'No.'

The president then turned to the visitor and said, 'All right, I'll talk to our chief about your case. Let's see what happens.'

The visitor rose from his chair and folded his hands. 'Please do something, sir,' he said, 'or I'll be left with no other option but to commit suicide.'

'Don't worry, we'll find a solution,' the president said. The visitor picked up his bag and threw a glance at Avinash, his eyes resembling those of a trapped creature, before walking out.

'What is the problem with him?' Avinash asked after the man left.

'Oh, nothing big,' the president said. 'We receive all kinds of visitors.'

Avinash got up from the chair. 'I think I'll talk to him,' he said. 'We'll meet later.'

'Don't bother. It's nothing worth discussing.'

'I'll come back,' Avinash said, leaving the cabin hurriedly. When he came out of the party office, he spotted the man walking towards the main gate. Avinash called out to him.

The man looked over his shoulder and stopped. He was a short, bulky middle-aged man with a round face and a mop of curly hair.

'I'm from *National News*. Can you tell me what's the matter that's troubling you?' Avinash asked.

The man thought for a moment and then smiled feebly. Avinash led him towards a concrete bench in the compound.

'My name is Arjun Kadam,' the man said as they sat down. 'I'm a filmmaker caught in a debt trap. I've made a film in Marathi, on farmers committing suicide due to crop failure and debts. It's an attempt to prevent farmers from ending their lives and it also suggests some ways in which the farmers can supplement their incomes and avert a financial crisis. The film released several months ago but it flopped at the box office. I'd taken a loan of ninety lakh rupees from a bank to make the film, and now the bank is after me to repay the loan. My condition is now like that of a debt-ridden farmer, and I'm very desperate.'

'But what help are you seeking from this political party?'

'Most of the leaders of this party are feudal lords who control the agrarian economy in rural Maharashtra. I'm requesting them to organize free shows of my film for the farmers, and I want them to pay me a small fee per show. By doing so, my film will reach the farmers in distress, and it will also help me clear my debt.'

He showed Avinash some documents that confirmed his plight.

'I'll write about this,' Avinash told him. 'But please don't think of ending your life.'

Kadam nodded and left.

Avinash went back to the party office and attended the press conference. After it was over, he met the president in his cabin and crosschecked the information.

'What he says is true, but it involves money,' the president said. 'The national president of our party will take the final decision.'

A few weeks later, after Avinash's story was published, Kadam called him to say that he was flooded with phone calls sympathizing with his plight. But nothing concrete emerged for several days. There were more meetings between Kadam and the party leaders. Then, nearly a month later, Kadam called Avinash again. 'A film producer who read my story has offered to finance a film,' Kadam said gleefully. 'He has given me an advance for the new film, and I've partially paid off my debt.'

'That's good news, but what happened to your idea of screening your previous film for the farmers? Did the party help you?'

Kadam chuckled. 'I've given up on that,' he said. 'They wanted me to show a documentary every time my film was screened for the farmers, and the documentary was a propaganda film about their national president's promises to work for farmers' welfare, so I declined.'

'What's your new film about? Are you sure it will click at the box office?'

'My new film is a mythological story about some regional deities,' Kadam said. 'And my producer is confident that it'll be a hit.'

Avinash was sceptical about Kadam's new venture but wished him success all the same.

Several months later, Kadam called Avinash and shouted jubilantly, 'The film is a hit in rural Maharashtra! I've cleared all my debts and am now making a profit.'

Avinash was speechless. 'Are you saying that people shunned a film offering free practical guidance for farmers in distress and are paying to watch a mythological film instead?'

'Yes! Can you believe it? Let's meet and celebrate.'

'There's no need for that,' Avinash said, 'but I must say that I'm surprised.'

Kadam laughed. 'It's absurd, but true. And the authorities at the temples dedicated to the deities in my film have organized a felicitation for me next week,' Kadam said. 'You are invited as well. I'll arrange for your transport, food and stay.'

'No, I'm not really interested in attending the event, but thanks. This whole episode is surreal.'

'Well, it's the bitter truth. Now that I have learnt my lesson, I'll make films only on commercially successful themes. Nowadays, there is ample scope for films on deities, especially the lesser-known ones,' Kadam said. 'I've decided to make more films and TV serials on these themes. After all, I have to survive in this man-made world which runs on money.'

A couple of days later, Avinash visited the party office again and met the president.

'I'll tell you something off the record, Avinash,' he said when all the other visitors had vacated his cabin. 'Why should our party spend money on such things? Kadam made the film voluntarily, and then it flopped,' he said. 'There's nothing wrong in us expecting him to spruce up our party's image. After all, we expect something in return too.'

Avinash shook his head. 'But most of your leaders run the rural economy and can change things on their own,' he said. 'And they get elected on farmers' votes.'

The president grinned. 'Yes, our leaders are wealthy because they belong to families that have built up the rural economy through cooperatives,' he said. 'And farmers happen to be members of our cooperatives. It's a give-and-take situation. They don't vote for free. The government compensates them for crop failures and suicides, and during the elections, the farmers also get sops.'

'But the compensation comes from public money. And most of your leaders belong to traditionally privileged communities that have received parcels of government land at nominal leases on which modern agricultural cooperatives and educational institutions are running and minting money.'

The president grimaced. 'We know that. Somebody had to build the nation up after independence and clear the social, economic and educational backlog,' he said. 'Nobody is asking who is responsible for so much developmental backlog that has piled up over the ages. Our traditional socio-economic structure was plagued with caste and gender discrimination, which benefitted a few communities. We're trying to ease the situation through democratic means. There is nothing wrong in us deriving monetary or electoral benefits out of it.'

'Even if it means indulging in malpractices?'

'The law is there to take care of that.'

'But its provisions are often tweaked to suit those in power.'

There was a pause in the conversation, during which the phone rang and the party president grabbed it, heaving a sigh of relief. After finishing the call, he pressed the call bell and the peon rushed in.

'What will you have?' the president asked Avinash.

'Nothing, thank you,' Avinash said. He rose from his chair and turned to leave as the peon walked out of the cabin.

'Please remember, whatever I've said is off the record—don't quote me,' the president said with an awkward smile.

When Avinash reached home that evening, he narrated the episode to his father.

Dagadoo shook his head. 'It has always been like this. Babasaheb used to say that our primary adversaries are the shetji and the bhatji, those who run the economy and those who lead religions,' he said. 'Things had started changing after the Constitution came into force. But over the years, the policy of prioritizing the profit-driven private sector at the cost of the welfare-driven public sector has widened inequalities. Besides, the political use of religions is leading to fanaticism, making matters worse.'

Avinash felt uneasy and insecure at his father's words, as if everything good was collapsing around him. What was even more worrying was that the common citizen, on whose shoulders the ivory towers of the shetji, bhatji and netaji were standing, was becoming more and more gullible, falling prey to emotive symbolism.

Filling in for Sanjeev, Avinash visited Mantralaya—the former's beat. It was a typical day at the state administrative headquarters. Employees were everywhere, working at their desks, chatting or carrying files. There were visitors in the corridors outside, some of them in traditional, rural attire. Avinash entered the cabin of a senior IAS officer, Anand Vyas. Tall, hefty and clean-shaven, Vyas was in his fifties and was wearing a white shirt and grey trousers.

'I'm familiar with your name,' Vyas said, looking at Avinash's visiting card. 'I read your newspaper every day and find your stories interesting. Tell me about yourself.'

After Avinash narrated his history briefly, Vyas said, 'I haven't come across anyone from your community working in a mainstream national daily yet. We have a few good officers from your community, though. There was an officer named Shivram Kamble from the Maharashtra Public Service Commission cadre working under me. He was so honest and efficient that during his annual appraisal, I wrote a remark in his confidential report that his performance was as good as that of an IAS officer.'

Avinash smiled. 'Oh, that's nice to hear. Where is he now?' he asked.

'He's a joint secretary in the higher education department. I hope he gets promoted to the IAS cadre. A team from Delhi is going to visit us soon; they'll probably look into it. You should meet Kamble before you leave.'

'That would be great!'

Vyas smiled, and then said, 'I joined the IAS with dreams of changing things for the better. There are limitations everywhere, but I do whatever is possible within my jurisdiction.' He paused for a minute and then continued, 'For instance, I'm trying to do something to improve the condition of the schools run by the government.'

'That's good,' Avinash said, suddenly recollecting his school days. 'Is it possible to form a network of government schools to impart some practical lessons to the students about expanding their worldview? For example, a programme where students from the city visit rural areas to see how farmers live and grow food. It would also help to have students mingle with people from different backgrounds living in different parts of the state or the country. Likewise, rural students could visit urban areas. Perhaps it could help the next generation experience the diversity in our culture, food, climate, social norms, religious thinking, methods of livelihood and many other things?'

Vyas stared at the ceiling for a while. 'It's an interesting idea, but rather utopian. Implementing it would be very useful in increasing knowledge and promoting fraternity. However, it's so gigantic and complicated a task in its scope that it's beyond my jurisdiction,' he said. 'Of course, I'll try to raise it at the appropriate fora whenever possible.'

'Okay. Would it be possible to hold emergency drills in schools, so that in case of a fire or a bomb scare, students can be evacuated without creating panic?'

'Yes, that's within my jurisdiction. I'll discuss this with my officers and work out a plan to make it mandatory in the entire state.'

Avinash nodded and after discussing some other issues, he left the cabin and went straight to the higher education department.

Joint Secretary Shivram Kamble was a man of few words and he was reluctant to speak to Avinash. He only opened up after Avinash said that he knew Vyas and also told him about his own background.

'I've also struggled a lot,' Kamble said. 'I used to walk five kilometres from my village every day to attend school.'

'Thank you for sharing that with me,' Avinash said.

'I've been trying to team up with like-minded officers to ensure that the tenets of the Constitution are implemented properly,' Shivram said. 'But the problem is that most of them are either resting on their laurels or are busy minting money by all means possible. There are very few who have the honesty, conviction and vision to do anything, but they are scattered and doing things on their own, and that has little or no impact.'

'Can there be a joint effort made by all these people?'

Shivram nodded. 'Networks based on religion, caste, region, language, ideology, gender and political affiliations do exist and play a role,' he said. 'But in our case, there is no such exclusive network. We'll have to reach out to honest and active people across caste and religions to implement the provisions of the Constitution properly.'

'Yes, there is a need to do it.'

Then, after discussing some other mundane matters, Avinash took his leave.

A few days later, he called on Vyas again and found him in a dejected state.

'I had called a meeting of some officials to discuss the question of emergency drills in schools, but ...' he trailed off. Then, after a pause, he said, 'You know the general tendency of government employees. Most of them wanted to scuttle the proposal. They showered me with excuses and tried convincing me that it was not a workable proposal.'

'So, what now?'

'You see how difficult it is to do anything new. They might seek help from unions or politicians to stall things, but I won't give up,' he said. 'I've called a meeting of key officials again next week. I've also intimated the minister and the chief secretary.'

Avinash felt uneasy. 'What if they don't cooperate?'

'Well, I'll try again and then ensure that a government resolution is issued and followed through.'

Avinash wished him success and left to visit the higher education department. Shivram was in high spirits. 'My name has been included in the list of officers to be evaluated for a promotion to the IAS cadre,' he said with a huge smile on his face.

Two days later, Avinash was leafing through various newspapers in the morning when he came across a headline in a prominent Marathi daily stating that a senior officer in the Mantralaya was facing an inquiry after allegations had surfaced of him misbehaving with some female staff. Avinash was shocked when he read that Shivram Kamble was the officer in question. The story claimed that the chief minister and the chief secretary had received anonymous letters accusing Kamble of harassing his female staff.

Avinash called Shivram, who expressed his anguish. 'This is a conspiracy to stall my promotion,' he said. 'I've asked them to call the victims to testify against me, but so far neither has anybody been identified as the victims, nor have they testified. I've already moved the National Commission for Scheduled Castes and Scheduled Tribes.'

Soon, various newspapers picked up the scandal, and Shivram was asked to go on leave. A committee was constituted under a senior IAS officer named Meena Gokhale to look into the case.

Avinash and Virendra met staff members of Shivram's department. All of them expressed shock over the allegations and vouched for his good behaviour. 'Our only grouse is that he's a workaholic and goes strictly by the book,' the women in his office told them. 'Otherwise, he's very courteous and decent. We don't know who has written those letters against him.'

Vyas was equally shocked by the allegations against Shivram. 'I've worked with him, and he's a gentleman. I don't think the accusations are true. The anonymous complaint appears to be a ploy to scuttle his promotion,' he said. 'But don't quote me on this. I've already been reprimanded by my seniors for writing that remark in his annual report.'

It was obvious that Vyas didn't want to stick his neck out on such a sensitive issue. He was already marginalized for straying off the well-beaten track followed by most of his colleagues.

'What about your proposal for the emergency drills in state government schools?' Avinash asked.

'We've issued a government resolution and next week, we're going to try it out in two schools in the city on an experimental basis. I hope it works out well. We can then replicate it all over the state.'

Avinash shook his head in despair. 'Actually, I was going to suggest another thing for the schools, but now I think I'd better not,' he said.

'What is it?'

'Well, I wanted to ask whether it's possible to teach school students how to swim and do basic first-aid procedures.'

Vyas nodded and narrowed his eyes for a moment. 'In rural and tribal areas, most of the students who live near water bodies know how to swim, but that is not the case in urban areas,' he said. 'The problem is that there aren't enough swimming pools in cities, and the number of students is huge.'

'Yes, but it can be done in a phased manner. Once a person learns to swim, the fear of drowning vanishes, and he or she never forgets how to swim. Every student can be trained, turn by turn, for say a week or two.'

'It's a good idea but very difficult to implement, given the size of the exercise and the logistics involved. Still, I'll keep it in mind.'

Avinash took his leave, wondering whether a student would ever step out of school armed with life-saving skills and a proper understanding of the phrase 'unity in diversity'.

A few weeks passed, and the scheduled emergency drill was conducted in two schools. The decision to extend it to all schools was still pending, but Avinash was happy that things were moving.

'We've at least made a beginning,' Vyas said when Avinash went to meet him. 'Now we're planning to extend it across the state.'

The phone rang just then and Vyas answered it. After listening to his secretary for a few seconds, he said, 'Send him in.'

The door opened and Prakash Agnihotri, a senior reporter from a rival newspaper, the *Morning Star*, walked in. He was a fair and bulky man with salt and pepper hair.

'How are you, sir?' he asked Vyas, and then stopped short at the sight of Avinash in the room. 'Oh! I'm sorry. I'll come some other time,' he said and turned to leave.

'No, wait,' Vyas said. 'Please, join us. I want to talk to you.'

Nodding, Agnihotri sat down; his branded yellow-and-white striped shirt, tucked in a pair of blue jeans, stretched across his belly.

'I'm glad that you came when Avinash is also here,' Vyas said. 'Do you remember you had called me up some days ago to say that I should not give any exclusive information to Avinash?'

Avinash was shocked. 'Oh! Is that right?' he asked.

Agnihotri looked rattled. He squirmed in his chair, folded his arms across his chest, resting them on his bulging belly, and tried to sit upright.

'I don't understand why a reputed senior reporter from a national newspaper would do something like this,' Vyas said. 'Is there a problem between you two?'

Agnihotri was red-faced. He seemed to be searching for the right words. Then, avoiding eye contact with Vyas, he finally said, 'No, no. There's no fight between us. It's just that …' Agnihotri trailed off. Then he cleared his throat and grinned. 'I sometimes get pulled up by my bosses for missing a story which Avinash writes first, and I have to follow up his stories,' he said.

'But getting pulled up for missing a story is common everywhere,' Avinash said. 'The best thing to do is to try not to miss a story and do something exclusive to score over your rivals.'

Agnihotri looked at Avinash and then at Vyas. 'Yes, I know, but sometimes it hurts, especially when my seniors praise stories written by someone like Avinash,' he said.

'"Someone like me"? What do you mean?' Avinash asked reflexively.

'Yes, what do you mean?' Vyas asked.

Agnihotri squirmed in his chair again, looking everywhere except at Vyas and Avinash. He looked down at his feet and then at the ceiling. There was a long, uncomfortable pause, after which he opened his mouth and said, 'Well … err … nothing. It's just that I'm senior to him in the profession, that's all.'

Vyas frowned. 'Seniority has nothing to do with such things,' he said. 'And you shouldn't try to stop me from interacting with him. Giving information to a media person is my prerogative. And please remember, I will continue to give Avinash information.'

Agnihotri smiled sheepishly. Then he got up from his chair and patted Avinash on the shoulder. 'No hard feelings. We're friends.

I must leave now as I have to meet someone,' he said and walked out of the cabin.

Vyas shook his head after the door closed behind Agnihotri.

'Do you think this was because of my background?' Avinash asked.

Vyas stared at him blankly for a moment. 'Perhaps,' he said. 'I don't know. But the fact remains that he has singled you out. And he might have said the same thing to some other officials too.'

Avinash felt terribly upset. 'It makes me feel uncomfortable,' he said. 'I'm tempted to think that it's the same old caste prejudice in a subtle form.'

'You may be right, or it could be that he's scared of the competition,' Vyas said. 'People from privileged families usually inherit a feeling of superiority, and they hate it when people they think are lower than them because of birth, compete with them. But don't waste your time and energy on such things. Just be better at your job than others.'

This experience was not new for Avinash. He longed for the feeling of belonging to a just world where he was not always required to remain on his toes.

He bade Vyas goodbye and walked out into the corridor. While passing by the urban development department, he saw a familiar face—it was Rustom, from the docks.

'Oh, what a pleasant surprise!' Rustom exclaimed when he spotted Avinash. He smiled and shook hands with him. 'It's truly a small world. How are you, sir?'

'I'm fine, and you?' Avinash asked.

'I heard that you quit the port job to become a reporter,' Rustom said and took him aside. 'I'm into the real estate business,' he said. 'I just met the urban development secretary regarding some approvals for a housing project.'

Avinash smiled and nodded. 'So, is your work done?'

'Almost done,' he said with a broad smile. Then, after a pause, he added, 'This officer is different.'

'Different?'

'Yes. He doesn't take bribes. But I'll tell you something only if you promise to keep your source anonymous.'

Avinash was curious. 'All right, what is it?'

Rustom came closer to him and whispered, 'He's clean at his job, but his wife is a painter, and he asks people like me to buy paintings from her at exorbitant prices. The payment is routed through a bank account, so everything is legal. She may even be paying tax on these transactions as it's white money. I've been asked to buy two of her paintings.'

'Oh! That's very clever,' Avinash said. 'How much are you going to pay for the paintings?'

Rustom smirked. 'I can't tell you anything more,' he said. 'In fact, I've not told you anything at all.' He picked up his briefcase and walked towards the elevator. But then he stopped and turned back. 'I am sorry about Mohan,' he said. 'He was your friend, wasn't he?'

'Mohan was my batchmate in the docks. But what happened?'

'You don't know? He died about a month ago.'

'*What?*' Avinash looked at him in disbelief.

Rustom shook his head in despair. 'He used to drink too much,' he said. 'He was a promising man and was minting money, but he couldn't manage his family life.'

Avinash was so shocked that he did not notice Rustom entering the elevator and leaving. He was soon lost in memories of his time with Mohan.

It was a typical working day at the docks when Avinash reached the Red Gate. The first shift had started, and the security personnel were checking vehicles and pedestrians as a matter of routine. Most of the trucks were carrying containers or dry bulk fertilizers.

Avinash spotted Kamble in his sparkling white uniform talking to a policeman. At the security office inside the gate, he saw Akash Deshmukh sitting at the check post as the gate inspector. He got up from his chair when he saw Avinash and beckoned him.

They shook hands and exchanged pleasantries.

'I heard about Mohan,' Avinash said. 'What happened?'

'It's very sad, the way he died,' Deshmukh said. 'As you know, he was making a lot of money, but there were some domestic issues that he wasn't able to handle. So, he turned to alcohol for comfort. His wife had filed for a divorce, and his parents thought he was hiding his income from them. During his last days, when he was promoted as a gate inspector, either his father or his brother would come here towards the end of his shift every day and snatch the cash he had collected throughout the shift from his pockets. He would get so drunk every day that his colleagues used to hire a cab and pay the driver to take him home. One day, he went missing and the next morning, his body was found on the pavement.'

'This is shocking,' Avinash said. 'It's difficult to believe that family relations can be so fragile.'

Deshmukh asked Avinash if he would like some tea, but Avinash declined the offer. Images of Mohan kept flashing through his mind. He was only pulled back to the present when Kamble patted him on the shoulder.

'I'm glad to see you after such a long time,' he said with a broad smile, shaking hands with Avinash.

'He found out about Mohan,' Deshmukh said.

Kamble shook his head sadly. 'He was a highly talented guy, making a lot of money,' he said. 'But he was an emotional fool.'

Avinash shook his head.

'Had he confided in us, we would've done something,' Kamble said, 'but he started avoiding our company and began drinking while on duty. We came to know about the situation only when things went too far.'

'He couldn't stand up to his parents and his wife. They were pulling him in opposite directions,' Deshmukh said. 'He probably took it to heart that the people he loved most had stopped trusting him.'

The three men fell silent. Then Avinash took their leave. He thought of visiting Mohan's family, but then he gave up on the idea.

Later in the day, he went back to the urban development secretary's office in the Mantralaya and sent his visiting card in through a peon.

'He's in a meeting right now,' the secretary's personal assistant said, asking Avinash to wait. There were a few visitors already waiting outside the cabin. Half an hour later, a couple of men walked out, and Avinash was ushered in. The secretary was sitting behind a huge table that had a thick glass sheet on it. There were piles of files neatly arranged on the table, with several pens and pencils stashed inside a mug and a couple of paperweights kept on top of some loose documents in front of him. He was in his forties, and was wearing a white shirt with red stripes and a pair of brown trousers. He peered over his glasses as Avinash walked in.

'I wanted some information about the changes proposed in the development control rules,' Avinash said after he'd introduced himself.

The secretary smiled very widely. 'We are still working on it,' he said. 'It'll take some time to draft a proposal to amend the existing rules. It's too early to disclose anything now, but I'll let you know.' He then opened a file and started reading it. A few minutes later, he looked up at Avinash, who was still standing there. 'Is there anything else?' he asked curtly.

Avinash smiled. 'Not really, but I've heard that your wife is a painter,' he said. 'I was wondering if I could meet her for an interview?'

The secretary looked shocked at the mention of his wife, but he collected himself promptly. 'What?' he asked. 'Who told you about her?'

'Just something I overheard.'

'Please have a seat,' the secretary said.

When Avinash sat down, the secretary laughed and, shaking his head, said, 'She's not really a painter; it's simply her hobby.'

He pressed a switch under his table, and the peon rushed in. 'What will you have? Tea, coffee or some fruit juice?' he asked Avinash.

'No, sir, nothing. I was just curious about your wife's art,' Avinash said.

'Well, there's nothing to be curious about, so you can forget it.'

Avinash left the cabin after that. Outside, the crowd of visitors had swelled considerably.

He walked through the corridor and descended a flight of stairs to meet Vyas.

'I forgot to tell you about my transfer to Delhi on deputation. I'm winding up things here,' Vyas said. 'We'll meet when I visit the city again.'

'Best wishes for your new assignment, sir,' Avinash said. 'But I must say, this is bad news for me.'

'No, no! Don't think like that,' Vyas said. 'Don't worry, we'll keep in touch. And there are some other very good officers in the bureaucracy as well.'

'What happens now to the changes you have initiated in the state government schools?'

Vyas shook his head. 'Since a government resolution has been issued, things will continue, but I don't know how soon the changes will get implemented,' he said. 'My successor will be dealing with it.'

Avinash took his leave and thought of following up on Shivram's case. He went and met the inquiry officer, Meena Gokhale.

'The probe against Shivram is still in progress,' she said casually. She was a chubby, fair-complexioned lady in her forties, wearing a cream sari with a red border.

'How many employees have testified against him?' Avinash asked.

She shook her head. 'I can't tell you that,' she said. 'The only thing I can say is that the inquiry is on.'

'I heard that he has moved the Scheduled Caste Commission, which has issued a notice to the government.'

'Yes, we have received the notice,' she said. 'He's free to move the Commission or the administrative tribunal to challenge the allegations.'

'He was shortlisted for a promotion to the IAS cadre ...'

'His name has been dropped from the list,' she said promptly. 'And now please don't ask me anything more.'

Avinash left her cabin and called Shivram, who did not have very good news.

'Neither are they conducting the hearing nor are they furnishing anything concrete to prove the allegations,' he said. 'There is no complainant who can testify either openly or on camera. They will, in all likelihood, withdraw the case after the central team evaluating the IAS promotions completes its work. I don't think I'll ever get promoted to the IAS cadre.'

Shivram was right. A couple of weeks later, once the IAS evaluations were completed, he was exonerated of all allegations for want of evidence.

CHAPTER 20

A week later, the artillery regiment organized its annual firepower demonstrations and invited the press. Gaokar asked Avinash to cover it as the reporter on the defence beat was on leave. Avinash was happy to go.

It was early morning, and there was a nip in the air in the army cantonment, which was located away from the city. There were hills and trees all around, and the sun had risen behind a wall of mountains on the horizon. A huge tent had been pitched in a clearing, offering a panoramic view of the landscape. The area was populated by army officers and cadets, and there was a flurry of activity a little distance away from the tent with some soldiers busy positioning the guns that were to be used in the demonstration. By the time a group of press reporters was escorted into the tent, everything was ready for the exercise. Over a public address system, an officer welcomed the gathering and identified each gun—they ranged from a 105 mm mortar and a 155 mm Howitzer gun to a 122 mm multiple-barrel rocket launcher. The officer pointed out the firing ranges in front of the guns. The targets, set up several kilometres away, were a series of white dots painted on the hills in different geometrical shapes.

The exercise began with the firing of the mortar and then moved to guns of higher calibres. The crew around each gun performed its task with precision, and the guns fired and recoiled with a loud thunderclap and a split-second gush of air that swept over the audience. When a target was hit, it raised a cloud of smoke and dust followed by the noise of a distant thud, like a bomb explosion. The exercise concluded with the multiple-barrel rocket launcher firing a series of missiles in quick succession. After the demonstrations, snacks and tea were served. A press release detailing the exercise and equipment used was also circulated.

As the officers became informal, many reporters went into a huddle with a major, who was the liaison officer. Avinash, meanwhile, was talking casually with a lieutenant colonel. After some time, the major approached the lieutenant colonel.

'Sir, I've received requests from some media persons for liquor bottles,' he said. Turning to Avinash, he asked, 'Do you need something?'

'No, nothing at all,' Avinash replied.

The major looked down at a list in his hand. There were several names on the list, some of them tick marked. 'You are?' he asked.

'Avinash Gaikwad, from the *National News*.'

The major glanced at the list again and put a cross in front of his name.

'I think it's wrong of them to ask for liquor bottles,' Avinash said.

The lieutenant colonel smiled. The name tag on his chest read 'Amar Singh'.

'You think it's wrong?' he asked.

'Yes, sir,' Avinash replied. 'Subsidized goods are meant for the soldiers.'

Singh smiled and nodded. 'I've read your work,' he said. 'Nice to have met you.'

At that moment, Singh was summoned by his senior officer and had to leave. Avinash also went back to the office and filed his report.

Two weeks later, Avinash received a call in his office. 'Is that Mr Avinash Gaikwad?' the caller asked.

'Yes, who's this?'

'This is Lieutenant Colonel Amar Singh,' the caller said. 'We met during the army exercise.'

'Yes, I remember,' Avinash replied.

'Can we meet somewhere outside tomorrow evening? I have some important information to share.'

Avinash agreed, and the next day, they met at a restaurant in the city for coffee. 'I can give you some sensitive information, but only on the condition of anonymity,' Singh said.

'Of course.'

'We are recruiting soldiers, but there are too many malpractices in the procedure,' Singh said. 'Some of our senior officers and the local doctor on the selection panel have roped in some serving soldiers to pick people looking to join the army from among their friends and relations so that the public doesn't have a chance. The physical tests and the answer sheets are tampered with in exchange for hefty bribes.'

'That's shocking. Isn't there an internal mechanism to monitor the process?'

'There is, and the information has been anonymously passed on to military intelligence and the higher-ups. But I'm cynical about punitive action being taken. The whole issue may be hushed up. I want this to stop, but I don't want to come into the picture.'

'I can do a story about this and keep you out of it, but only if I have proof.'

Singh shook his head. 'Well, I don't have anything concrete in my hands, and I can't use my office to get proof. If they come to know about it, I'll be doomed. The brigadier is a very smart and resourceful person. He'll go to any extent to either silence you or win you over.'

'Don't worry about that,' Avinash said. 'But I need some evidence to raise doubts about the recruitment process.'

There was a long pause before Singh spoke again. 'All right, I'll try to get something, but please keep my name out of it. And don't contact me on my office phone. I'll give you the number of an acquaintance who owns a shop. Just leave a message with him and don't reveal your real name or profession. If I want to contact you, I'll call on your office landline from a public phone.'

Avinash agreed to the conditions and Singh gave him a number. 'Okay, if I need to contact you, I'll call on this number and say I'm Ashok Chakravarti, a friend.'

They parted ways after that and about a week later, Singh called Avinash to fix a meeting. They met again at a different café, where he handed some documents over to Avinash.

It took a couple of days to get a formal appointment with Brigadier Inder Kumar. After passing through various security cordons and pickets, Avinash reached the brigadier's office in the army cantonment. Everything appeared to be in order. The roads, the building and the potted plants in the veranda were neat and tidy. The colours of the regiment, its totem, the national emblem and the flag were prominently displayed. Outside the brigadier's cabin, a long mirror was fixed to a wall. A brass plate with the brigadier's name hung on the door to his cabin. A sentry ushered Avinash into the cabin, which was neat, cold and silent like a sterile operation theatre.

There were numerous trophies and miniature models of war machines on the shelves, while various insignias and photographs of army officers decorated the walls. A miniature model of an artillery gun was kept on a huge table, behind which sat the brigadier, dressed in his crisp uniform. He was fair, tall and robust and had a thick handlebar moustache.

'Welcome, young man. Please, have a seat.' The brigadier's stiff face broke into a measured smile for a brief second. 'What can I do for you?'

Avinash sat down in a chair. 'Sir, I wanted some information about the ongoing recruitment of soldiers,' he said.

Kumar nodded. 'Yes, we are recruiting soldiers as per our requirements. But it's a routine process; there's nothing special about it,' he said curtly. 'What would you like to have? Something hot or cold?'

'Nothing, but thanks for asking,' Avinash replied. 'I've received information that there have been irregularities in the recruitment process.'

Kumar looked stunned for a moment, but he quickly collected himself and burst into laughter. 'Who told you that?' he asked. 'No, no! Everything is by the book. If anything goes wrong, we're here to handle it.'

'Well, there was a signal from the army headquarters raising questions over the recruitment process,' Avinash said.

'No, no, no!' Kumar raised his voice and shook his head. 'Someone has given you wrong information.'

'Sir, I have a copy of the document,' Avinash said. 'I only came here to get your version of the story.'

There was a long pause, and the expression on Kumar's face changed from hubris to suspicion. 'There's no such thing,' he said, narrowing his puffy eyes. 'You may leave now.'

'Sir, I also have some papers from the military intelligence. If you don't want to react, it's up to you. I'll say that you refused to comment,' Avinash said and stood up to leave.

The brigadier gestured for him to sit down again. Then he stared at him blankly for a moment. 'What do you want?' he asked.

'Only your comment on the recruitment process.'

'I don't have to answer your questions,' the brigadier said sharply.

'That's all right. If you don't want to comment, that's your choice,' Avinash said.

'Tell me something—who gave you this information?' the brigadier asked.

'Sorry, I can't tell you that,' Avinash said, pushing his chair back and standing up.

'Wait.' Kumar rose from his chair and approached him. Laying his hand on Avinash's shoulder, he smiled. 'Why do you want to write about this?' he asked. 'There are a lot of things happening everywhere. Write about those instead. Just forget this. It's a trivial thing, which will be sorted out internally. It's not worth your time.'

'Sir, respectfully, I'm the best judge of what is and isn't a waste of my time.'

The brigadier nodded. 'All right. What do you want?' he asked. 'I'll make you happy. You can ask for anything—cash, premium liquor, something from the defence canteen,' Kumar offered. When Avinash did not respond, he winked and asked, 'Girls? You can have beautiful, clean girls. Even Russian girls.'

Avinash felt resentment building up inside him but he controlled himself.

'Take your time,' the brigadier said with a smile. 'Let me know. We can be friends.'

'Sir, I'm a journalist, not a blackmailer,' Avinash snapped and walked out of the cabin.

He contacted some other army officers, including the official spokesperson, and wrote a story that appeared in the paper the next day.

He left a message for Amar Singh at his friend's shop, but there was no response.

A few weeks later, a court of inquiry was announced by the army headquarters. Avinash left another message for Singh at the shop, but again, he heard nothing. He called again and the shopkeeper told him that the message had been conveyed but that Singh was very busy and would get back when free.

Subsequently, Brigadier Kumar and a handful of other officials were indicted, and a CBI probe was recommended. Transfers and suspensions ensued. Avinash followed up on the story intermittently, reporting whatever information he could get.

Months later, he finally received a call from Lieutenant Colonel Singh.

'Jai Hind,' Singh said. 'I must thank you; there is some good news. The army headquarters has changed the recruitment process. The existing panels, comprising local army officers and doctors, have been replaced with panels made up of officers and doctors from Delhi and other cantonments. The names of the panellists are to be announced at the last moment to ensure neutrality and pre-empt malpractices,' Singh said.

'That's good,' Avinash said.

'Yes, and I hope things will improve now. Thank you again.'

'Sir, I only did my job, just like you did yours. It was my duty, and I draw a salary for doing my job,' Avinash said. 'But for you, it was risky. Let's just hope the correction in the system works.'

'Yes, that's true. Just one more thing—please don't call me in the future and don't mention my name to anyone. They already suspect my hand in leaking the information about this scandal. I'm being marginalized, and I don't think they'll ever promote me to a colonel. But I don't mind—I've served the nation by fighting this battle. The only difference is that as a soldier, my battlefield was not on the borders but within my country, my regiment.'

'Thank you for being honest and brave,' Avinash said.

'I'm a soldier, brother, and my life is dedicated to the nation! Jai Hind!'

'Jai Hind, brother.'

As he hung up, Avinash recollected his time as a dock employee willing to expose wrongdoings. He also remembered several people with different backgrounds and professions, like Ramachandran, Shivram Kamble, Amar Singh and even Patwardhan, who had been relegated to the margins, like Singh. In Shivram's case, caste prejudice had invited the wrath of his seniors when he was being considered for a much sought-after promotion. Ironically, the immediate trigger for his marginalization was the fact that an upper-caste senior officer had praised him too much. In Ramachandran and Amar Singh's case, it was not caste but moral uprightness that made their seniors marginalize them. Amar Singh was a soldier fighting enemies within the country—his own seniors and colleagues—risking his career and, ultimately, paying the penalty by not being promoted. Indeed, principled behaviour had nothing to do with any caste or religion as there were people of different temperaments everywhere. The fact was that upright people were a miniscule minority willing to face difficulties as they had chosen the path of righteousness of their own volition.

About a month later, acting on a tip-off from one of his sources, Avinash requested Gaokar to allow him to visit a tribal region. Gaokar agreed, and Avinash travelled to a hilly tribal hamlet in northern Maharashtra that lay along the state's border with Madhya Pradesh and Gujarat. It was summer and the landscape in front of Avinash was almost barren, like giant waves of brown earth frozen in time. He was walking on a snaking, uneven path that rose and fell along the contours of the hill. There were a few trees scattered on the hills and gorges, casting faint shadows on the ground. No houses or human beings were in sight. The silence was punctuated by the chirping of birds flying overhead and the buzzing of insects. The ground rose under his feet, breaking his pace, until he reached a clearing. He stopped to catch his breath under a tree. Putting a couple of pinches of oral rehydration powder from a packet into his mouth, he drank some water from the bottle he was carrying. On the other side of the hill, he could see a cluster of thatched huts surrounded by some trees. As he made his way down, he spotted some movement in the cluster, with a few tribals coming out of the houses and standing under a tree, looking at him. By the time he reached the spot, more tribals had come out. Most of them were grey-haired elderly men and women with wrinkled, dark-skinned faces and curious eyes. There were a few half-naked children among them too. They were all thin and barefoot and stood waiting silently.

'My name is Avinash. I work for a newspaper in the city,' Avinash introduced himself to the group, folding his hands in greeting. 'I'm looking for Khilpya. I was told by someone from Khadakpada hamlet that Khilpya's son died in a government hospital, and that he had to carry the dead body for about fifty kilometres on his shoulder to reach home.'

'Khilpya? Yes, yes,' one of the tribal men nodded and started walking away, gesturing for Avinash to follow. After they passed several dwellings, the tribal man stopped in front of a house and hollered Khilpya's name.

A man appeared at the door and stood with his hands on the door frame, viewing Avinash with suspicion. He was thin and dark-skinned, and wore only a pair of black shorts. The elderly tribal told him about Avinash, after which they entered the house. It was cooler inside, providing some respite from the heat outside.

'I'm Khilpya,' the man said. A thin woman, wearing a blouse and a sari that was wrapped around her waist, was rocking a baby sleeping in a cradle fashioned from a sari hanging from two wooden poles. A half-naked boy, about five years old, the contours of his ribcage visible, was standing near her. Some groceries and utensils were lying in a corner near an earthen fireplace.

Avinash introduced himself and asked, 'What do you do for a living?'

'I'm a farmer,' Khilpya said. 'During the monsoon, I grow paddy and ragi. After the monsoon crop, with the rainwater flowing down the hills, there is no scope for agriculture. So, for the next eight months, we migrate in search of work as farm labourers or road diggers and return home before the next monsoon season arrives.'

Gradually, more people from the hamlet gathered around Khilpya's hut, the number of children outnumbering the adults.

'There are so many children around. Don't you think that you should plan your families more carefully?' Avinash asked.

The tribal who had escorted Avinash nodded. 'You're right; we should limit the number of children, but a major problem is that all the kids don't survive,' he said. 'I had nine children, but only four have survived.'

'I had three kids, only two are left now,' Khilpya said.

'What happened to your son?' Avinash asked.

'He was younger than this one,' Khilpya said, pointing at his son. 'We were preparing to migrate when he fell sick. We took him to a tantrik in Khadakpada, leaving this one here with our neighbour. The tantrik baba gave him some holy ash and herbs, but despite several visits to Khadakpada, there was no improvement. Then we took him to a primary health centre about twelve kilometres away. The doctor was not available there, and the nurse directed us to the district hospital at Nandurbar. We went there, but the doctor referred us to the district hospital in Dhule and provided us with an ambulance.

'When we reached the hospital in Dhule, the doctors admitted him but said that his condition was very critical. The next morning, they declared him dead and asked us to take the body away. When I asked for an ambulance, or whatever other vehicle they could provide, to return home, they said nothing was available and that I should arrange my own transport. I had no money, so I picked up my son's body, put it over my shoulder and walked home with my wife, who carried the baby. In the evening, we buried our son.'

Khilpya sighed. His wife, who seemed to be listening to him, continued to stare blankly, her eyes glassy. 'We are jobless and hungry this summer because we could not migrate in time with the others,' he said.

'But why didn't you take the sick child to a doctor in time?'

'Because the doctors would've admitted him to the hospital, and we would've been compelled to stay with him for the duration of the treatment. This would have prevented us from migrating for employment and we would have lost out on wages, besides incurring extra expenditure on food and stay during his treatment.'

Avinash looked around and suddenly realized that most of the people around him were either elderly or very young. The youth had already migrated in search of livelihood. He knew that despite heavy rainfall in the hilly tribal regions, in the absence of watershed development or dams for irrigation, all the water flowed downhill to the catchment areas of faraway dams near cities. Consequently, after the monsoon, tribals had to migrate in order to work.

He collected some more information, took some photographs and retraced his steps. He visited Khadakpada, and then went to the primary health centre and the hospitals at Nandurbar and Dhule. While the tantrik was not available—he was out looking for some herbs—the primary health centre was waiting for a doctor to be appointed to their facility. At both the hospitals, doctors blamed the child's death on the delay in hospitalization and complained about the shortage of staff, medicines, equipment and amenities.

The day the story was published, Chief Minister Vikasrao Patil called Avinash. 'I read your story in today's paper,' he said. 'Is this true?'

'Of course it is, sir,' Avinash replied. 'You can ask someone to verify it, or you can pay the tribals a visit personally.'

'Hmm, let me see what can be done.'

A few hours later, Avinash received a call from the deputy chief minister, Balasaheb Naik. 'It's very shocking,' Patil said. 'It's also difficult to believe, but I trust you since I know you. We'll do something about this.'

Within a couple of days, various government officials and elected representatives visited the Dhule and Nandurbar districts, with some even visiting Khilpya. A week later, Deshmukh and Patil addressed a meeting of government officials, including doctors from the region. It was announced that tribals accompanying their undernourished or sick children to government hospitals would be served free meals and compensated for their loss of wages in order to encourage them to seek early medical treatment. A recruitment drive to appoint more medical staff as well as to procure medicines and equipment was also announced.

When Avinash informed his parents about the development, Dagadoo was elated. He patted him. 'I'm glad that you've become a journalist,' he said. 'You've just done a priceless thing, which is much more important than making money or earning a livelihood.'

Godavari was dumbfounded.

'You did not want him to become a journalist,' Dagadoo pointed out.

'Well, my concern was that he should first take care of his parents properly and then do whatever he likes,' she said. 'Anyway, it's good that because of your efforts something positive has happened in the lives of such marginalized people. God will bless you.'

'God?' Dagadoo exclaimed. 'Have you forgotten that we were not allowed to enter temples despite our satyagraha at various shrines? The agitation at that temple in Nashik lasted for about six years, but it was all in vain.'

Curious to learn more, Avinash decided to visit the temple in Nashik.

❀

A few days later, he was standing in front of the temple in Nashik that his father had referred to. Built by a general during the Peshwa regime, it was bustling with activity. Ascetics and devotees were clanging bells, praying and performing rituals. The tourists visiting the temple were paying obeisance and admiring the meticulously carved black stone architecture.

A plaque installed near the main entrance of the temple informed visitors that a satyagraha led by Dr B.R. Ambedkar had been organized at that very spot to demand entry for Dalits into the temple. As Avinash read the plaque, he remembered that his father was a foot soldier in Dr Ambedkar's social movement. He entered the temple courtyard and approached a priest standing nearby and talking to some devotees.

'I'm looking for Swami Sunil Maharaj. I'm a newspaper reporter,' he said.

The priest sent a messenger to the swami who was living in an old building adjacent to the temple complex. After a while, the swami arrived and greeted Avinash with a smile. He was clean-shaven, bald, round-faced and hefty, and was dressed in saffron robes. On his forehead was a tilak in red and white.

'Do you want to perform some ritual?' he asked.

'No, I just wanted to talk to you,' Avinash said. The swami took him to one of the rooms located in the building skirting the compound wall of the main temple. After some small talk, Avinash asked him about the significance of the plaque.

'I played a crucial role in getting it installed. It marks the prolonged historical agitation led by Babasaheb Ambedkar, demanding entry into temples for all Hindus, irrespective of their caste,' the swami said. 'My grandfather barred the untouchables, including Babasaheb Ambedkar, from entering the temple. During the six-year-long agitation, there were intermittent riots as well.'

'Do you think your grandfather and other orthodox Brahmins were justified in shutting out Babasaheb and the other Dalits?'

The swami thought about it for a few moments and then smiled. 'I think they made a mistake by not opening the temple doors to Babasaheb,' he said, 'because the protest continued for years. Ultimately, though, Babasaheb gave up his efforts to reform Hinduism and years later, he converted to Buddhism. I think he might not have rejected Hinduism if his demand had been granted.'

'So, you think it was a mistake which can't be undone?'

'Yes, and as penance, I've decided to finance the education of fifty Dalit and tribal school students till they finish their graduation.'

Avinash smiled. 'I'm going to write this story,' he said. 'I hope you won't face any problems because of it.'

'Please go ahead and print it. There is no problem. Now anyone can enter the temple, but the problem is that Babasaheb's followers who converted to Buddhism still don't come,' the swami said. 'We are willing to welcome them and perform rituals, but now they are not interested. So, we cooperated with the government to install the plaque that acknowledges Babasaheb's historic satyagraha.'

After spending some more time with the swami, Avinash left the temple complex.

When the story was finally published, a couple of priests stormed Avinash's office.

'So! You are the Avinash Gaikwad who wrote that temple story,' fumed an elderly priest dressed in saffron robes. His head was clean shaven, except for a tuft of hair at the back. 'I'm the son of the priest who stopped Ambedkar from entering the temple, and I think it was the right thing to do.'

Avinash had been expecting some backlash and had already received many calls since morning. Some callers appreciated the swami's gesture, while some criticized him for disagreeing with his ancestors.

'But I've only published what Swami Sunil Maharaj said,' Avinash pointed out. 'What's wrong with that?'

'Who is Swami Sunil Maharaj to say anything?' the priest shouted. 'He's my nephew and a priest, yes, but he can't speak on our behalf. Traditions must be followed, and there was nothing wrong in shutting Ambedkar and his people out of the temple.'

'What do you want me to do now?' Avinash asked.

'Retract the story and publish an apology,' the priest said. 'We'll see what to do with Sunil Maharaj.'

'If all the priests of the temple take a collective stand against Swami Sunil Maharaj and the temple trust issues a written statement, we'll publish it.'

'Who are you to tell us what to do?' the second priest, a younger man, shouted. 'Apologize for what you've written.' The elderly priest nodded in agreement, clenching his teeth.

'I can't, not unless the swami retracts what he said or the temple trust issues a statement,' Avinash said

'All right, if you want something in writing, I'll come back with a written statement after the trustees and priests meet tomorrow,' the elder priest said and walked out with his companion in tow.

For the next several days, Avinash waited for the priest to arrive with a written statement, but he never did. When Avinash called up Swami Sunil Maharaj, he said that majority of the priests and trustees had decided not to issue any statements as it would open a Pandora's box of trouble and trigger a huge backlash from several quarters as times had changed.

A week later, the swami called Avinash. 'I received a call from the leader of the National Bahujan Party to thank me,' he said. 'The party has also offered me a ticket for the upcoming general elections, but I don't know what to do.'

'Swamiji, I have nothing to say on this issue. It's entirely up to you to decide whether you want to join politics or not.'

The swami was quiet for a moment. 'I'm in two minds,' he said. 'Not only am I a novice in politics, but at the temple, even though my fellow priests have not formally contradicted my stance on Ambedkar, I'm being sidelined.'

'I can only say that your stance on temple entry is progressive, legal and moral,' Avinash said. 'But whether to join politics or continue as a priest, that's a call you'll have to take yourself.'

Months later, Swami Sunil Maharaj contested the elections but lost miserably. 'Neither my community nor the progressive-minded voters from other communities supported my candidature,' the swami said. 'I've been marginalized by everyone.'

Avinash was stunned.

Years passed. New reporters were recruited and Avinash became a senior to many in the organization, but he was not given a decision-making position. There were pressures and limitations, but he tried to make the most of whatever freedom he had at his disposal. Two new newspapers were launched, creating a severe shortage of staff at the *National News* as many people from the editorial department quit their jobs for the sake of higher salaries and designations.

During a meeting to discuss how to manage the workload and yet score over rival newspapers, Jai Singh told Avinash, 'Our seniors in Delhi are thinking of promoting you.'

'Me?'

'Yes, your performance is good, and there aren't that many senior reporters left,' Singh said. 'You may have to lead a team of reporters for state-level stories and coordinate with our other offices as well.'

'I was not expecting this,' Avinash said, 'but I'm willing to accept the challenge.'

'Good! We're pinning our hopes on you.'

The promotion was a boost to Avinash's morale. It meant he would have more say in editorial matters and be able to plan and execute stories.

When he reached home that evening, he told his parents about the impending promotion. His father was exhilarated. 'I'm so proud of you!' he said. 'This situation is in your favour, and you should make the most of it. I've always told you that honesty and hard work make for an invincible combination.'

Godavari, who was cutting some vegetables, looked at Avinash. 'Are they going to increase your salary?' she asked.

'Yes, of course, but that's secondary,' Avinash replied.

She nodded and resumed her work.

A couple of days later, when Avinash had finished his work and was about to leave, Jai Singh called him into his cabin. When he entered, the editor got up and closed the door.

'There is a small problem with your promotion,' he said, sitting back down.

'Problem?'

The editor avoided making eye contact with Avinash and looked at the ceiling instead. 'There is no issue with your capability,' he said, 'but there are some people who are not comfortable with your promotion.'

'Who? And why not?'

'Well, keep it between you and me,' the editor said. 'I won't take any names, but a delegation of four reporters who are to be assigned to you, came to meet me. They said they don't want to work under you.'

'Why not? Do they have a problem with my background?' Avinash asked.

'No, they didn't say that,' the editor said, still refusing to look at Avinash.

'Then what is it?'

'Well, they said that you're a bit reserved and don't socialize enough,' Singh told him. 'And that you're very strict in terms of work ethics, deadlines and quality of writing.'

Avinash smiled. 'What do you think?' he asked.

'We've worked together for years, and I've never had any problem with you. I'm delighted with your performance,' Singh continued. There was a long pause, after which he said, 'I talked to our seniors in Delhi about it, and they'll take the final call.'

'No problem. I'm happy with what I'm doing right now,' Avinash said.

The next day, Singh called him to his cabin again. 'Good news! Our seniors have put their foot down in your favour,' he said. 'Those who were uncomfortable with you have been told that you are a senior not only in the industry but within our newspaper as well, and that your performance is outstanding. So, there is no question of going back on the decision to promote you.'

It was a rare occasion for Avinash because for once, his work was being formally acknowledged.

'But that doesn't solve the problem,' the editor said. 'All four of them have resigned, and two of them have already joined some other newspaper. The other two are on notice period as there are opportunities available in new media houses.'

'Oh.'

'You realize what this means, right?' Singh asked. 'Until we find new reporters, you'll be working alone in the bureau.'

Avinash closed his eyes for a moment and thought over it. Then he smiled. 'Yes, it means I'll be heading a team comprising only one person, and that's me,' he said. 'It's not a problem but an opportunity to prove myself all over again. I'm looking forward to taking on our new rivals single-handedly. It'll be fun!'

'That's the spirit,' the editor said. 'I wish you the best! And of course, we are here to help. We'll build up a new team.'

That night, Avinash could barely sleep because he kept wondering why people were not willing to work under him. Did they have a problem with his background? Was it a case of subtle casteism? Or was it his uprightness?

The next morning, Avinash woke up with a mild headache. The city, visible from the threshold of his house, was perpetually undergoing a metamorphosis. The buildings were becoming taller and were enclosed in glass walls with decorative facades. Sprawling malls and office complexes had mushroomed in places previously occupied by factories. Away from the flight paths of aircrafts, sparkling skyscrapers stuck out like huge glass shafts sprouting up from the uneven concrete jungle of square and rectangular blocks, dwarfing neighbourhood structures. The pace of the swirling traffic had slowed down as the density of vehicles increased, causing bumper-to-bumper traffic even on newly constructed flyovers.

Avinash sat on the threshold. The city was the same urban habitat that had fascinated him as a child—but not anymore. It appeared superficial and synthetic, like a bouquet of beautiful plastic flowers of different colours in a fantasy world.

The same city had attracted his father, who had been desperate to escape the tyranny of caste in his village. Indeed, the city had offered him employment and an opportunity to ensure that his son joined an English-medium school. The brutal caste prejudices prevalent in their village were missing in the city. The caste fault lines were stealthy and less important than those in rural areas because the city was a huge marketplace filled with strangers who were all busy making money. One had to travel with strangers in public transport or come face to face with them in public places, and there was little or no time to think about caste.

Yet, caste prejudices had not really ended. The discrimination was very much alive, albeit in subtler forms. Whenever the opportunity arose, the sleeper cells in the brains of the orthodox were reactivated to rekindle the caste hierarchy that determined a person's worth on the basis of their birth rather than their individual talent.

By converting to Buddhism, Avinash's family had slipped out of the clutches of the divinely ordained caste system enshrined in ancient Hindu holy texts. The Constitution of independent India outlawed untouchability and provided affirmative action, thereby enabling education and employment. But Babasaheb's core followers who embraced Buddhism had to wait thirty-four years to be formally accommodated in the central government's reservation policy. Nevertheless, while there was a spectacular change in their lives within a couple of generations, the situation was changing for the worse.

They had to now overcome the influence of the orthodox bhatji to a large extent by converting to Buddhism, but there was no escape from the clutches of the shetji. The traditional communities involved in trade and industry, along with domestic and multinational corporates, were dictating the template of modern living. The free-market economy had devastated all the constitutional safeguards for education and employment in government institutions by increasing privatization and universalizing the contract system dictated by the modern shetji. The appropriation of constitutional provisions continued unabated, abandoning the idea of a welfare state.

In the race to amass wealth, the value of noble qualities had been entirely discarded. The corrupt and the gullible people with their herd mentality had become the foot soldiers of mercenaries and fanatics. Celebrities were creating artificial needs by promoting unnecessary products, while politicians were helping businesses at the cost of the welfare of the masses. This was despite the fact that business and politics both survived only with the support of the masses. Moreover, some of the best brains in science and technology had abandoned wisdom and were helping greedy businessmen and politicians. Humanity was being pushed towards destruction by the invention of technologies that mostly added to the wealth and power of a few, making the masses poorer still and turning them jobless and helpless, and by increasing the inventory of tools of destruction.

Nevertheless, the voice of reason was still alive, although it was too meek to raise the bar of understanding among the masses. Sensible people still existed, irrespective of their lineages, and were doing their bit. Avinash remembered the honest and compassionate people he had encountered in his life. They were all from different backgrounds, but they had been relegated to the margins, their voices stifled by those with power and wealth. The situation had worsened, with a large number of people being brainwashed by the template of life prescribed by politicians, businessmen and religious fanatics, transforming them into organic robots—machines in flesh and blood.

He remembered people like customs officer Ramchandran, IAS officer Anand, Joint Secretary Shivram Kamble, Lieutenant Colonel Amar Singh and Swami Sunil Maharaj, who were from different backgrounds, but were all marginalized. Their marginalization was not because they, except Shivram Kamble, belonged to a lower caste. It was because they challenged the status quo and wanted to change things for the better. It was because they spoke the truth to power. In the case of Shivram Kamble, it was his caste and his honesty both, and put together, it was not a desirable combination.

Were morality and altruism becoming a stigma, like untouchability?

The result was a tumultuous ride towards the devastation of human values and of the planet itself. The evolution of humanity from barbarism to civilization was being reversed as violence, hatred, war and destruction had become the popular solution for solving disputes. With the wise, selfless and compassionate people relegated to the margins by mercenaries intoxicated with wealth and power, not just human lives, but the entire planet was on the edge. Could this be considered 'progress' made by the most intelligent animal on the planet?

And considering the global village from the ancient social perspective, the Vaishya (traditional businessmen) category, in connivance with the intellectual elites and the modern-day rulers elected in democracies (unlike the Kshatriya monarchs), had become the most powerful category of economic imperialists dominating vital socio-economic, political and religious areas, including scholarship, technology, education, employment, cultural practices, food habits and communications. The other lobby trying to dominate the global village was led by the religious or ideological fanatics engaged in hatred, violence, war and, at times, terrorism. The death and destruction they caused was justified by them on the pretext of religion, ideology, politics and economics. It seemed that everything noble was collapsing.

Then again, if humans were pushing the entire world towards a catastrophic end, no other living being but the humans themselves had the capability to reverse the trend. Would the voice of reason ever be able to assume centre-stage and peacefully neutralize the juggernaut? Who else could instil sense in the boisterous modern shetji intoxicated with wealth, the power-hungry netaji and the orthodox bhatji, irrespective of his religious hue, before it was too late?

Was there a way to raise the bar of understanding and enable the common people to transcend man-made barriers, which they willingly or inadvertently supported, to get a proper perspective of the world and their responsibilities towards Mother Nature, in order to save themselves, the future generations and the planet from extinction?

'Don't you have to go to work today?' Godavari asked, pulling Avinash out of his reverie.

'Yes, I have to,' Avinash said, getting up and throwing a glance at the city that had fascinated him once. With a renewed resolve to face yet another challenge lined up before him, he entered the house. He knew he had to keep running, even if it was to remain stationary and keep his conscience intact.

ACKNOWLEDGEMENTS

I am grateful to my family and those who helped me shape my thoughts and actions. I am also obliged to those people across caste, gender and religion who demonstrated that combating the immoral and the illegal was the right thing to do, even if it meant being slighted.

I am thankful to my literary agent, Anish Chandy, for finding me a publisher as well as updating my knowledge about the world of publishing. I am grateful to HarperCollins India for accepting my proposal to write this story based on real incidents. I am especially thankful to Bushra Ahmed for making some crucial suggestions that helped shape the book.

ABOUT THE AUTHOR

Rakshit Sonawane was born in Bombay on 13 May 1957. He is a first-generation learner from an erstwhile untouchable family that converted to Buddhism. His father, Dhondiram, worked as a watchman and was a foot soldier in Dr B.R. Ambedkar's social movement, while his mother, Runjabai, worked as a maidservant. The family initially lived in Wadala and then shifted to Ghatkopar. After completing his schooling, Sonawane worked in a factory as a casual labourer for two years. Post this, he joined the Bombay Port Trust (now Mumbai Port Authority) as a tally clerk, recording cargo operations for seven years. Simultaneously, he attended college, securing a bachelor's degree (in 1979) and, later, a postgraduate degree (in 1981) from Bombay University's Department of English. He also studied journalism and law, and became a newspaper reporter in 1985. Since then, he has worked in several English newspapers like *Mid-Day*, *The Indian Express*, *The Times of India*, the *Lokmat Times* and *The Free Press Journal*. He has also written articles for various periodicals and contributed to online news portals like Firstpost and News 9.

HarperCollins *Publishers* India

At HarperCollins India, we believe in telling the best stories and finding the widest readership for our books in every format possible. We started publishing in 1992; a great deal has changed since then, but what has remained constant is the passion with which our authors write their books, the love with which readers receive them, and the sheer joy and excitement that we as publishers feel in being a part of the publishing process.

Over the years, we've had the pleasure of publishing some of the finest writing from the subcontinent and around the world, including several award-winning titles and some of the biggest bestsellers in India's publishing history. But nothing has meant more to us than the fact that millions of people have read the books we published, and that somewhere, a book of ours might have made a difference.

As we look to the future, we go back to that one word— a word which has been a driving force for us all these years.

Read.